LACAN'S FOUR FUNDAMENTAL CONCEPTS OF PSYCHOANALYSIS

LACAN'S FOUR FUNDAMENTAL CONCEPTS OF PSYCHOANALYSIS

AN INTRODUCTION

DR. ROBERTO HARARI

TRANSLATED BY JUDITH FILC

OTHER

Other Press
New York

Library of Congress Cataloging-in-Publication Data

Harari, Roberto.
   [Cuatro conceptos fundamentales de Lacan. English]
   Lacan's four fundamental concepts of psychoanalysis : an introduction /
by Roberto Harari ; translated by Judy Filc.
      p. cm.
   ISBN 1-59051-082-8 (pbk. : alk. paper)
   1. Lacan, Jacques, 1901- Quatre concepts fondamentaux de la psychanalyse.
2. Psychoanalysis. I. Title.

BF173.L14623H3713 2004
150.19'5'092–dc22

2004005587

To Jacques Lacan, atypical psychoanalyst, master of reading

Contents

Prologue

It's a dismal thing to think of being master when one was never disciple.

F. de Rojas, *La Celestina*

Even though the purpose, scope, and thematic choices of this book have been made explicit quite often throughout the text, indicating the pertinence of their being heard as reiterated by the same emitter, it is important to detail the circumstances, the juncture, that made this book possible.

As you will see, the work responds both in style and organization to its oral origin—the book constitutes the transcription of ten classes taught between April and August 1986 at the Center for Psychoanalytic Education (CPE) of the General San Martín Cultural Center, an agency of the Buenos Aires City Government. It is worthwhile highlighting the unheard-of character of the CPE, locally and maybe even worldwide. In 1984, under the protection of the return of democracy in Argentina and with the enthusiastic and unconditional support of the then brand-new secretary of culture for the city, Dr. Mario O'Donnell, a heteroclite group of psychoanalysts gathered to work *ad honorem* at the San Martín Cultural Center.

This endeavor was actually the result of a proposition made by Dr. O'Donnell as a response to an offer the psychoanalytic institution Mayéutica-Institución Psicoanalítica had made to him to collaborate with his secretariat. The proposition involved a manifold challenge. To begin with, since it should obviously be a pluralist endeavor, the CPE—coordinated by this writer—summoned qualified colleagues who had never shared a working space before to join the project. Yet this was not the only factor creating uncertainty. Such space had to be built on nonconventional bases, insofar as the CPE posited not the classic, predictable paths taken by (and within) the analytic institutions, but the enactment of the links between psychoanalysis and culture, on the one hand, and the special consideration of the diverse nature of the Cultural Center's audience, on the other. Such diversity is due to the fact that the San Martín Cultural Center opens its doors gratis to anybody interested in the activities held there, regardless of their education, level of information, or professional training.

At the San Martín we received the frank and generous support of the *Licenciado*[1] Javier Torre, who conferred to his work as director of the Cultural Center an impulse and creativity that rendered the Cultural Center one of the most significant of its sort worldwide, due to its power of appeal. I am deeply grateful to Dr. O'Donnell and Lic. Torre, as I am to my colleagues in the CPE's organizing committee and to the numerous guests who continually added to the center's prestige. At least as important to the CPE were the attendants to our activities. Without the enticement of a certificate, with no predefined program, without the promise of specialized training, they fill seats, floors, and access hallways with truly outstanding constancy, attention, and interest. They are without a doubt the true instigators—and main addressees—of the following pages, since they have never ceased to encourage me to give the classes taught at the CPE a publishable form (and even cordially insist that I do so).

Finally, if this endeavor became possible it was thanks to the Lics. Andrea Gómez's and Alejandra Cowes's invaluable collaboration, the first

---

1. Title given in Spain and Latin America to those who finished a five-year undergraduate degree. (Translator's note)

one transcribing the lectures, and the second one editing the transcription for publication. To both, also, my sincere thanks.

I would also like to point out that only a few parts were deleted from the original, since my goal was to preserve the original conditions of its enunciation. The titles of the chapters represent the major topic of discussion during each class.

To conclude, a vow: that the reader will validate this Introduction as an acceptable attempt to establish with as much rigor as possible in the kingdom of lights—which is not that of the Enlightenment—the incomparable richness of the postmodern reading of Freud processed by Lacan. Such a reading, clearly sustainable for each psychoanalytic concept, is radically (*raigalmente*) put to the test when dealing, as we do here, with its very foundations.

Buenos Aires, June 1987

Helix and Quadrangle: Psychoanalysis and Its Fundamental Concepts

I want to thank you all for being here, since I never expected to have such a large audience; on my part, it will compel me to work arduously so that you continue to come. I don't believe such a large audience constitutes solely an acknowledgment of my own abilities; it also acknowledges Lacan's teaching. Throughout our ten meetings, I will engage in an introductory discussion of some of the themes Lacan developed in his Seminar 11, *The Four Fundamental Concepts of Psychoanalysis*.[1]

You will forgive me if I start with a truism, but sometimes redundancies are not superfluous. Of course, the view I can offer you of Seminar 11 is obviously partial, since on the one hand, a seminar such as this is impossible to encompass in ten meetings, and on the other, such

---

1. That was its title when it appeared in published form in 1973. Its original title had been *The Foundations of Psychoanalysis*. Regarding this change, J. Allouch considers that it is "far from accepted that the concept constitutes a foundation in Lacan's view" [in "Lacan *censurado*" ("Lacan Censored"), *Littoral*; La torre abolida, Córdoba, 1986, p. 11]. In a far less Manichaean way, M. Marini states, "Lacan now speaks of concepts, now asks himself whether psychoanalysts do not live in 'deceit' ('*la impostura*'), and he is leery of the relations between psychoanalysis, religion, and science" (*Jacques Lacan*, Belfond, Paris, 1986, p. 201). Due to the slant taken in our exposition, it will be easy to justify (*fundamentar*) the reason for our choice.

reading will be, inevitably, my own approach to the text. What follows is a guiding principle to our reading: there is no exact or literal reading, but rather themes I consider crucial and about which others might say, "How is it that he has barely touched on that point, or that he has skipped that other one?" They will be right, as well. In any case, it is a principle whose function is to warn you as to what the development I intend to display in front of you will be like.

We may briefly situate the moment when Lacan teaches this seminar, both chronologically and in terms of the course taken by his teaching. To do this, we need to consider the politics of psychoanalysis, and particularly Lacan's part in such politics. His role toward the official entity, the IPA,[2] was indeed revulsive, repelling. He thus starts this seminar by referring to the "excommunication" he suffered on the part of the IPA. His use of such a term is certainly not random, since through its introduction he instantly refers to the religious question. We will see later how he will focus psychoanalysis on its relations with religion and science from the start, trying to identify, if possible, and delimit the respective epistemological borders, to say it along with Gaston Bachelard.

In any case, what is at stake here is whether psychoanalysis has anything to do with the order of science. If it does, the question is what that relation must be, in the imperative mood. But let me return first to the political question. Lacan is indeed expelled from the IPA, and at the same time, thanks to the good efforts of those who promote his expulsion, he is forbidden to continue with his seminar at the *Hôpital de Sainte-Anne*.

Lacan is then successfully welcomed at the *École Normal Supérieure*, a university institution. He had very good friends there, such as Claude Lévi-Strauss and Louis Althusser, who were then very interested in Lacan's teaching, going as far as using psychoanalytic categories to process their own revision of Marxist theory. Now that we can find their books again among us,[3] you can see both in *Reading Capital* and in *For Marx* how Althusser makes use of notions such as overdetermination,

---

2. International Psychoanalytic Association.
3. Harari refers here to the return of democracy in 1983, which resulted in the end of censorship. (Translator's note)

displacement, and condensation—notions he takes directly from the teachings of Freud and Lacan. Althusser thus introduces the whole scaffolding of his rereading of Marx's work, basically, of *Das Kapital*.

These and other good friends will make it possible again for Lacan to have a large audience before which he considers crucial to develop no more and no less than a thematic referred to the foundations. This choice involves raising what he calls the nodular question about analytic practice, analytic praxis (a term that has also Marxist roots), namely, What is it that founds our praxis? What is it that prevents it from becoming a sort of thaumaturgy, of magic, something that works but for reasons that cannot be determined? For many things do work. The question is whether he who makes them function knows the causes of such functioning, and whether he knows why a certain produced effect was actually produced. Such knowledge would allow analysts to establish a certain logic, a certain rigor different from an effect based, we could say, on transference, an effect that, in one way or another, and because of the place we occupy, we may obtain with doubtful effectiveness.

Look how there appears here—and let's pay attention to the number— "The four." This number is a constant and defining operating principle in Lacanian teaching. Some believe that it's number three, but others, and I among them, believe that it's not the empirical "Oedipal triangularity" that basically gives support to many of Lacan's conceptions, but rather it's number four that has primacy. I don't want to start pointing out the respective arguments for both positions, but if one traverses Lacan's teachings one may see how, in various moments and paragraphs, this way of arranging data and concepts of analytic experience in four categories produces a very peculiar effect. Lacan obtains a logicization— if I'm allowed to use a neologism—particular to the analytic field.[4] To talk about "four concepts" entails conceiving them in a certain homogenizing level. It seems that this, certainly, does not go along with the positivist eagerness to define a science by means of a sole formal and

---

4. Yet it would not be banal to recall this quote from Lacan: "A fourfold structure can be always demanded from the unconscious in the construction of a subjective ordering" ("Kant con Sade," *Ecrits II*, Siglo XXI, Mexico, 1975, p. 346). [English translation: "Kant with Sade," trans. J. B. Swenson, Jr., in *October* 51, Winter 1989.]

abstract object. For instance, what does psychoanalysis study? It is usually said that it studies "the unconscious,"[5] just like that. The pertinence of a science in the positivist mode will then always entail the existence of a singular theoretical object—situated also within the praxis—that defines the specificity of such a science. Lacan names instead four concepts, as they say at the dance halls: four concepts four[6]; four, and not just one. Besides, these concepts articulate in such a way that they may constitute the foundations—the *fundamental*—of what supports the operational field of psychoanalysis.

I will write these four concepts in a particular way, offering you a schema that may be didactically inconvenient to bring up at the beginning. Yet I want to do it, mainly to intrigue you and to see if this proposition will be fulfilled or not throughout the ten classes. It is a table that attempts to broaden the question of the four concepts, indicating a form of relationship among them that I believe to be significant. I will gradually give the reasons for this.

The four concepts displayed in this particular way are:

Unconscious	Repetition
Transference	Drive

In the first pages of the seminar, Lacan will say that one of the requirements a science must fulfill is that of being able to put the whole of its specific field of knowledge in formulae. Granted that there can be formulae for anything, and that does not indicate that the said discipline is scientific, far from it. It doesn't matter; to those of us who acknowledge ourselves as indebted to Lacan's teachings, trying to elevate concepts (fundamental or not) to the category of elements that may be articu-

---

5. "*El, o lo, inconsciente*" in the original. In Spanish one can differentiate between a masculine article, *el*, and a neuter article, *lo*. The use of *lo* would not imply the existence of an entity called "the unconscious," as does the use of *el*. (Translator's note)

6. The author refers to announcements of different sorts that used to be made at the dance halls, repeating the number before and after the noun, to entice the audience. (Translator's note)

lated in terms of what could be called an algorithm comes naturally. What is an algorithm? This term, which psychoanalysis drew from mathematics, gives us the possibility to work with some letters and organize them in a sort of regulated slippage, obtaining productive effects of knowledge by means of these formulae.

Let us then play one of these serious games:

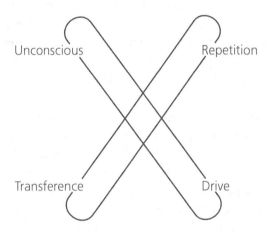

We articulate unconscious with drive, and repetition with transference, which does not imply in any way that this is the only possible relation. We may identify in these lines that we assume as symmetrical (but which leave a vacant place) a gap represented by a "little symbol" often used by Lacan, which is quite useful. Let's see how it is used in a formula, in this case, that of the *fantasme*[7] ($ \mathcal{S} \lozenge a $). The lozenge, which reads as "cut of," or "desire for," indicates a series of linking operations between the two connected terms. For instance, if we take it apart according to a horizontal axis, in the bottom part we'll have 'V.'

In logic, this is the disjunction symbol (either . . . or . . . ; or). To go back to what we were stating before, we write $\mathcal{S}$ or object *a*, in one sense or the other. Later on we will look at the differential figures of disjunction more closely, according to Lacan's reformulation.[8] Let us

---

7. I opted for the French term instead of the English "phantasy" in order to preserve the specificity of the Lacanian concept. (Translator's note)

8. Cf. Chapter 9.

try now to understand what stems from the lozenge that Lacan calls punch (literally, *poinçon*) even if sometimes it will appear as *losange*[9] because it resembles a lozenge. It seems that such literality, apparently, did not convince the translators. Although the drawing resembles a lozenge, the punch, the instrument, is linked to a particular mark used by silversmiths that testifies to each artisan's singularity. By means of the punch a kind of signature is stamped whereby one may even tell the place and year of coinage of each piece. The punch, therefore, holds a very conspicuous spatial-temporal location and order of singularity. I believe that by using the term *punch* Lacan wants to convey precisely this, and not just a figurative little lozenge. The lozenge constitutes a phenomenological description while what we're interested in here is in recapturing the value of uniqueness the punch transmits. I repeat: in our schema there remained a punch in the site of articulation of the four concepts. In dividing it we obtained a "V," which we will call disjunction. If now we superimpose the upper part, "Λ," we are faced with the complementary logical operation called conjunction.

Speaking precisely from the perspective of logic, what we just said would be an aporia, that is, a noncategorical enunciation that admits even its opposite. However, it does not invalidate the system by trivializing it. If in logic one says "A is not B" and "A equals B," one says nothing. This, logicians say, trivializes the whole. There is no possibility to discriminate anything. Even so, students could reach a sort of compromise, in the sense of accepting that there exist both strong negations, where disjunction is absolute, and other, weak negations which may endure aporias, which is our case. There is disjunction, but that doesn't preclude the existence of conjunction. In a different manner, there is $\mathcal{S}$ or a, but there is also $\mathcal{S}$ and a. Proof of this is that, if one took the graphically higher operation included in the punch, one might say: the subject is its object a ($\mathcal{S} \wedge a$) in the writing of the *fantasme* ($\mathcal{S} \lozenge a$).

By means of such writing we may grasp the fact that the subject does not face an object—as philosophers usually say. We may understand instead how the object constitutes the deputy of the subject itself; the object is the very subject, as its amputated part. The subject does

---

9. In French in the original. (Translator's note)

not face the object, as if it were a dimension referred to a distant and different other. Rather, the subject will come to be that object *a*, whose nature we will explore more thoroughly later on. Let us know for now that it is that which Lacan considered his "only invention" in psychoanalysis, which as we may appreciate, is a strong statement that we must consider very seriously.

In this first stage in the breaking down of the punch, we have already marked two operations. We may, however, cut vertically and we will be left with something that will read mathematically like this: more than, ">," less than, "<." If we take them to a nonquantitative categorization, these symbols mean the following: if it is more, that it implies, and if it is less, that it is de-implied. In other words, it accounts for the dimensions of implication and de-implication between terms. The more implies the less; the less is de-implied with respect to the more.

All the relations we are considering are established solely by positing the existence of a punch amidst the four concepts. This analysis is not part of Lacan's text, for it is just my personal way to attempt to organize the Lacanian formulations. On the other hand, I understand that we may use another notation that is frequently utilized in expositions such as this one, and place it on the punch:

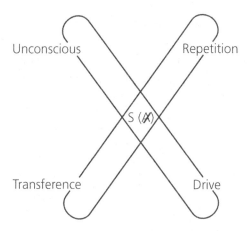

This writing—S (A̶)—means "signifier of the lack in the Other." The Other, the place of the signifier, of the symbolic for Lacan, is the A. Yet the inconsistency of the Other, the lack, is what makes the helix "work." If it weren't because there is something here that indicates the incompleteness—and, therefore, the lack—of the Other, none of these concepts might exist.

This said, we can think of other relations for which I will attempt to lay the foundations in the course of our classes. Besides the previous articulations, we will then find, through a shift, another way in which Lacan has accustomed us to put various psychoanalytic notions to work:

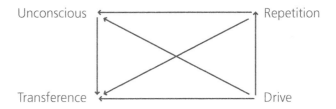

Using this schema, we obtain a quadrangle as a result. We will see the reason for the directionality of these arrows, which support the postulation that states that the fundamental and defining concepts within the field of our praxis are four, and not only that of the unconscious. If this schema works and these four concepts are indeed fundamental, we will have to remember that any foundation gives rise to the beginning of a construction. If we put the cornerstones in place, we will then be able to derive other concepts from these, not fundamental ones anymore, yet not, for that reason, less implicated in our operational field.

Let us take, for example, the transference, of which this seminar will say that "it is the enactment of the reality of the unconscious." If we draw an arrow from the unconscious toward the transference, we will find the analyst:

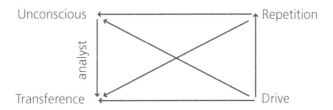

The analyst is the one who offers his being as support for the phenomenon of the transference. The enactment of the reality of the unconscious, such is the transference, and there is the analyst. Still, this reality is also, decisively, sexual reality. We can see how the drive inscribes itself in the unconscious insofar as it is partial—all drives are partial by definition, and there is no totalization of drives. The reality of the unconscious is above all sexual; here then is the libido qua drive inscribed in the unconscious. Drawn from drive to unconscious, we find one of the fundamental coordinates in psychoanalysis, namely, sex:

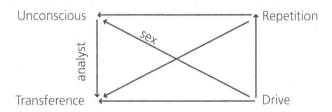

Let us not forget the other variable, that is, death. I don't want to posit anything pansexualistic; in this regard we should make clear that since Freud, undoubtedly, we can say that everything can be sexualized. This does not mean that everything is sexual, as some stubborn critic pretends to have him say. But let us continue: now, we will draw a line from repetition toward the unconscious. That line will testify to something we will develop later, namely, what Lacan calls, using a Greek term, the *Tuché*. This term denotes the action of nonautomatic causality (which Lacan confronts with *Automaton*) given as chance. Said in a different way, it is chance as cause that, due to a certain form of repetition, inscribes itself, via the *Tuché*, in the unconscious (since the latter does not exhaust itself in the signifying reference, as we shall see):

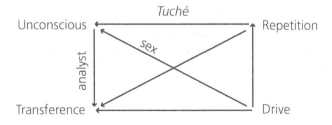

This is a table that we will gradually develop and have as a referent in all our meetings. Today I only wish to present it so that we will be able to refer to it once and again. To continue, we find another arrow that goes from the drive to repetition. Among other items related to the drive, this seminar will tell us about its circuit—such is the title of one of its chapters. This circuit follows the paths, the meanders, of repetition, since it constitutes a recurrent turning around object *a* (one of whose readings is the object of the drive). Here, object *a* imbricates in, or straddles (*se encabalga*), the articulation drive-repetition. (To be more precise: another of the readings of *a* is that of the object-cause of desire):

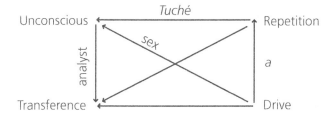

We've got another arrow, namely, that which goes from repetition to transference. This one does warrant our special attention, because it is here that one of the more traditional deflections in clinical psychoanalytic practice appears. Such a deflection is produced because of the dulling (*achatamiento*) of transference brought about in the name of a repetition conceived rather as a reproduction of the same. It is a move made by the analyst and it consists mainly in interpreting through the question of the same: here, now, and with me, equals there, then, with that one.

Most members of the IPA share[10] the following: that transference is repetition. What this seminar will attempt to demonstrate, drawing from notions of Kierkegaard among others, is that it is possible to produce a concept as complicated as that of repetition with difference, or that there is no repetition, precisely, without difference. On the other hand, the slant of the reproduction of the same implies only the trans-

---

10. The term used in Spanish, *comulgar*, means "to share" in a figurative sense, but its literal meaning is "to receive Holy Communion." In this way, Harari follows up on Lacan's connection between psychoanalysis and religion. (Translator's note)

ference that we will call imaginary along with Lacan, namely, that transference forged in terms of the problem of the mirror stage:

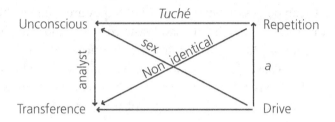

Now, due to Lacan's peculiar reading of Freud's text *Inhibitions, Symptoms, and Anxiety*—basically, in his 1962/63 seminar on *Anxiety*—and to the way in which he reworks the Freudian concept of inhibition, we may place this term—*inhibition*—in the articulation between drive and transference:

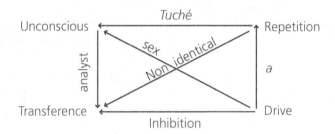

The inhibited drive is the aim, as Freud teaches us. It is the drive that does not reach consummation, in that the latter involves corporal *jouissance*. This drive stops in what concerns its aim, even if it sustains its object. This way of defining inhibition differentiates this notion from that of the drive that does reach its aim, on the one hand, and from sublimation, which is akin to it, on the other. Once we have located the notion of inhibition, we will finish the table I conceived a while ago and still judge convincing. I think, as I said, that this table may account for the articulation that gradually emerges from the elaboration of the "four concepts" in Seminar 11.

There is another important point to tackle in this introduction, namely, that of *fundamental concept*. Unfortunately, the new translator of Freud into Spanish, José Luis Etcheverry, caused us to lose this idea when, in his translation of *Instincts and their Vicissitudes*[11] (*Pulsiones y destinos de las pulsiones*), he wrote *basic concepts* (*conceptos básicos*).[12] Words for Lacan possess a meaning, insofar as they are not mere "ways of saying." It is not the same then to say "basic concept" and "fundamental concept." In Seminar 20 he will scan the term and turn it into funda-mental, thus alluding to a sort of veil that would cover the mental[13]; but already in Seminar 11 there is an acute reference to the cabalistic (from Kabbala, the mystic dimension of Judaism) origin of this term when he says that "*fundamentum* has more than one meaning, and I do not need to remind you that in the Kabbala it designates one of the modes of divine manifestation, which, in this register, is strictly identified with the *pudendum*."[14]

The term *pudendum* denotes private parts (*partes pudendas*)—or, as the dictionary states, shameful—known as "those of the generation" (*las de la generación*). The term *fundament*, then, articulates something of the union, so that the four concepts will be able to seek support in this search for sexual relation. Lacan thus retrieves the Freudian term *Grundbegriff* (we know Lacan works with the Freudian categories in a very strict way).

I will now read to you the beginning of Freud's *Metapsychology* because of its epistemological rigor. This work opens up with a famous manifestation of how the said fundamental concepts are constructed. In this opening, countless questions are answered that are still a concern for psychoanalysts as well as for some epistemologists who consider themselves authorized to give an opinion on psychoanalysis. I have

---

11. The Amorrortu edition of the Spanish translation from which the author is quoting follows the organization in volumes of the *Standard Edition*. I will add the corresponding pages to each quote in brackets. (Translator's note)

12. S. Freud, *Obras Completas* (*O. C.*), Amorrortu, Buenos Aires, 1977, vol. 14, p. 113. [p. 117. James Strachey also translates as "basic concepts."]

13. This is a pun on the Spanish word *funda*, that means "cover." (Translator's note)

14. J. Lacan, *Las cuatro conceptos fundamentales del psicoanálisis*, Barral, Barcelona, 1977, p. 17 (partially modified translation). [The English version of the quote corresponds to Alan Sheridan's translation in Jacques Lacan ([1973]1998). All quotes from seminar 11 will be taken from this translation.]

with me Laplanche and Pontalis's French version of the *Metapsychology*. We are particularly interested, as we said, in *Instincts and Their Vicissitudes*, where these authors did take *Grundbegriff* literally as fundamental concept. That is how we can understand that the title of Lacan's seminar is indebted to Freud's work, even though he won't say it (his mentioning of *Grundbegriff* notwithstanding).

The text then states the following: "We have often heard the following demand formulated to us . . ." This is important, for it marks a kind of unique bond between the analyst and those who demand that the analyst give reasons. There isn't a symmetrical relationship, but somebody, from the place of the Master, pressures the analyst—placed in the role of a trembling slave—to give his reasons. It is in fact characteristic of the scientific tribunal to formulate the following demand: "A science must be constructed on concepts fundamentally clear and neatly defined." As I see it, such an intention refers to Descartes' rationalist conception concerning clear and distinct ideas. This conception greatly differs from the set of relations implied by the punch, which are themselves undoubtedly very conflicting, rather aporetic. They are relations that must endure ambiguity, and the categories we must use to reflect on psychoanalysis are precisely of this kind, without, of course, falling into the opposite extreme, that is, the lack of discriminating rigor.

"Clear and distinct" ideas don't work in psychoanalysis, among other reasons because psychoanalysis, a practice, is construed on words and, that being the case, it is predestined, in Freud's terms, to polyphony.[15] Montaigne used to say it: words belong half to the one who says them and half to the one who hears them. Those who believe there is only one frozen meaning for each word confuse the lexical meaning (that of the dictionary), or words that are provisionally fixed, with what happens in and through the interlocutory, evocative dimension, which has little or nothing to do with what the dictionary says. One thing is communication based on lexicon, and another thing is the phenomenon of speech. I pointed out this same matter a year ago, in this same place, when we reflected on "Función y campo de la palabra y del lenguaje en

---

15. S. Freud, *La interpretación de los sueños*, O. C., *op. cit.*, vol. 5, p. 346. [*The Interpretation of Dreams*, p. 353.]

psicoanálisis."[16] The ambition for clarity, definition, and distinctiveness refers to an order that wants, maybe in a shamefaced way, to constitute a sort of metalanguage that will explain speech. A supralanguage, a language of language where the condition of ambiguity, of polysemia, of diversity of meanings (which even the dictionary offers, to the extent that sometimes, as Freud himself had detected, it may offer one sense for a word, and then its opposite), that which is only alluded, as I was saying, is irremediably lost. Freud detects this diversity in his essay "The Antithetical Meaning of Primal Words,"[17] but the fact is that this characteristic of words is not limited only to primitive terms.

Think simply of the word *réplica*.[18] Somebody formulated a *réplica*, and therefore contradicted that which he heard. This is one possible meaning. Another person, instead, made a *réplica*, which might mean that he faithfully copied a model, an exactly opposite sense—it is not something that one contradicts, but something that one intends to copy literally. The option one chooses will depend on the context and the way in which the term is used, but this example serves to demonstrate that this feature is not limited to a primitive stage of language, since it happens every day in our own language (an example that may be generalized). We need to acknowledge this in order to realize that the metalinguistic pretension is quite hard to maintain. That is why Lacan's teaching sometimes becomes complicated, because he does not give out definitions, which is what we want to cling to when we are trying to learn something new. It isn't hence a problem encountered by a particular reader, but something that emerges as a structural effect of Lacan's conception.

Some psychoanalytic dictionaries appear now and then that attempt to narrow the possible meanings of a series of concepts. In this respect,

---

16. Published in English as "The Function and Field of Speech and Language in Psycho-Analysis," *Écrits: A Selection*, trans. Alan Sheridan, Tavistock Publications, London, 1977. The parenthesis that follows in the original refers to a specific translation problem of the Spanish edition that does not occur in the English version. (Translator's note)

17. S. Freud, *O. C.*, *op. cit.*, vol. 9, pp. 143–153 [pp. 153–161].

18. The following example of contradictory meanings for the same word does not work in English as it does in Spanish. The meaning of *réplica* in the first sense is "reply," but its meaning in the second sense is "replica." (Translator's note)

the seminar asks whether the object of current physics is the same as the object of seventeenth-century physics, that is, when physics was born. If it isn't, that sole fact indicates that the term *physics* does not connote the same thing in different epochs. Such pretension on the part of science should be presented back to it from a psychoanalytic perspective.

We may then be able to validly raise the following question: What science is that which remains as a sediment after the impact of psychoanalysis? How does the scientist take up the challenge involved in the postulation of the Freudian unconscious? The same question is valid concerning philosophy, undoubtedly, because, what kind of a philosophy is that which is based only on data stemming from consciousness and does not take into account the subject's split?

We should then follow the path Lacan himself set out when some very troublesome students, who wanted to get rid of him by calling him a "bourgeois," demanded that he say what psychoanalysis could do for the revolution. Lacan answered, "You tell me what the revolution can do for psychoanalysis." This was a very smart, psychoanalytic way to answer, whereby he obviously did not satisfy the students but placed them in their right context. For everybody is always asking psychoanalysis to be this or that, to give answers to this and that, always accusing it, in sum, of lacking in something or other; which is absolutely right, since that is what it is all about, substantively.

We talk about the signifier of the Other's lack; then, psychoanalysis always lacks, for it deals with the lack, which certainly cannot be "solved" with complements in the manner of the biological, the social, and so many other facets that psychoanalysis should supposedly have and of whose absences it is accused.[19] Through this sort of belief in the unitary one forgets in the end that it is possible to conceive something in a certain way because something else is left aside, something that will thus be redefined. If we did not carry out this task of epistemological differentiation, the result would be a huge chaos. It is what one obtains, after all, with "integrating" proposals based on concepts such as "wholism"

---

19. Is "the social" the sacralized multiplication of individuals, or the detection of the determination we receive from the field of the Other?

(*todismo*) or the unitary. This is certainly no more than the Imaginary's fascination.

Going back to *Instincts and Their Vicissitudes*, you can see that in Freud's view, the issue of clarity and distinctiveness is an exogenous demand. He writes that "in actual fact no science, not even the most exact, begins with such definitions. The true beginning of any scientific activity consists rather in describing phenomena." The first point, then, is by no means to start from a definition, but on the contrary, to constitute a grouping of phenomena. One may "reply"[20] that, in any case, this description of phenomena follows an ordering (besides the fact that such phenomena are themselves involved in relations), and that such ordering follows a specific criterion. This is inevitable. The applied criteria may be rapidly charged with being prescientific or ideological in the best of cases. Freud recalls the fact that "even at the stage of description it is not possible to avoid applying certain abstract ideas to the material in hand, ideas derived from somewhere or other but certainly not from the new observations alone."[21] They are taken from another place, which means that in order to found a certain notional field that may sustain and account for a praxis, we need to resort to a theoretical import, that is, to take something from a different place and build a new field.

Specifically, Freud developed a system of theoretical references that Lacan saw as his mission to update, to render contemporary. If in Freud's case the terms were imported from physics and biology, in Lacan's case they originated at first from linguistics (and in a parallel way from logic) and later on from topology. This does not mean that Lacan was a logicist, a linguisticist, a topologist, etc. It implies only that nothing is born out of nothing. Even this formulation is wrong; if I say, "is born," I am taking for granted that the antecedent belongs to the same genus as the consequent. The newborn belongs to the same genus as its parents. To say that a science is born is a mistake—we should rather say that "it starts." In this sense, Althusser pointed out that Freud is a son with no

---

20. See note 18. (Translator's note)
21. *Instincts and Their Vicissitudes*, p. 117. (Translator's note)

father, because he admits no precursor.[22] When Lacan starts to revise the fundamental concept of the unconscious, he will also say that there are a number of predecessors, but that there was no unconscious before Freud. The word had been used in many contexts by a variety of authors, but none of them constitutes an antecedent that may enable us to say, "it was all, or part of it, already in . . ."

Theoretical import serves to found new fields. This is what Freud is telling us, namely, that there are abstract ideas that can be taken from here or there and that do not come from the present experience. This affirmation is very important as a refutation to all forms of empiricism, to the belief that practice in itself carries a form of wisdom of its own. Such an assumption is a total aberration, for, what is the wisdom of a practice in itself? Is it the practice that generates ideas, or are the ideas what makes practice "speak"? I think I am being faithful to what Freud conveys to us when he refers to "such ideas."

We must then specify which are these ideas that are "abstract and brought from somewhere else," will later "become the basic concepts of the science, [and] are still more indispensable as the material is further worked over." He then says that such ideas "must at first necessarily possess some degree of indefiniteness."[23] Such indetermination, I might add, is precisely what renders them impossible to define in a clear and distinct way. The seminar fosters, in turn, the concept of approximationism.[24] It indeed upholds an approximation (to "the reality to be grasped") through the construction and elaboration of the concept, but with the caveat that the design of such a concept can never be fully finalized. There does not exist a concept that can be completed once and for all. If we fixate it, we kill it.

---

22. L. Althusser, "Freud y Lacan," in AAVV *Estructuralismo y psicoanálisis*, Barral, Barcelona, 1977, p. 17. (We have partially edited the translation.) [*Writings in Psychoanalysis. Freud and Lacan*, ed. Oliver Corpet and François Matheron, trans. Jeffrey Mehlman, Columbia University Press, 1999.]

23. *Instincts and Their Vicissitudes*, p. 117. (Translator's note)

24. This concept was developed by Gaston Bachelard in his book *Essai sur la connaissance approchée*, and it refers to the use of approximation in the pursuit of scientific knowledge. (Translator's note)

This is precisely what Lacan denounces with such rigor, vigor, and lucidity, that is, what has been the fate of Freud's teaching in the hands of the post-Freudians. It becomes necessary to put things in their place—if psychoanalysis is constantly relying on the garglistic (*gargarística*), echolalic repetition of Freud's isolated concepts, such concepts will be of no use whatsoever. We must then renew psychoanalysis's wager but not just with Freud's quote, because if we do that, it will end up being a coin so common that—to use another of Lacan's allegories—it will circulate so much from hand to hand that its value will be erased (as happens with currency in times of high inflation).[25] The fate of psychoanalysis may resemble that of the coin if we don't establish an epistemological surveillance, as Bachelard (who is also the creator of the notion of approximationism) puts it. Lacan thus enrolls in the best lineage of French epistemology—that of Gaston Bachelard, Alexandre Koyré, Georges Canguilhem, and, finally, Michel Foucault and the already-cited Althusser. The reading of all these thinkers will give us some guidelines on the most decisive coordinates that marked Lacan's vast theoretical corpus.

Freud then specifies an indetermination that renders the clear apprehension of the content of conceptualism impossible. We may appreciate here how anybody who will accuse Freud of biologicism, physicism, and so on, shows that he has not grasped Freud's postulation, his complete break with the universe of inherited notions. For instance, when he introduces concepts such as the forms of energy to describe the psyche, it is obvious that Freud is simply resorting to a convention.

Constraining ourselves to use conventions involves using them without believing them to possess an ontological character, that is, that things "are" literally like that. Believing in such ontological nature would imply the conviction that a discipline must faithfully copy a presumed reality. Who supports this notion? Empiricism fosters this type of view. The "secrets" of analytic theory, launched once again by Lacan, may allow us instead to come into contact with a psychoanalysis that will not pre-

---

25. The author plays here with the Spanish idiom *moneda corriente*, whose literal meaning is "common coin" but whose accurate translation is "commonplace." I used the literal translation to respect the author's intention. (Translator's note)

tend to faithfully copy (*calcar*) anything from the psychological experience, that is, a psychoanalysis that does not remain at the level of the ego convictions accepted by everybody but sustains the revulsive effect of the Freudian discovery beyond the "truths"—falsities—of common sense that are usually attributed to our discipline.

What Freud tells us is that the relations "one believes to have guessed before being able to have knowledge and offer proof" actually preexisted one's hypothetical discovery. In other words, it is thanks to our theoretical work that we may actually discover phenomena. It is due to a (bad) empiricist education that we affirm that experience conveys to us a form of wisdom. Freud tells us the exact opposite thing. Such empiricism is what leads to the frequent, almost indignant accusations brought against Lacan, through "questions" such as, Where are the patients? Is this psychoanalysis? What is this man talking about in his contrived style?

What Lacan is conveying is not in the order of the psychological and it results, therefore, in our being able to preserve the field Freud bequeathed to us. That is why it seems so unscientific a style—in an ironic sense, having in mind science's claim to the transparency of its discourse, which leaves no room for misunderstandings. When Lacan stylistically carves with his punch (his style), he draws a radically heteroclite path with regard to a psychoanalysis that cherishes the ambition, in any case, to adhere to the designs of positivistic science. We say this, furthermore, without forgetting the rigor he intends to convey to us in an integral way through his "matheme."

Faced with this introduction, you might also ask, Are we going to talk about psychoanalysis, or are we going to stick with the doctrinal foundations? It's just that there is no other way to talk about psychoanalysis than relying on these concepts. I believe an introduction like the one I just presented is inevitable in order to tackle the first fundamental concept. Lacan will say about the unconscious something more and something else than what we repeat tirelessly. He will call it "that part of the psyche that does not recognize negation nor logic, that is ruled by displacement, condensation, etc." He will thus not only account for the already classic formula, "the unconscious is structured like a language" (*lo inconsciente es estructurado como un lenguaje*) (I suggest that we enounce it in this way, and we will see why later on), but he will also introduce with his notion of the unconscious the nature of what he will call "temporal pulsation." This is a novel concept, as Lacan mentions in the report he submits to the *École Normal Supérieure* with the content of his lectures for the year 1964.

Temporal pulsation—a term we will attempt to analyze next class— allows us to better understand the formulations that postulate that the unconscious is not a second sense that would authorize the analyst to engage in a sort of therapeutic Ping-Pong. If we suppose that the unconscious is a mind with a false bottom, what is at stake here is not, anymore, the analysis of the discourse that is subject to temporal pulsation. In this way, the notion of the unconscious qua fundamental concept is lost. In any case, what Lacan is saying is that the analyst acts like the hermeneutist who will always find a second meaning to things. This, of course, is not psychoanalysis, as is neither Ping-Pong nor hermeneutics.

QUESTIONS AND ANSWERS

I am often asked about object *a*. I will try to specify two or three traits without going into detail. So that the concept will not remain so vague, we will "approximate" it. This object is undoubtedly something different from the object that the Anglo-Saxon psychoanalysis in particular posits as the one involved in so-called object relations. The latter alludes in general to the ways in which a behavioral bond between two practically co-present persons is understood. In this way, according to how one person gets along with the other one, it is usually said that the relation is predominantly oral, anal, etc.

The clinical history of the Wolf Man situates a concept, namely, that of the small thing that may be detached from the body (*lo pequeño separable del cuerpo*).[26] Freud locates it and builds an equation: penis–

---

26. S. Freud, *De la Historia de una Neurosis Infantil, O. C., op. cit.*, vol. 17, p. 78. [*From the History of an Infantile Neurosis*, p. 81.]

feces–child. He will even add later "money" and "gift"[27] as terms that are equivalent within the unconscious due to their peculiar nature of being "the small thing detachable from the body." We can "naturally" understand why the child is part of this equation, since its birth involves its biological separation from its mother. We can also understand why the feces. Yet, what about the penis? There is no effective and processed castration. As a consequence, this sole circumstance breaks the intelligibility we thought existed so far.

In other words, we are faced with something detachable but that in fact does not detach itself. What is indicated is that the penis refers here to an order of loss defined within the Symbolic, and not to an actual loss, whereby a piece of the body would be amputated from it. It refers then to something that may fall, or be lost, that may or may not have a realistic loss as its grounds, but that, insofar as it has fallen, is located within the register of the Real, in a first approximation. (We will return to these specifications when we deal with the question of the gaze and of the object of the drive.)

The voice and the gaze are the objects *a* Lacan adds to the list of "pieces" left of the Other. That means that what is left from the relation with the Other—the relation in which we are constituted—is transformed into, becomes a relation with, the variances of object *a*. This is something that has nothing whatsoever to do with an interhuman bond, it is a relation with something that may not even be patently manifest or present; for instance, the gaze located in that painting, that is looking at me. The gaze, therefore, is not in the eye. Lacan will thus disassociate the eye from the gaze, stating that the latter is an object *a* that, being "outside," determines me qua desiring subject.

As we have already said, Lacan ratifies object *a* as his "invention," his decisive contribution to psychoanalysis. I believe his modesty is excessive in highlighting just this notion. There would be much more to say about object *a*, but what I have said is at least indicative. It is

27. S. Freud, "Sobre las trasposiciones de la pulsión, en particular del erotismo anal" ("On Transformations of Instinct as Exemplified in Anal Eroticism"), *O. C.*, *op. cit.*, vol. 17, pp. 125–133.

certainly about a loss, and the attempt at a reencounter with what has been lost through this object *a*. This means, finally, that the assumed relation with the object is not a relation with something new but it is always built on the trace or stroke (*trazo*) of an object constituted as lost. This seminar thematizes the list of objects *a*. Lacan names the breast, the excrements, the gaze, and the voice. You may find a relatively different list in "The Subversion of the Subject and Dialectic of Desire in the Freudian Unconscious," in *Ecrits I*.[28] What I have said is very "telegraphic," but we will have a chance to get into this topic in depth later on.

Q: Regarding Lacan's relationship with science, with respect to the non-relation between the latter and a certain object in order to define it from there, my question is whether it is really like that, since one might confuse object with concept. One thing would be to posit that the four fundamental concepts relate to four objects, but that is not what it is about, there are differences. In a way, that would be a positivistic reading. I ask myself then the following, when Lacan differentiates himself from science, is he doing so by identifying it with this positivistic reading, or does he recognize also other possible epistemological readings posited from the scientific perspective that claim that science constructs its objects from its concepts, that is, through differentiation? It is Khun's case, applied to physics, chemistry, etc. He establishes precisely that each scientific paradigm constructs its own world. What Galileo saw, Newton didn't. His objects had changed with the change in his conceptual framework. You can then establish different criteria of truth, and we would have to see whether the debate that emerges between science and psychoanalysis is not connected mainly to the fact that science is identified with positivism, and not with other trends. I don't know how Lacan sees this.

A: That is a very good question. It would take too long to answer it, but I can make at least a few comments. Freud starts his *Constructions*

---

28. In Seminar 10, *La angustia* (*Anxiety*) (unpublished), Lacan included the (lacking) phallic object as a fifth form—or "stage"—in the constitution of *a* (June 1, 1963). [I have not been able to find an English version of this seminar. The article mentioned is included in the English translation of *Ecrits* already cited.]

in Analysis with that apparently naive way peculiar to him (which actually possesses a considerable depth), pointing out that a common criticism of psychoanalysis is that which says, more or less, "Let's flip a coin; if it's heads, I win, if it's tails you lose." It is said that the analyst proceeds in this way when he considers that if the analysant (*analizante*) accepts an interpretation, the interpretation is true, and if he doesn't, he is resisting because the interpretation is true. What Freud wants to posit is whether our criterion of truth, following Khun's paradigms, has to be local, that is, has to refer to our discipline.

If we then take as our basis the question of interpretation, we find that there are "yeses" for a multitude of motives, and "noes" for a similar amount, to the extent that if there is an effect of truth in the interpretation, Freud will discover it through the subsequent associations of the analysant, and not through the specific yes or no. For if somebody locates the analyst in the locus of the ideal in the transference, that person will say yes to anything the analyst says, and that yes does no more than foster a definite stagnating place in the transference. If the analyst doesn't realize that this is what is actually happening, he will think that everything is working out and going in the right direction, when the analysant is actually situated in an idealizing stagnation. If, on the contrary, the analysant is taken by negativism, that is, he is saying no to everything (which may sometimes occur due to the passion of hatred), his desire weakening, the analyst may think that his behavior is entirely wrong.

Our field is a praxis and is not, therefore, constrained to theoretical consistency. Yet there is even more, for Lacan says, "truth has the structure of fiction,"[29] which refers to the fact that the speaker, insofar as he is such, fictionalizes. This is clearly connected to the field of literary fiction. Could one say about a novel whether or not it is true? Wouldn't it seem, in any case, that a different dimension is generated here? Of course, but you may say that this is a lateral answer, since through it we would end up stating that psychoanalysis is, after all, something of the order of the

---

29. J. Lacan, "El psicoanálisis y su enseñanza" ("Psychoanalysis and Its Teachings"), in *Ecrits II, op. cit.*, p. 174. [I have not been able to find an English translation.]

literary, namely, an artistic practice. Nonetheless, interpretation is not true or untrue in itself. Lacan speaks of "effects of truth." This means that what is important is that interpretation may provoke the truth in the analysant to emerge. Yet in addition, to make matters worse, truth (and this is another aphorism) is half-said. This means that the demand to the patient that he "swear to tell the truth, all the truth, and nothing but the truth," is nothing but an illusion created by juridical discourse. Truth is, precisely, not-all. It will be barely half-said, and this is decisively due to the action of primal repression. If somebody does not say all, or says not-all, it is not a matter of good or bad will.

As you can see, there is a series of variables that may or may not enter easily into the question of regional rationality—a position that Althusser also maintained at some point, and I think that at least in this issue it would coincide with Thomas Khun's conception of paradigms. The "latest" Lacan, for instance, the one of the 1975 lectures and interviews, regarding the issue of whether or not psychoanalysis is a science, stated at the Massachusetts Institute of Technology that it is actually "a practice."[30] In a text I worked on in my 1981 book *Del corpus freudolacaniano (On the Freudian-Lacanian Corpus)*, I tried to reflect on the meaning of such a position. Why did he say "a practice" and not "a science"? What could seem like a chaotic, nonregulated practicism was not that at all. Since Lacan never used words without reason, I resorted to the etymological dictionary. "Practice" comes from the Greek *praktikós*, which means, first, "to act," and second, "to converse." This becomes very clear in Portuguese, since *prática* means both practice, as we understand this term in Spanish, and conversation (*plática*).

Well, Lacan will go so far as to tell us even more, namely, that it is in this *space* of "practice" where, maybe, the only crucial difference between psychoanalysis and a trait of scientific discourse that extends from such a discourse to others is promoted. Yes, because it is the only place where somebody is asked to endure his own silly prattle. One of the most common statements made by analysants is, "I don't come here to talk

---

30. J. Lacan, "Conférences et entretiens dans des universités nord-américaines," *Scilicet*, 6/7, Seuil, Paris, 1976, p. 53. [I have not been able to find an English translation.]

about stupid things, but, look at the things I'm coming up with! This is not a problem, really, with the problems I have, to talk about such a thing!" It seems that there is an impulse to talk about "serious" and "important" things as defined by the analysis of content, when Lacan maintains that psychoanalysis is actually a practice of *bavardage*,[31] that is, of drivel, of *bêtise*,[32] of silliness.[33]

There precisely lies Freud's challenge, what is remarkable about the operational field he founded, in saying exactly this: "Come in, talk, and say silly things. That is how we will reach the core of your being." It is there that we may grasp how it is not a question of becoming metaphysical, of speaking of deep and very serious things in order to discover precisely what takes place in the uniqueness of an existence. When Lacan returns to the Freudian unconscious he insists repeatedly on this dimension of the stumble, of the fault, the crack that is generated within the homogeneous manifest discourse thanks to that "sillerile" (*tonteril*) irruption of the unconscious.

Another reference that relates to this question may be found in the unpublished 1969/70 Seminar 17, *El revés del psicoanálisis* (*The Other Side of Psychoanalysis*). In this seminar Lacan introduces the question of the four discourses, namely, that of the Master, that of the Hysteric (*lo Histérico*),[34] that of the University, and that of the Analyst. Lacan situates science on the side of the discourse of the Hysteric (*lo Histérico*), with which he means that it incites to knowledge. In this way, psychoanalysis results from the relation of the hysteric's desire (*el deseo de la histérica*) with Freud's desire, as Lacan expresses it in *The Four Fundamental Concepts of Psychoanalysis*. The hysteric (*la histérica*) is that who,

31. In Seminar 25, November 15, 1977 (unpublished).

32. In Seminar 20, *Encore*, Seuil, Paris, 1975, pp. 16–18. (The Spanish translation confuses "silliness" with "nonsense" (*necedad*) [*The Seminar of Jacques Lacan. On Feminine Sexuality, The Limits of Love and Knowledge. Book XX, Encore, 1972–1973*, trans. Bruce Fink, W. W. Norton, New York, 1998, pp. 13–15. Fink translates *bétise* as "stupidity or nonsense."]

33. Both terms in French in the original. (Translator's note)

34. As he will say in Chapter 2, Harari respects here Lacan's spelling so that the term *hysteric* is rendered neutral, *lo Histérico*, the condition of being hysteric, as opposed to *la histérica*, the feminine adjective, which would allude to a woman. Such a difference cannot be appreciated in English. (Translator's note)

even with the refined intrigue displayed by her usual way to behave (where the classic seduction feature usually becomes manifest), arouses the will to know from her place of nonknowledge (*no-saber*). In this sense I think this formulation is interesting, because rather than saying that science has answers, it says that if science fulfills its goal, it will rather stimulate the will to know what is still unknown (*no-sabido*).

Another free association on this matter: in Seminar 25, *Momento de concluir* (*Moment to Conclude*) (the second to last), Lacan enounces: "I had formerly said, 'I don't search, I find.'" With this phrase taken from Picasso and located almost at the beginning of Seminar 11, Lacan refuses to be labeled a researcher, because psychoanalysis is not about searching for something but about a haphazard encounter produced thanks to the *Tuché*. What matters is not what one went searching for but what appeared in an untimely way. That is how it happens with love, as I think we all know. It appears around the corner when one least expects it. I do not search, I find. Yet in *Moment to Conclude* Lacan rectifies: "Now I do not find, I search." This phrase was uttered in front of the Sorbonne's Law School audience, when Lacan was searching with the rings of string, trying to shape his teaching in terms of the Borromean knots. It seems that he had changed his attitude to one of somebody who wants to research the connection with a new field, albeit in terms of a very unique status assigned to the Borromean knot, as Lacan said of the latter that it was not a model (a simile or representation), but the structure, the Real. We can start to see here, I think, the problematic situation brought about by a statement of this caliber. I think that one way in which science takes up the challenge of Freudian subversion is by asking how a certain science is constituted, taking into account the fact that there is "desire of the . . ." (as Lacan will say). A new science emerges then in reference to the question of the subject, which is not that of subjectivity. Fine, there is, hence, the desire of the analyst. And what about the physicist's desire? The problem is that at the beginning a science, whichever it would be (it doesn't matter here if it is positivistic or not) is asubjective. It tries to minimize, or even to get rid of, the subject factor (which implies the subject's split). In Seminar 17, Lacan says ironically that science is an ideology of the suppression of the subject. This is an indirect attack to the alleged antinomy science/ideology. He also points out in that seminar that what is crucial in science—namely, to eliminate the subject—is an ideology, and that psychoanalysis is posited as a reintroduction of the subject dimension science is still trying to set aside.

Q: This is very complex, even polysemic, because on the one hand it's like that and on the other it's the opposite. In a way, Lacan also tries to eliminate subjectivity, as does science. What differentiates them is what happens to the subject. For Lacan, the subject is not related to subjectivity, and for science, subjectivity would be the opposite of objectivity, even though within science also objectivity is ceasing to be considered as that which is on the side of the object, and being thought as, for instance, the intersubjective.

A: I agree, but there is another point to consider, which is how the analyst is produced. The analyst is produced in the training analysis, in the analyst's own analysis. At one time Lacan will write "Training, analysis," by which he means that all psychoanalysis actually produces a psychoanalyst. This does not mean that each analysant will become a professional analyst, will make of analysis his way of life, but it does mean that whoever has undergone analysis has fulfilled the "requirement" that enables him to modify his subjective position. He could, if he wished, offer his being as support for transference phenomena, since he has transformed his listening conditions. This differs undoubtedly from the ways in which a scientist is constituted. Lacan will hence also insist on the fact that psychoanalysis is transmitted above all in a one-to-one situation, since what is privileged is the analyst's analysis. We thus highlight a differential aspect in the production of analysts, unlike the production of scientists. In the latter the scientist's being is not questioned as a constitutive sine qua non.

In sum, without wanting to close the matter, I will make another observation. Whether we want it or not, psychoanalysis has a marginal character, its condition is to be inside-outside, to be accepted-rejected systematically. Even though your kind consideration does not confirm this, I believe that present-day resistance against psychoanalysis is addressed particularly against Lacan. In a way, Freud is more or less accepted today because he has been washed and rinsed. Now, to refute this exclusively marginal character, we must note that psychoanalysis possesses the scientific ideal of the search for logical rigor, something the structure of psychoanalytic doctrine shares with science but, for the reasons we have just discussed, does not seem to be inserted within the field of what we may call science, be it positivistic or not. In other words, that such an affirmation includes also other trends, such as Khun's version of science, or that of the French productivist-historicist epistemology. To conclude, I would like to add that the fact that a particular field originates in the same status as a certain order (in this case, the scientific order) does not mean that it must be subsumed to that order.

Language, the Unconscious: The Cause, the Temporal Pulsation

In our previous meeting we presented a general introduction to Lacan's Seminar 11, positing some possible relations among Lacan's four fundamental concepts of psychoanalysis. Before I start to unfold in some detail the first of these concepts, I would like to return to a pending matter that stemmed from the very interesting exchange we had last class. This debate was truly productive, thanks to your participation, and it hinged on the relation between psychoanalysis and science. We pointed out how Lacan stated that the order of science substantively attempts to produce the same thing as psychoanalysis in the following sense: how the Real can be influenced—besides being induced—by the Symbolic. It is certainly a "tendentious" reading ("tendentious" in a positive way), because it strives to account for the primacy of the Symbolic order over the Real, a debatable issue, since stated in this way, it may suggest a reduction of the Real to the Symbolic, something that is certainly false. Yet regarding the analyst's goal, the problem lies in how to tackle the Real via the Symbolic. Thus is our praxis founded and its operational field legitimated.

There is another important concept whose consideration would serve to conclude our quick incursion through the articulation between science and psychoanalysis, namely, the analyst's desire. This idea cannot be found in Freud by any means. It belongs exclusively to Lacan's production, and the latter will attribute such relevance to this notion as to postulate it as the pivot of psychoanalysis. In other words, this concept denotes centrally what authorizes the support of a cure. Some, making a gross mistake, pretend that this concept corresponds in Lacan to what other authors since Freud have called countertransference. Nevertheless, it is necessary to note that where the conceptualization of countertransference ends—in the original: *Gegenubertragung*, reciprocal transference[1]—the analyst's desire appears. Freud's concept points to something of the same caliber—reciprocal, imaginary. Where reciprocal transference ends, then, there starts Lacan's conceptualization of the analyst's desire. If we translate this into a graph, we may establish an ideal limit:

Countertransference   /   Analyst's desire

Countertransference is that which stems from the analyst as a response, and hinders the latter's ability to listen to the analysant. The analyst's desire, instead, allows for analysis to develop, to endure, to get out of its impasses; in short, it allows analysis to circulate. The analyst's desire hence combats countertransference.

We must not confuse the analyst's desire with the desire to be an analyst, nor with the desire of a certain analyst who has a name and last name. It is, says Lacan, an objectifiable function. In any case, we could point out that it is the analysts' desire, namely, the desire to occupy that unique site which is that of being the support for the analysants' transferences.

In Seminar 8, entitled *La transferencia* (*Transference*),[2] Lacan tells us where this desire of the analyst is rooted. He writes there that "it is a stronger desire, it is a desire of death." In a somewhat cryptic way, this

---

1. R. Harari, *Textura y abordaje del inconsciente* (*The Texture of the Unconscious and Its Approach*), Trieb, Buenos Aires, 1977, pp. 211–212.

2. Or, to be more precise, *La transferencia en su disparidad subjetiva, su pretendida situación, sus excursiones técnicas* (*The Transference in Its Subjective Disparity, Its Pretended Situation, Its Technical Excursions*) (unpublished); the quote is from the March 8, 1961, class.

statement means that there is a desiderative dimension to the analyst—where we run into his specific sublimation—which is present in the fact of deciding to tolerate such a place. There is at stake here something more important than attending to the Other's desire. One may very well ask, Is the analyst concerned first of all with responding to the analysant's desire? Since desire is the desire of the Other, one might argue that the analyst's desire is a desire just like any other, and hence obsequious. Yet the ability to direct the cure will lie, conversely, in not responding to such a desire, by means, or in terms, of that desire of the Other, thus conquering the opportunity to articulate with the maintenance of the analyst's place.

For this is a place that, insofar as it is the place of the practice of the Real, is an impossible one. It can be constantly sustained, and it is precisely due both to the weakenings and to the return to that place that such a place may exist. Let us put it differently: if the analyst believes that he is an analyst all the time, one might affirm that he is immersed in a belief of paranoid overtones, due to the megalomaniac situation in which he recognizes himself and to his parallel certainty in his own identity. If he admits instead that countertransference hinders the analyst's desire, he will be able to fall once again into such a desire. Of course, this is a necessary albeit not sufficient condition. The four discourses (we will not expand on this right now) also enable us to understand how the analyst will inevitably occupy, besides his own place, the place of the Master's discourse, that of the Hysteric's discourse (*lo Histérico*), and that of the university discourse. The analyst wishes to seem what he is not, which implicates neither his subjectivity nor his affects, not even when he takes the place of the first-person pronoun who takes charge of the utterance—when he interprets from the place of the countertransference and only produces confessions that have little or no role in the direction of the analytic cure. For if we resort to the use of countertransference as an exception it is because of a tactical maneuver that is part of a strategy.

The analyst's desire entails a structure of interpretation in which the analyst "immerses" himself. In this way, he maintains no relationship whatsoever with an ineffable, unobjectionable, emotional countertransference. This desire goes against the belief that the analyst must orchestrate, and must operate with, the affects related to unprocessed remnants of his training analysis, which would lead one to think, undoubtedly, that such analysis has not "succeeded." In sum, countertransferentialists make the best of a bad thing. And deontologically, this . . .

Finally, to put a temporary end to the matter of science, we may recall that Lacan remarked that there is something decisive around the creation of psychoanalysis, namely, Freud's desire, articulated, certainly, to the hysteric's desire (*el deseo de la histérica*). In this regard you must have noted that in reference to another issue about hysteria I said, following the Lacanian spelling, *discours de l'Hystérique*, discourse of the Hysteric (*lo Histérico*), so that we may avoid the simplistic equation hysteria-woman.[3] Such a relation is linked to the origins of psychoanalysis but not to a biological sex, far from it. To write the prevalent trait of the discourse of the Hysteric we resort to the following matheme (used from Seminar 17 on):

$$\frac{\$}{a} \; \underset{\longleftarrow}{\overset{\longrightarrow}{}} \; \frac{S_1}{S_2}$$

impotence

"The" (*lo*) hysteric as agent addresses S_1, a Master signifier, to ask him or to inquire about a knowledge (*saber*) (S_2) concerning object *a*. The barred subject ($\$$) does not purport to a hysteric (*una histérica*), but to any desiring subject who asks the Master about a supposed knowledge (*saber*) about the object. This little matheme supports Lacan's reference to a discourse of the Hysteric (*lo Histérico*) and not of the obsessive, the phobic, or of any other clinical type we may think of. It is not a question of nosography, of pathological profiles, but an attitude regarding the discursive link at stake. To that end, it doesn't matter whether the patient *is*, for example, hysteric or obsessive; what matters is that the analytic device works. If it works, it must hystericize the analysant without using any particular maneuver.

By virtue of the analyst's desire as support, with its falls, its weakenings, and so on, the hystericization of the analysant takes place regardless

---

3. See note 34 in Chapter 1. (Translator's note)

of his particular pathology. In this way, the analysant will take the position of the inquisitive, the demanding one, which is indicated by the bar crossing the S. Lacan states that the origin of psychoanalysis has been the encounter between Freud's desire and the desire of his hysterics (*histéricas*), even if it isn't Isabel de R. or Emmy de N.—not those hysterics in particular but the condition of the Hysteric (*lo histérico*) that is structured from the questioning, the interrogation of the Master concerning his knowledge (*saber*).

Sometimes the Hysteric (*lo Histérico*) will even try to expose the castration of the Master himself by using arguments such as, "What you're telling me is of no use to me. It's not like that; you're always harping on the same thing." Those kinds of references have as their goal the undermining of the comfortable knowledge (*saber*) the Master pretends to have. That is why they have been, and still are, so enormously useful to the history and progress of psychoanalysis. The homologous unsatisfied desire of the Hysteric (*lo Histérico*)—and chronologically, of the hysterics (*las histéricas*)—is hence crucial to sustain the unusual "origin" of our discipline.

Having cleared up the matter of science in its relation to psychoanalysis (obviously, within the limits of this course), we will start with the first fundamental concept, that of the unconscious, so as to follow the order Lacan suggests. This is the classical fundamental concept of psychoanalysis, and I pointed out to you last time that it should not be considered the only one, since there is a reason why the seminar, in a dissenting way, postulates four of them. You will recall that we had stipulated certain links among them both in terms of a sort of helix similar to DNA and of an arrowed quadrangle. Well, circa 1964, speaking about the unconscious again while trying to say something new after Freud was quite daring; that is to say, if one meant to sustain a project that would not consist merely of a naive, reproductive, echolalic procedure. In our previous meeting I noted that we can all easily enounce different traits of the unconscious. We certainly repeat them acritically, in a descriptive way. We might even say that a certain vulgarized version of the unconscious is already part of the cultural heritage of a somewhat educated person. The matter lies then in what it is that Lacan will contribute to this concept that is both original and productive.

In the first place, we may advance a negative answer, that is, that the unconscious is something neither primitive nor primal. It is not the same as the subconscious either. We may find an example of this last meaning in a book many of us know, namely, *La Argentina del siglo XXI* (*The 21st Century Argentina*) by Rodolfo Terragno,[4] where the term subconscious is used.[5] The use of "subconscious" apparently does not respond to the fact that the author ignores that this is about the unconscious. It would, therefore, bear witness to a slip originated in the Enlightenment stance that permeates the whole book. Such a viewpoint tries to assume the existence of a subconscious, which means a diluted and diminished, a pale consciousness to which the actual consciousness may be superimposed or offered as alternative.

On the other hand, the term connotes that we are not dealing here with an active and efficient agency, but with a not very powerful one. Evidently, this view does not jibe with the more tragic and torn notion of the subject posited by psychoanalysis. The latter is not pessimistic, as some suggest; it simply takes into account the fact that the subject is not the master of his motivations. It does not subscribe to the belief that we are always going toward a promissory future, even if this may happen transitorily. In this sense, Lacan was quite skeptical. Proof of this is that in 1975 he affirmed that one of the effects of his teaching was to demonstrate that there is no progress, as what is gained on the one hand is lost on the other.[6] This is another way, finally, of lucidly taking castration into account.

The Freudian discovery involves calling attention to the crucial determination, the effective force of that which we will call *the unconscious (lo inconsciente).*[7] We should explain the reason for the neuter article. I may seem to be a perfectionist, but we must recall Freud's motto: "One starts by yielding in the matter of words and never knows where one might end." I vote then for *the (lo)* unconscious instead of *the (el)* unconscious. It is my impression—and this is also Etcheverry's view—

---

4. An Argentine politician, member of the Radical Party. (Translator's note)
5. R. Terragno, *op. cit.*, Sudamericana-Planeta, Buenos Aires, 1985, pp. 18–19.
6. J. Lacan "Conférences . . . ," *op. cit.*, p. 37.
7. See note 5 in Chapter 1. (Translator's note)

that *Das Unbewusste,*[8] translated as *lo* in Spanish, lends the term a very different sense from the one it has if we translate *el.* The crux of the matter lies in the substantification, the reification that occurs when one says *the (el)* unconscious.

In choosing *lo* I indicate that I may take certain aspects, certain angles, certain viewpoints of an object without exhausting all its facets. *The (el)* unconscious, on the other hand, usually evokes the bottom of a sack where elements, instincts, and affects lie. Many analysts hold these odd conceptions, founded on an idea of something that is receptive to more and more elements that enlarge this sort of depository. What will Lacan highlight as the fundamental trait of the unconscious in order to avoid this deviation into a "double sack"[9]? What he points out is already present in Freud, so that he only needed to look into the latter's texts with sagacity and intelligence. The Freudian concept concerning the mode of existence of the unconscious is *Gedanken,* that is, thoughts. We are dealing, therefore, with unconscious thoughts.

If we say the *(lo)* subconscious, the *(lo)* infraconscious or other similar terms, it is easy to postulate, at the same time, a relation of heterogeneity between that which this designation denotes, and consciousness, for instance, conscious thoughts on the one hand, and brutal instincts— "sub," "infra"—on the other. What Lacan remarks is that Freud claimed the existence of a relation of homogeneity between these orders. In this way, the unconscious is not heteroclite with respect to the *(lo)* conscious—there are dimly distinctive rules pertaining to each one, but not a substantialist difference. This decisive specification begins to stress a concept that will make its way in the Lacanian explication, namely, that of the signifier.

In this way, the chapter of the seminar entitled, *"El inconsciente freudiano y el nuestro"* ("The Freudian Unconscious and Ours") practically opens with the classic aphorism, "The unconscious is structured like a language" (*El inconsciente está estructurado como un lenguaje*). I

---

8. S. Freud, "Lo inconsciente," *O. C., op. cit.,* vol. 14, pp. 185–186. ["The Unconscious," p. 186.]

9. I am using here the same term Alan Sheridan uses to translate the French word *besace* (see note 1, Chapter 3). (Translator's note)

will suggest some changes to this statement. First, we will substitute *lo* for *el* unconscious. In addition, our language has a by no means small nuance for which we must be grateful and that French lacks, that is, the difference between *ser* and *estar*,[10] and this is an opportunity to make use of it. We may therefore affirm that it *is* (*es*) structured like a language. So instead of saying, "The (*el*) unconscious *is* (*está*) structured like a language," we will say, "The (*lo*) unconscious *is* (*es*) structured like a language." Now, we can see here how a paradox emerges. Indeed, the usual difference between *ser* and *estar* lies in the fact that transitoriness is a feature typical of *estar*, and permanence of *ser*. Here lies the paradox: If I transcribe "*está* . . . ," it suggests something finished, that "is done" (*ya está*). If I say instead "*es estructurado*" ("is structured"), I connote the idea of a dynamia, of a processing, so that *ser* and *estar* invert their typical meanings. Moreover, we must at least pick up this reference to productivity as the distinctive, elementary, and basal note about what the unconscious is. If we translate "the (*lo*) unconscious is (*es*) structured like a language," we are not dealing with something that has already been completed.

I thus retrieve first of all a defining element that Lacan does not fail to point out, namely, the synchrony of the unconscious; synchrony as opposed to, and not as excluding, diachrony. Synchrony means simultaneity—without *chronos*, without time. We may infer from the preceding statements that the steering of the cure is not limited only to what is already structured, insofar as it originates in the remote, diachronic past—that is, that belongs to the order of the successive. In claiming that the unconscious *is* (*es*) structured, we establish the idea of processing in the bosom of the chains of signifiers instead of the idea of a full, completed depository where we only have left, as a praxis, the extrac-

---

10. These are two forms of the verb "to be" that are used to indicate different meanings. *Ser* is used to express unchanging characteristics, provenance, etc., for instance, "*Ella es rubia,*" "She is blonde." *Estar* is used to convey states of mind and temporary conditions, for instance, "*Estoy muy cansado,*" "I'm very tired." The form *ser* is also the auxiliary verb used to conjugate the passive voice. This is the sense to which the author alludes here. At the same time, and this is part of the author's argument, *estar* is used in conjunction with the past participle to indicate the result of an action or change, as in "*la puerta está cerrada*" ("the door is closed"). This use of *estar* may give a sense of unchangeability. (Translator's note)

tion of the elements lying at the "bottom." The "*es*," in this case, entails the postulation of the space of the present as a possible novelty.

When he approaches the concept of the unconscious, Lacan points out (as was his view at the time) that if there is a pilot science of which we may draw notions and methods for the construction of our discipline, it is linguistics, which does not imply, of course, that psychoanalysis *is* a form of applied linguistics. In our last meeting we alluded to this topic when we mentioned Freud's own borrowings stated at the beginning of *Instincts and Their Vicissitudes*. It is necessary to draw notions and methods from other fields so as to found the order of a knowledge that is just emerging. Initially, Lacan wagered his attempt at formalization through linguistics when he said about the unconscious that it was "structured like a language." He does not argue that the unconscious is language, as some have wanted to impute to him. Rather, he highlights the relationship of "like a," whereby common structural laws are shared by the unconscious and by language— a homology that may enable us to apprehend the mechanisms of the unconscious. From there on, pondering the structural dimension of the unconscious (which is not, I repeat, linguistic) starts making sense.

We should point out now an objection I heard, not for the first time, when Lacan explained this topic in Caracas in 1980. A Venezuelan psychoanalyst replied to him that, according to Freud, the unconscious consists of representation-things, and the preconscious of representation-words. He reproached Lacan for ignoring this Freudian reference and for reducing everything strictly to the condition of the word. There seemed indeed to exist a clear-cut difference between both conceptions [what Freud postulated may be found in Chapter 7 of *Lo inconsciente* (The Unconscious)]. This analyst's reply sounded very consistent, but the problem is that he confused signifier and word, and nobody says that they are the same thing.

The signifier may be a word, but it also possesses, among other alternatives, a corporeal embodiment, as proved by the symptom. Is the signifier—and a signifying chain—not that which is em-bodied (what becomes flesh)?[11] This is what we verify when Freud interprets his

---

11. The word used by the author is *encarnarse*, and in scanning it he obtains *en-carnarse*. *Carne* in Spanish means "flesh." (Translator's note)

analysant's chest pain based on a phrase about a certain affront that she had experienced as if it had been a stab to the heart. Another similar example with the same patient—Cecilia M.—refers to the way in which a phrase she endured felt like being slapped, and it brought about an alleged "trigeminal neuralgia."[12] We may draw a very long list of possible signifiers I once called "crystallized syntagm."[13] Several terms with a bodily reference are crystallized that bear among them a solidary relation, and become flesh.[14]

The mechanism of hysterical conversion circulates in this way. This signifier, therefore, is not a word either in the sense of something audible or within the order of interlocution. On the contrary, it is a silent and censored way in which something strives to be said, keeping nonetheless its disguise as bodily conversion. More precisely, Freud says that the unconscious—this is what schizophrenia indicates—is concerned with treating the word as a thing. In this way, the word is treated in its strict signifying aspect. The confusion emerges actually when it is affirmed that the unconscious is structured by images, an exclusively fantasmatic conception of the unconscious as is, for example, the Kleinian conception. From such perspective, Kleinian psychoanalysts often criticize Lacan due to a poorly processed comprehension of what the differentiation between the concept of the signifier and its diverse phenomenic manifestations implies. They hence insist on the fact that the unconscious is constituted by images and the preconscious by words.

Instead, Freud highlights the nonheteroclite, as we said before. He will thus write in Chapter 5 of *Lo inconsciente* (*The Unconscious*) that what is specific of such an instance is the primary process, which consists of two operations—displacement and condensation—that are also present, albeit dimmed, in the workings of the preconscious.[15] Freud never says that these operations cancel each other, or that there exists a different type of legality that is categorically other. If, as a mere

---

12. S. Freud, *Estudios sobre la histeria*, O. C., vol. 2, pp. 188–194. [*Studies on Hysteria*, pp. 176–181.]

13. R. Harari, *El objeto de la operación del psicólogo* (*The Object of the Psychologist's Operation*), Nueva Visión, Buenos Aires, 1976, 2nd ed., pp. 53–62.

14. See note 11. (Translator's note)

15. S. Freud, O. C., *op. cit.*, vol. 14, pp. 185–186. [p. 186.]

phenomenologist, he stated that we are dealing with the image in one case and the word in the other, he would face a number of difficulties, since it is well known (the semiologists have studied it quite well) that the image presents some unsolvable problems.[16]

For instance, where do we cut an image? What is the discrete, discontinuous, separable aspect of the image? What happens is that the image possesses a different kind of legality from that of the word, due to the indiscernible nature of its terms. To the immediate intuition, the image seems easy to articulate—we can divide it, bisect it, and we think we can identify the last elements that constitute it. These, however, have nothing to do with phonemes, which are objectifiable and do not depend, as does the image, on each person's perspective. How can we then structure what is indiscernible?

Neither within the unconscious are we dealing with a relation of mere homophony, that is, between words of a similar sound. Many of the examples we read in Freud's work and we use in our everyday clinical practice are homophonous, others are not. Faced with this situation, one might fall into the trap of the meaning or, conversely, establish a different kind of signifying connection. Let us take part of the classic first chapter of *The Psychopathology of Everyday Life*, to which Lacan has returned so often. In that chapter Freud recalls how he forgot the name of the painter of the frescoes at the Orvieto cathedral, Luca Signorelli, and remembered instead, by substitution, Botticelli and Boltraffio, while realizing that he was doubly mistaken. Between Signor*elli* and Bottic*elli* there exists an evident homophony, and that contributes to the appearance of one term in the other's stead. Now, *Bo*tticelli also emerges, through association, by means of a place called *Bo*snia (actually, Bosnia-Herzegovina). Herzegovina and Botticelli are not in a relation of homophony even though a signifying connection does exist:

16. VARIOS, *Análisis de las imágenes* (*Image Analysis*), Tiempo Contemporáneo, Buenos Aires, 1973.

And since there is no connection from a strictly homophonous perspective, we must consider Bosnia-Herzegovina as *one* signifier.

: *one* signifier

There is a concatenation here from the point of view of contiguity, what in rhetoric is called metonymy, a term Lacan incorporates. This process, this operating principle, claims Lacan, is the same one Freud has called displacement.

As you can appreciate in these few remarks, the problem of the signifier is quite more complex than Ferdinand de Saussure shows. The latter was the one who started this matter when he pointed out in his *Curso de lingüística general* that the signifier is the acoustic image of a word (or sign).[17] This formulation entails from the beginning the problem of the acoustic tied to that of the image. Lacan, in turn, will offer a different, much stranger definition of the signifier. He will say that the signifier "is what represents a subject for another signifier."

In our previous meeting we recalled that despite our being used to definitions, Lacan is implacable in their regard. He demolishes them with hermetic sayings that are, on top of that, circular and paradoxical, as we shall see. Lacan warns us then that the subject does not possess signifiers located in that *cul de sac*[18] to which we referred before. He notes that, on the contrary, the subject is an effect of the signifier. To clarify this statement, he makes a detour by alluding to Claude Lévi-Strauss's *El pensamiento salvaje* (*The Savage Mind*).

It is worth digressing a bit here. This work by the French anthropologist is related, in the same connective style as Bosnia-Herzegovina, to another text by the same author, namely, *El totemismo de la actualidad*

17. F. de Saussure, *Curso de lingüística general*, Losada, Buenos Aires, 1967, pp. 129 ff. [English edition: *Course in General Linguistics*, Wade Baskin, trans., McGraw-Hill, New York, 1965.

18. In French in the original. (Translator's note)

(*Totemism*).[19] I believe both works constitute an indispensable reading for any psychoanalyst. Some hasty readers took from *Totemism* only the critique Lévi-Strauss expresses about Freud's *Totem and Taboo*. The anthropologist states that what Freud affirms there is erroneous, since it cannot be verified from an anthropological perspective. We may, however, think of *Totem and Taboo* as nothing but a primal myth, and Lacan helps us do so. We are talking here about clinical practice, not about anthropology, and that is why this is a datum that recurs systematically in our everyday practice.

Returning to the issue that interests us here, let us say that Lévi-Strauss shows in *Totemism* that we may pick elements from nature—animals or plants—and elevate them to the category of signifiers in order to organize sets. If, for instance, we apply this procedure to kinship structures, we may say that if I am born from a certain father and mother, I will be a white bear. If I am a white bear, such membership will grant me a certain place in relation both to those who are white bears and to those who are not. It might give me the chance, or force me, to look for a wife within my own clan, or contrariwise, if there is a prohibition to do that, it will thrust me into exogamy. There is, therefore, a system of relations that preexists the birth of the subject and places him in a position with no chance of escape, because that system of relations constitutes him, shaping his own relations.

A signifying order exists logically prior to the subject, who "is entered" into this system—the subject does not incorporate it, as the theory of language acquisition maintains. The topic of language acquisition pertains to developmental psychology, and has nothing to do with what the foundation of a subject by the signifier implies. Such a theory, without accounting for the fact that the subject is an effect of the signifier, confines itself to pointing out "unobjectionably" how the subject "learns how to speak." The subject then is what represents one signifier for another signifier—a formula that, as we can see, is very similar to the preceding one. As a consequence, related definitions emerge, namely, that of the

---

19. C. Lévi-Strauss, *op. cit.*, Fondo de Cultura Económica, México, 1964 and 1965, respectively. [Chicago: University of Chicago Press, 1966, and Boston: Beacon Press, 1963.]

subject and that of the signifier. It could not be otherwise, since what it attempts to specify is that both refer to a homogeneous order.

A conception such as this one definitely surpasses the idea that one holds within oneself images, words, or whatever, since this conception is an imaginary reference by someone who recognizes himself as an I. Instead, the subject is nothing but an effect of the signifier once he has been seized by that order Other, which preexists him and calls for him in an unappealable way. To say it along with Heidegger, it is not that I speak, but that I am being spoken. I think I speak, but when I do, I have no choice but to appeal to all the conventions of a language I have neither created nor determined. If I modify them globally in the semantic and syntactic fields, it will very likely be at the cost of schizophrenia. Yet what a letdown! Schizophrenia also follows the rules of language when, for instance, it creates neologisms.

There is a very graphic example of what Lacan wants to demonstrate when he points out the splitting that takes place when one counts oneself as someone who is part of a certain set when one is, at the same time, the person who recognizes oneself saying that. Such is the case of the child who states, "I have three brothers: Pablo, Ernesto, and me." Since the child is naming the three brothers, we can maintain that it is a discourse of an Other. It becomes necessary here to distinguish between an order of the statement and an order of the utterance, which somehow collide, without canceling the phrase's truth effect—the three are being counted, and there is an I who counts.

Let us move on to another example of incorporation *into* language, that is, that of "the boy—meaning himself—wants" something. When the child says this, it might be that he is reproducing verbatim something the mother said to the father. We may detect here something similar to what can be frequently noticed in the delirious form of schizophrenia, when comments such as "They are reading my thoughts" or "They are stealing my thoughts" are uttered. It is indeed the case, since thoughts are primordially the Other's. In these instances, the collapse brought about the loss of sameness, of the patient's imaginary identity. It is, therefore, as if thoughts "returned" to their place of origin, to the realm of the Other.

In relation to the concept of the unconscious there is a very striking and subversive matter—that is what this is about, the subversion of the subject[20]—that Lacan uses as a point of departure, namely, that of the cause. Here we must follow Lacan's reasoning to the letter, line by line, and linger particularly over the philosophic discussion regarding the notion of cause since, to my knowledge, a series of hindering misinterpretations exist as to such notion. I will make two specifications on this topic. (If you read the entries on cause and causality in a dictionary of philosophy, you will get a preliminary overview of this issue.)

The seminar distinguishes first between "cause" and "law." It remarks that concerning the law there is no major objection in endorsing it. When the idea of cause is raised, conversely, there is always something in the middle that does not work. There is a sort of missing link (my term) that indicates a fault in the intelligibility of the cause. Lacan offers the following example: movement, the phases of the moon, affects the tides; the phases are their cause. This is something well known that can be recognized and stated. Yet somebody like Hume may appear who will entirely call into question the existence of the cause. He will say that a connection exists between two facts—one happens before and the other one afterward—but to affirm that one engenders the other would mean falling into a trap, confirmed by the introduction of the word *cause*. Hume concludes that only simple successiveness exists.

"The Etiology of Hysteria" is a truly remarkable text that helps us understand how Freud thought about the question of the cause. In certain observations made as he writes, with apparent naïveté, but with a considerable rigor indeed, Freud teaches us that analysants are almost always victims of a reasoning of the type *post hoc, ergo propter hoc* (after something, and hence because of something), which is precisely that to which Hume was referring. It is a common belief that since a certain event *b* took place after an event *a*, it is *a* that engendered *b*. We can detect this type of reasoning very clearly among our analysants, especially when they are positing causal relations that do not belong in the imaginary-symbolic code of reality. Freud advances even the idea that

---

20. J. Lacan, "Subversión del sujeto y dialéctica del deseo en [lo] inconsciente freudiano," *Escritos I*, Siglo XXI, México, 1976, pp. 305–309. [English translation: "The Subversion of the Subject and Dialectic of Desire in the Freudian Unconscious," in *Ecrits: A Selection*, trans. A. Sheridan, W. W. Norton, New York, 1977, pp. 318–322.]

hysteric susceptibility and hyperirritability are due to a slippage between cause and effect.

Freud wrote three texts between 1895 and 1898, namely, "The Etiology of Hysteria" (the one I have already quoted), "Sexuality in the Etiology of the Neuroses," and "Heredity and the Etiology of the Neuroses."[21] In all of them we may verify how Freud will unravel in a plain and sometimes "medical" style that which Lacan will theorize admirably many years later. Freud explores whether there are accidental, specific, determining causes, in short, a myriad of possible causes. Yet what is most interesting, in my view, is the passage where Freud asserts that causality must be conceived as a genealogic tree. It is undoubtedly in comparisons such as this one where the mark of genius is sealed, that is, a tree where even—see what he is thinking—the members of the same family intermarry. In this schema, Freud foresees the linkages that may exist among the various factors.

I was amused when I came across this again a few years ago, when I was already familiar with Lacan's work, because what Freud suggests is in the order of what Lacan elaborated within, or from the perspective of, the graph theory.[22] In this way, and after the apparent Freudian candor, the determining character of the sexual is established, and with an example that admits no less than the eventuality of incest. The text is prior to any allusion to Oedipus, which only takes place around October 1897. Freud was elucidating the way in which sexual determination plays a role, even though his orientation back then was more empiricist (the occurrence of the patient's seduction during her childhood, the consequent mounting of excitation, and so on). On the other hand, this sexuality that comprises the possibility of marriage among the members of the same family is, undoubtedly, a very different thing from the initial seduction theory.

---

21. *O. C.*, *op. cit.*, vol. 3, pp. 141–156, 185–218, and 251–276 [191–221, 263–285, and 141–156].

22. R. Wilson, *Introducción a la teoría de los grafos*, Alianza, Madrid, 1983, pp. 64–82. [Originally published in English as *Introduction to Graph Theory*, Academic Press, New York, 1972]

These precedents say much more, in my view, about the way in which Freud apprehended the question of causality than the famous complementary series. At universities, save for meritorious exceptions, professors tend to assign the corresponding chapters in the *Lecciones introductorias al psicoanálisis* (*Introductory Lectures on Psychoanalysis*) to illustrate the Freudian conception of causality.[23] Yet this way of thinking about causality by means of the genealogic tree already possesses what Lacan will thematize by stating that there is no cause but that of what limps, that is, of what isn't working, what isn't going well, in French, *ça [qui] ne marche pas.*[24] There emerges here the dimension of the cause along with a question, namely, what is it that doesn't go well? We will mathematize it in the following way: Α, a notation that Lacan uses to write the unconscious.[25]

Besides postulating the dimension of the cause, such a question implies that the unconscious must be posited in relation to the dimension of *hiatusness* (*hiancia*), a neologism created by Tomás Segovia, the translator of Lacan's *Ecrits* into Spanish, in order to transpose *béance.*[26] What exists and is mentioned in the Spanish dictionary is the term *hiato* (hiatus), that is, gap, crack, and within the same semantic field, *hiante*, a verse in which hiatuses, cuts, may be identified. Relating cause and *hiatusness* (*hiancia*) entails arguing that the unconscious is located within an order of the cut, of the slit, and of a consequent closing.

The fact is that one of Freud's presumed—and truly brilliant—naïvetés claims that psychoanalysis has as its goal to block mnemic lacunae. We may start to transpose this affirmation into a graph in the following way:

---

23. S. Freud, *O. C. op. cit.*, vol. 16, pp. 316–333 [pp. 339–357].

24. The pun with the verb "to limp" works both in French and in Spanish but not in English. (Translator's note)

25. J. Lacan, seminar 10, *La Angustia* (*Anxiety*), *op. cit.*, class of January 13, 1963.

26. Alan Sheridan translates *béance* as "opening." However, I have respected Harari's use of the Spanish neologism in this translation. (Translator's note)

In a discontinuity of the type land-lacuna-land,[27] psychoanalysis would advocate the establishment of a continuous order:

If we consider the word *lacuna* as a literal, not a metaphoric signifier, the blocking of mnemic lacunae postulates as its first step the identification of certain cuts. We are then faced with the hiatusness (*hiancia*):

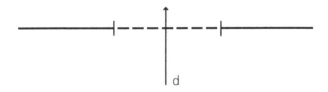

In these places where there is a cut we may observe an opening through which the order of desire will filter:

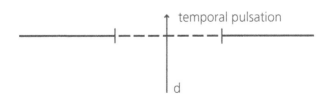

The dimension of the cause appears as a question about that which bursts in unexpectedly. We should recall here that if the unconscious alludes to a regime that resists, its appearance, therefore, will not be simple or direct. In general, it emerges through an effect of surprise or astonishment—as Theodor Reik had once pointed out, Lacan recalls. The moment of the opening—when the lacuna, the cut, is produced—is regulated according to a temporal pulsation. Indeed, the opening is immediately succeeded by a closing:

27. In Spanish, the word *laguna* means both "lacuna" and "lagoon." (Translator's note)

The presence of the unconscious is fleeting. That is why we cannot in any way conceive of it as a sort of extended second meaning that would authorize the steering of the cure in the manner of Ping-Pong. According to this view (which we discussed last class) the unconscious is always hidden "under" every act, where the corresponding unconscious fantasy is lodged; this constitutes, typically, the Kleinian approach. The logical conclusion, of course, is that everything may be interpreted.

With more pertinence and rigor, Lacan indicates certain sparkling moments that may be remarked, for example, through a scanned intervention. *Scansion* is another term Lacan draws from poetics and linguistics, which consists, for instance, in the following operation:

re-cutting (*re-corte*)

I have written, precisely, a word that indicates what scansion means, namely, a recutting (*recorte*), a cutting again.[28] "Scansion" means that the unconscious is neither a co-meaning nor a coextensive meaning that is constantly present. It is not a different meaning words possess that the analyst may use to play with them, since it relates to the fact that, in the first place, the subject remains as if "trampled on" by the signifier. The subject can't be quite sure of himself when the field of the Other appears under the shape of what Lacan calls the unconscious, that is, the discourse of the Other. We will sometimes find a fairly common mistake—it will be said that the Other is the unconscious. This is not the case. The unconscious is the discourse of the Other. The Other, in its strict sense, is the site of the treasure of signifiers. The metaphor must be understood literally. We may think of a virtual chest where signifiers "are," even though it obviously does not denote an empirical space, a *res extensa*, as Descartes would put it.

Going back to the temporal pulsation, we must note that it constitutes a time of emergence where that which is not going well may appear. "This is not what I wanted to say," the analysant will say. "Why did this come out of my mouth (*por qué me salió esto*)? It must be

---

28. This play on words is untranslatable. In Spanish, *recortar* literally means to cut out, and a *recorte* is a cutout. (Translator's note)

because . . ." References will emerge later on to all the causalities that may occur to him, the same ones, in fact, that philosophers have systematically classified. Immediately afterward, Lacan's argument will rely on Freud, affirming that the unconscious is not what determines neurosis. Could we say that the latter is determined by humoral problems, or by something connected to biology? No, for the scope of the Freudian statement indicates that what the unconscious does is show the hiatusness (*hiancia*) through which neurosis connects with something of the order of the Real:

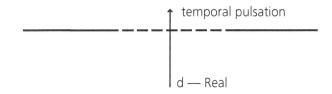

Hence, the real of desire. This thesis might seem heretic because we generally tie desire to the signifier, which does not belong to the register of the Real, of course, but of the Symbolic. Yet we must be able to account for the reason why Freud says that desire is indestructible (a characterization written in passing in *La interpretación de los sueños* (*The Interpretation of Dreams*).[29] If desire is indestructible—that is, the Real is irreducible—that means that it outlives the subject. This does not mean that the subject owns his desire, but that desire owns him. Even if he dies, desire continues. It uses a relay system and endures in other subjects. Within the order of the transindividual, we must not confuse this fact with reincarnation, metempsychosis, or anything like that. It means simply that we must think of desire in terms of the desire of the Other.

In this way, when in "The Function and Field of Speech . . ." Lacan defines the unconscious as transindividual,[30] he is asserting precisely that the unconscious traverses the subjects, thus conceiving of an order

29. *O. C., op. cit.*, vol. 5, pp. 545–546. [p. 553. There is another reference to this feature of desire in a footnote on p. 604.]

30. *Escritos I, op. cit.*, p. 79. ["The Function and Field of Speech and Language in Psychoanalysis," *op. cit.*, p. 49.]

that neither is situated nor can be located in any mind. As the author will ironically observe elsewhere, the unconscious is not a little man, a homunculus located in the mind. Since it entails a long-lasting dimension, desire possesses the traits of a duration other than the biological duration of a certain individual. Concerning duration, Lacan will add another point, namely, that of the terms that constitute what he calls logical time, opposite to (chronological) duration. Logical time encompasses:

1. The moment of seeing

2. The stage of understanding

3. The moment to conclude

This is how Lacan describes it in "El tiempo lógico y el aserto de certidumbre anticipada,"[31] an essay included in the *Escritos*.[32] The author returns to this exposition in Seminar 11 and in many other occasions. In the seminar he states that duration founds things, for a thing is that which remains identical to itself during a certain amount of time. Such definition is certainly fairly elementary. We need instead an operating principle that will account for the pulsation, for the heartbeat or the blinking of the eyes, of the vanishing appearance of the unconscious in such a way that we may be able to corner it in a non-"thingist" (*cosista*) temporal dimension. In actuality, if we reflect on such a pulsation in terms of the causal hiatusness (*hiancia*), we will not have any trouble. It is the passage from the moment of seeing—the irruption of the event, of the formation that dumbfounds—and the terminal moment, that of the immediate closing that we know as the moment to conclude. Then the stage of understanding will come:

31. "Logical Time and the Assertion of Anticipated Certainty: A New Sophism," trans. B. Fink and M. Silver, in E. Ragland-Sullivan, ed. *Newsletter of the Freudian Field*, vol. 2, 1988. (Translator's note)

32. J. Lacan, *Escritos I, op. cit.*, pp. 21–36.

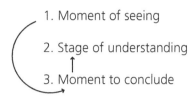

1. Moment of seeing

2. Stage of understanding

3. Moment to conclude

Even if it seems obtuse, this conception bears inestimable consequences for clinical practice. For instance, this is what happens with the conceptualization of the Freudian *Ducharbeitung* (working-through) beyond the famous Anglo-Saxon insight.[33] Insight may connote the moment of seeing—"inner vision"—but as a notion, analysts go as far as to use it to sustain facts such as the long duration of the sessions, since, they say, that is how the analysant will understand what has emerged, what he has internally seen.

Conversely, Lacan teaches us that a moment to conclude may precipitate the stage of understanding. In other words, cutting the session, for instance, may favor, stimulate, and propitiate the stage of understanding outside the session. Yet again: the session does not end with its cut. If we claimed otherwise, we would be attending only to chronological time. The session continues, and Freud said this to us crossing all the tees: When a person is in analysis, his whole life is placed in relation to this situation. Analysis is not limited to what happens during the classic fifty minutes, which, on the other hand, do not respect the time of the unconscious. When the International Psychoanalytic Association (IPA) reproached Lacan for conducting short sessions, pointing out that others should not do what he did, he answered, "Do what I do, do not imitate me." As you can see, this is an aporia worthy of his clinical perspicacity to face the demand.

Short sessions are usually condemned with the argument that the unconscious needs time to speak at length. We might ask ourselves then, which time are we talking about, logical or chronological? It is in this differentiation that the cut relies, insofar as it precipitates the possibility for the stage of understanding. The other psychoanalysis functions

---

33. In English in the original. (Translator's note)

in the manner of the question, How are we going to end the session if the analysant has not understood yet? which conveys an obsessive, symmetrical, domesticating idea, namely, that everything in analysis must be understood. This way of thinking derives from the University discourse.

What takes place in such ideology is that the subsequent time— that which, they say, would allow for the working-through to take place— succeeds in neutralizing or sterilizing those interpretations that disturb the analysant's subjective position. We may characterize this time that the other psychoanalysis wants to devote to the assimilation of inter- pretations within what Lacan very cleverly called the "horror of the act," of the analyst's act. It is as though we were apologizing for what we have said, even though—or because—we have verbalized something that bears an effect of truth. There occurs then a phenomenon of attenuation, of sedation of the beneficially subversive effect of the analyst's speech (*habla*).

The emphasis on the working-through thus understood results in a sort of punctual remembrance on the part of the analysant who in the following session will have in mind, will rememorate, will carry out a whole exercise that will be as much, or more, about learning new imagi- nary meanings than about a true analysis. In this situation, the analysant will express something of this sort: "I already know all that about my- self, but look at what is still happening to me." Let us recall what Freud taught us in the case of little Hans, namely, that a good analysis is not remembered.

If, on the contrary, we believe that our goal is to provide the analysant with an increasing number of meanings—meanings upon meanings—the failed analysis is reduced to remaining in the same neu- rotic dimension for which the analysant is consulting us. In actuality, the problem lies in the fact that the analysant does not lack meanings but wants to face the possibility of nonsense, and in helping him in his effort lies our role. The issue of the duration of the sessions—of the cut— goes beyond claims about the amount of time. In this way, we will find practicing analysts who will demand that certain things not be inter- preted at the end of the session to prevent the analysant from leaving in anxiety. It is true that we must know how to administer anxiety—

the psychoanalyst's task is not an exercise in sadism. Yet elevating such a claim to the status of a universal law reduces psychoanalysis to a mere habit that tends to preserve good manners.

If we do not disturb the status of the analysant, we establish a pseudoanalysis that may last years and years with nothing taking place except the admittance of more and more imaginary meanings. This task will have an excellent outlook (*panorama*)[34] (we might say, an excellent psychological map), but it is empty speech (*habla*), as Lacan points out in the *Discurso de Roma* ("The Rome Report")[35]—an empty speech in which the analysant is not at all implicated nor questioned in his being.

QUESTIONS AND ANSWERS

They ask me whether what I have just recounted articulates only with the cutting of the sessions. Definitely not. The problem lies in finding the reasons for the cut insofar as it is an efficient resource for the analyst, for we need to clarify what serves as foundation for the analyst's praxis—this is undoubtedly what Lacan posits in the seminar—by questioning each of the elements that comprise it.

There are other aspects to keep in mind. One of them is that of the caretaking function (*maternaje*), related to the conception of the analyst as container, that is, the one who, in the manner of the mother–child relationship, covers up, offers a sort of cover (*cobertura*) to the person in analysis. For instance, an analysant considered that she "had the week covered" because she had sessions Mondays, Wednesdays, and Fridays. I tried to break that imaginarization by cutting the (suspiciously "balanced") periodicity that validated this type of assumption.[36] The analyst's role is not that of being a container, but as Lacan used to say, that of being the semblance of the object-cause of desire.

---

34. The word *panorama* in Spanish means both "panorama" and "outlook," and thus the play with the word *map*. (Translator's note)

35. The jargon designation for "The Function and Field of Speech . . ."

36. R. Harari, "El desengaño . . . o el desamor" (Disillusion or Lovelessness), *Discurrir el psicoanálisis* (*Pondering Psychoanalysis*), Nueva Visión, Buenos Aires, 1986, pp. 182–190.

We must aim for the analysant to articulate himself to his desire, not to new meanings. That is why we often try (why not) to generate the void characteristic of the object-cause of desire by means of silence. In relation to Kleinian analysts, one tends to value silence—and hence words—more. When we speak it is only because we have something to say. A container tries instead to acknowledge what the analysant is saying. This attitude is not exclusive to Kleinians but is also present in the modern versions of self psychology (e.g., Heinz Kohut, as we can see in his books *Análisis del self* and *La restauración del sí mismo*).[37] Kohutianism, along with the trend inspired by Anna Freud, insists on creating a favorable condition prior to the installation of the analytic artifice. In my view, this trend is linked to the theme of maternal care and mental health. We cannot, we must not, forget the Anglo-Saxon origin of Margaret Ribble, John Bowlby, and all those who highlighted the importance of the mother in all of what concerns the child's emotional balance.

Establishing the possible link between the empiricist tendency (always dominant in the "island" and its by-products) and the caretaking function (*maternaje*), almost ironically designated as "container," may then be a valid path toward elucidation. There are those in our country who also follow this Anglo-Saxon course—they attend to this hypothetical maternal function of covering up, covering, and protecting. If they succeed in exerting this function, they will also attain at the same time the certain infantilization of the analysant.

When one conducts a cure, and wagers, in the Lacanian manner, on time to understand and not on understanding in the speculative mode, there is an ethics at play. Such an ethics will apprehend what it might mean to forget the sessions and the sessions' so-called topics in a different way, for working-through does not depend, as one might naively think, on coming back to a certain issue again and again. If the working-through has occurred, therefore, we will only find out *après-coup*, a posteriori,[38] as Lacan has taught us. A very elementary datum on this

---

37. English original editions: *The Analysis of the Self: A Systematic Approach to the Psychoanalytic Treatment of Narcissistic Personality Disorders*, International Universities Press, New York, 1971, and *The Restoration of the Self*, International Universities Press, New York, 1977. (Translator's note)

38. In French in the original. (Translator's note)

topic will emerge in the analysant's discourse when a problem so far dramatically insistent dissipates unexpectedly. For instance, when the analysant says to us, "I spoke about . . . for so long! It was a big deal for me, and then one fine day it disappeared. I try to trace what happened, what you said to me, what I said . . . and I really don't know." There lies the analytic effect. This is not the case when the analysant says, instead, "I understood that that time, when my father beat me, my mother came, and . . ." I show it *in extremis* so that you may grasp that a working-through such as this one has no other fate than serving to build lovely castles in the air.

Q: Could you explain the term *working-through* as it appears in Freud, and what Lacan has to say in that regard?

A: It would be good to read "Recuerdo, repetición y elaboración" ("Remembering, Repeating, and Working Through").[39] We might note here that the term *working-through*—which is the translation of *Durcharbeitung*, as I already mentioned—must be differentiated from that which appeared in the old Spanish version of Freud's works as "*elaboración onírica*" (oneiric working-through) as the proposed translation of *Traumarbeit* (literally, dream work). Nonetheless, working-through (*elaboración-perlaboración*) is also a matter of work, yet certainly with different consequences from those derived from the mere act of dreaming. In short, the analytic artifice consists in putting the analysant to work by establishing the rule of free association, knowing in advance that it will be transgressed. If we focus the question on the Freudian text, three elements stand out, namely, those of the title. That is the case also with "*Inhibición, síntoma y angustia*" ("Inhibitions, Symptoms, and Anxiety"). What do these articulations imply? Lacan taught us not to process these concepts separately but to attend to the suggested triangulation.

Durcharbeitung is translated as working-through in the English version. Lacan, in turn, will name it "the work of the transference."[40] If

---

39. S. Freud, *op. cit.*, vol. 12, pp. 145–157 [pp. 145–156].

40. J. Lacan, "*La dirección de la cura y los principios de su poder*," *Escritos I*, *op. cit.*, p. 261. ["The Direction of the Treatment and the Principle of Its Power," in *Ecrits. A Selection, op. cit.*, p. 236.]

this is about relational triangulation, we shouldn't be afraid of replacing the act of remembrance with that form of repetition as act that is called acting-out within analysis.[41] The analysant repeats and does not remember, says Freud; he repeats even so as not to remember. Concerning the character of variance or invariance, we must point out that an acting-out disturbs the subjective status much more than a symptom. In any case, we will only find out a posteriori, when the analysant will comment, "How could I do something like that? I can't believe it. I knew while I was doing it that I mustn't, but I couldn't stop. It was as if I were another."

Whether we like it or not, the symptom comes adorned, invested with a series of meanings and imaginary causal relations. A way to understand the work of the transference is to take into account that there may be transference without analysis—this is precisely a definition of acting-out according to Lacan. The issue here is not to work in the manner of the other psychoanalysis, which penalizes and punishes the acting-out both through interpretation and by setting limits to what it calls an attack on the setting. In this case there is a use, or abuse, of repression, but not precisely of the one psychoanalysis conceptualized.

Working-through, in sum, is not just a matter of mental work, since thus isolated it is close to obsessive rumination, if we look at it from the perspective of a cognitive formulation of the search for memories. The work of the transference is what allows for the triadization of the unavoidable relation, that is, that between remembering, repeating, and working-through.

Finally, we must take into account that the Other is historical; in changing, it has frequently produced a psychoanalytic *vulgata* as a precipitate. The problem, therefore, may be formulated thus: How can we disturb the status of a subject without falling in the *vulgata* whereby the Other is already basically neutralized? Hence, if we have in mind what

---

41. In English in the original. This term always appears in English in the original, and it is differentiated from the term *pasaje al acto*, the Spanish translation of "acting-out" in "the other psychoanalysis" but which corresponds here to the French *passage à l'acte*. I am following Sheridan here, maintaining the French term. (Translator's note)

we had already discussed concerning the fact that we cannot define present-day physics with Newton's concepts (for Einstein came in later), we may draw a parallel by pointing out that after Lacan's teachings we cannot continue to claim that analytic practice remains unalterable.

Freud's desire opened up the problem, but we cannot keep sustaining psychoanalytic terms in the same way as he did when he surprised people greatly by making an interpretation concerning incest. Over the years, these topics have come to be part even of journalistic popularization. The idea is that we may recover some of the singularity, and not the generalization of that historic Other. Singularity may very well return through a repetition in act. It is necessary to locate the terms in a different way, since in the usual version remembering appears as good and repetition in act as bad, as pathological. When we transfer this to our clinical practice, the implication is the censorship of the acting-out. The latter, in sum, is to be expected in every analysis, regardless of the difficulties it entails. Finally, we must highlight the *passage à l'acte* as another variant of the action, of which Lacan offered a detailed account.

Q: In relation to what Freud wrote about thinking causality as a genealogic tree and what Lacan said about the fact that there is no cause but the cause of that which isn't going well, when both of them speak of cause, to what kind of causality are they referring?

A: In Freud's manifest discourse it seems that he is trying to understand, as a clinician, what is happening to the patients, and why they get sick. In Lacan, rather, the formulation is stated around the desire of the one who is wondering about the cause. It is also the Freudian desire, however, that leads him to inquire beyond that *post hoc, ergo propter hoc*, that mere human successiveness of events that the analysants view as a causal relation. Using the instruments Lacan offers us, we may conclude that both authors ask themselves about the same thing, namely, about the desire of the one who inquires about the cause. In this way, we may see their fields consolidate.

The topic of the cause is a crucial one. Notice that if we thought that neuroses are caused by the lack of a certain hormone, we might cure them by administering it to the patients. The cause defines the therapeutics at stake. If, on the contrary, I claim that there is an interlocutory causal dimension responsible for the silencing of certain crystallized syntagms, then we need to talk in order to cure.

The way we understand causality will determine the type of assistance we will offer. In Freud, the question of the cause coincides temporally with his introduction of the term *psychoanalysis* to account for a practice different from those recognized by the medical field. His search was oriented toward the question of how to sustain the analyst's desire beyond the usual medical causalities, the well-known impasses reached by the medical field when it attempted to account for the etiology of the so-called mental disorders.

Q: What is the difference between *passage à l'acte* and acting-out?[42]

A: It's a vast topic. We will make a short detour. Seminar 10, *La angustia* (Anxiety), is one of the places where such a difference is processed. It is written there that the *passage à l'acte* consists in a fall, followed by an exit from the scene (*abandono de la escena*). In Dora's case, for instance, the act of slapping Mr. K. and her sudden and immediate flight constitutes an exit from the scene.[43] This "falling" prevents the interlocutory dimension from continuing to be at play. A typical *passage à l'acte* is suicide. In the latter we may sometimes recognize a physical crossing (*atravesamiento*) in the exit from the scene. In this way, the modality of suicide that participates in the dimension of what is known as defenestration is very common. Literally, this means to throw oneself out the window (out the *finestra*).[44] Such a crossing of space in the exit from the scene, where the subject identifies completely with object *a*, is one of the specific ways to fall. A classic example of (unsuccessful) defenestration is that of the young homosexual woman (Freud's failed

---

42. In English in the original. (Translator's note)

43. S. Freud, *Fragmento de análisis de un caso de histeria* (*Fragment of an Analysis of a Case of Hysteria*), O. C., *op. cit.*, vol. 7, p. 87 [p. 93].

44. In Italian in the original. (Translator's note)

patient) who tries to commit suicide when she identifies with object *a* in the face of the censorship of the paternal gaze.[45] Anyhow, we must specify that in this case there is, it is true, an exit from the scene, but what also happens is that the young woman's father decides to take her to Freud to start an analysis. There was *passage à l'acte*, but this was also, aporetically, an acting-out.[46] There appeared a way to induce the generation of an analytic situation through the other, with the consequent question.

If the acting-out is related to motility, it is also related to a certain provocative challenge, with an aggressive dimension impossible to conceal. We cannot avoid thinking about this, however, as a weakening of the analyst's desire, which stops functioning in the right way. It is as if the analysant were saying, "What you're unable to hear, I will rub it in so that you will have to acknowledge it; if not, there will be no way for you to sustain your analyst place." Such an occurrence consists in a provocative exhibit yet with the maintenance of the scene. Whether it is an acting-out or a *passage à l'acte*, the analyst will only know afterward, never through a phenomenological description. In short, it is always a dimension of repetition that will seal either one thing or the other, or one thing and the other.

Finally, we should articulate certain notes about the act, taking into account the fact that Freud remarked that the crucial act is the parapraxis. The parapraxis is actually a successful act.[47] It is the one through which the truth of a subject is half-said; it is through there that the pinch of truth seeps through, infiltrates. Lacan will go as far as to say that the only nonfailed act in a strict sense is the *passage à l'acte* of the suicide, because it has no return and no polysemia. What is left is the final letter, "To the coroner." Beyond that it is the perfect act, for it has no alternative

---

45. S. Freud, *"Sobre la psicogénesis de un caso de homosexualidad femenina"* ("The Psychogenesis of a Case of Homosexuality in a Woman"), *O. C.*, *op. cit.*, vol. 18, pp. 142 and 154–155. [pp. 148 and 161–162].

46. R. Harari, *"Caída de un querer"* ("A Love's Fall").

47. Harari plays here with the literal meaning of the Spanish term for "parapraxis," i.e., *"acto fallido,"* or "failed act." (Translator's note)

and it succeeds in erasing a signifier at play that represented the subject himself, now identified with object *a*.

There would be much more to say about this conceptual family, going over the various Freudian case histories, for example. These are novel concepts, due in particular to the recuperation of the positivized aspect of the acting-out. This is the item that utterly reverses the way to understand the acting-out in relation to the perspective of the analysis of the setting and the attack on the setting, which is the one highlighted undoubtedly by the official psychoanalysis.

3

Hoop Net and Tuché[1]

We begin today with a brief return to the issues developed before, proposing an elementary, not a topological, schema. This schema is not a slit of the sort Lacan presents in his latest seminars. It is simply a didactic tool that serves to delimit the fields opened with the conceptualization of the unconscious and of the second fundamental concept Lacan proposes in Seminar 11, namely, that of repetition.

We repeat a graph, but repetition—and we can thus advance one of Lacan's concepts—is not the reproduction of the same, but repetition with difference. In our last class we drew a schema referring to Freud's conception that psychoanalysis aims at blocking mnemic lacunae. The diagram represented the profile of a land surface, a cut where the lacuna[2] would be located and then, again, a land surface:

―――――――― ― ― ― ― ― ― ― ― ――――――――

This is an apparently puerile schema, but it is in fact quite precise. For the moment, it makes clear that we need at least three elements to contemplate the structure of analytic practice:

---

1. I am following here Alan Sheridan's translation of the French word *nasse* (*nasa* in Spanish). As we will see later, Sheridan translates *besace* (*alforja* in Spanish, the figure Lacan compares to that of the hoop net) as double sack. (Translator's note)
2. See note 27, Chapter 2. (Translator's note)

1	2	3

We don't see an oscillation of the presence of 1 and its absence through 2, but the return of 1 in 3. As you can see, it is not a punctual return. There exists here the presentation of a discontinuous order; it is the first point we need to take into consideration. The discontinuity is marked by the appearance of the lacuna, taking the Freudian simile literally. This schema allows us to introduce, in a way, the concept of repetition, but I won't dwell on this for now. Instead, I will take advantage of this lacunar circumstance to help understand the schema that will appear later on, namely, the one Lacan calls the hoop net.

The hoop net is a fishing device whose structure can be opened and closed. It comprises a sort of funnel and a mobile closing in the base. Lacan comments on the difference between the hoop net and the double sack. If we adopt the latter image we will fall into the same mistake Lacan criticizes in Freud, that is, to conceive the psychic apparatus as a closed system, like a sack where we throw elements, contents, feelings, instincts, and/or, finally, objects. There is no such sack, specifies Lacan: "You may picture it to yourselves as a *hoop net* (*nasse*) which opens slightly at the neck and at the bottom of which the catch of fish will be found. Whereas according to the image of the *double sack* (*besace*), the unconscious is something kept in reserve, closed up inside, in which *we* have to penetrate from the outside."[3] The hoop net is therefore in disjunction with the geometry of the sack characteristic of the double sack:

Hoop net   V   Double sack

The hoop net possesses a crucial trait, namely, the fact that it opens and closes, appearing as a structure with mutating borders in which the hole predominates. It aims thus to represent a topic we tackled last

---

3. J. Lacan, *Los cuatro conceptos* . . . , *op. cit.*, p. 150 [pp. 143–144 of the English edition].

meeting, that is, the temporal pulsation of the unconscious. In this way, such a concept encompasses the whole schema, which we might designate as the hoop net in the lacuna:

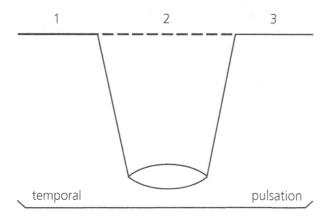

The word *pulsation* refers to the simplest example, namely, that of the pulse—the presence of a heartbeat, the absence of a heartbeat, the presence of another heartbeat. It is not an infinite absence, for the third moment delimits, sets a boundary to the second one. Now, to say temporal pulsation is somewhat redundant. If the pulsation would not unfold in time, it could not exist. That is how we may understand Lacan's view of the unconscious as a moment of opening followed immediately by a moment of closing:

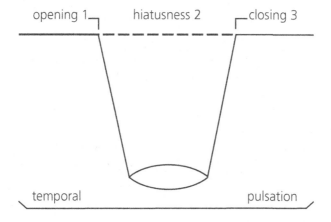

Freud's mnemic lacuna gradually transforms into this gap the hoop net marks that we will call hiatusness (*hiancia*). We should recall that this is a neologism related to the verse divided by hiatuses (*hiante*). The hiatusness entails another tripartite structure tied to the void generated in relation to the action of the cause. Lacan used to point out that the cause is that which always leaves something unexplained, bringing about a gap. Between the cause and its effect there appears something undetermined, indefinite, an empty gap we will call hiatusness (*hiancia*). We have already pointed out that it is here where Lacan posits one of his most original ideas, one of his unheard-of contributions about the unconscious, namely, the concept of hiatusness. The effect of cut, of gap and opening marked by the hiatusness ties it to the unconscious on the one hand, and to the cause on the other:

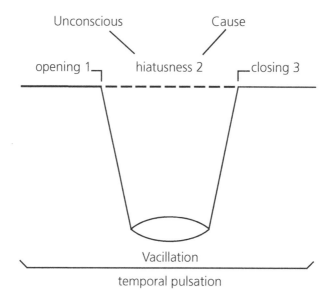

The hiatusness (*hiancia*) is a cut and also a vacillation, for the status of the subject is disturbed at the time the hoop net of the unconscious opens. The former remains in a state of vacillation, as we already said, "trampled over" by the order of the signifier. That is how the status of the certainty of the subject, the "I am what I am," "I know what I'm like," "I only say what I want to say," "I know what's happening to me," "Who better than myself can know about myself," and so on, will collapse. It will all crumble when the astonishment (*anonadamiento*) produced by the appearance of the unconscious bars[4] the subject in what concerns his certainty.

After the previous class was over, it was important to me that one of you informally asked me one of those questions that seem so simple but are the hardest to answer, namely, What is the unconscious? This question allows me to show that, faced with the request to define the unconscious, Lacan will take the path of the hiatusness in order to affirm a feature of being.

What is it? The question pertains to what in philosophy is called ontology, that is, the chapter that refers to the being. The seminar will then place the unconscious in a status that is neither that of being nor that of not being. It will say that the unconscious belongs to the order of the nonactualized (*no realizado*). In other words, neither the unconscious is (*es*), nor it is (*es*) not, but it *is* (*está*) in a state of becoming (*en estado de realización*). That is why the unconscious is structured like a language—it entails a statement that refers to being that is said using *ser* with the sense of *estar*.[5]

As we have already noted, there is a paradox, an inversion between *ser* and *estar* when we use one or the other in the phrase "the unconscious is structured like a language." Such a formulation using the verb *ser* supports the status of the nonactualized, the status of becoming (*siendo*). This idea is one of the defining issues in this seminar. Furthermore, the latter notes that this status has nothing to do with the unreal, the disreal (*desreal*), or anything of the sort. In signifying that which is in a state of becoming, Lacan denotes that it does not end, nor will end in the future. In this way, this opening—which acknowledges and calls for a closing—indicates that the unconscious is not a concluded entity. The huge clinical implication of such a conception is obvious, namely, that psychoanalysis does not consist in the analysis of childhood, or of what was closed at some point. On the contrary, what this notion values is the synchronic character of the unconscious structure. It will hence respond to a question that ap-

---

4. Harari refers here to the barred S, Lacan's notation to designate the subject. As Lacan puts it in *The Four Fundamental Concepts of Psychoanalysis*, "I symbolize the subject by the barred S . . . in so far as it is constituted secondary in relation to the signifier" (p. 141). (Translator's note)

5. See note 10, Chapter 2. (Translator's note)

pears in the seminar about the ontology of the unconscious—there is no ontology, for what we maintain is of the order of the pre-ontological. The status of the unconscious is, therefore, pre-ontological:

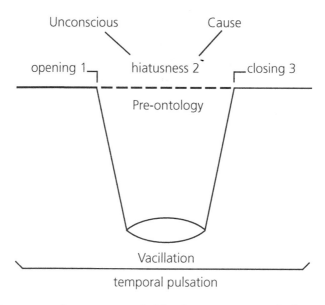

This answer shows a remarkable cleverness typical of Lacan's wide knowledge. In a way, he takes the stance of what has been called negative ontology, which is somewhat homologous to negative theology. For a negative theologist, attributing any trait to God already constitutes a way of setting limits to Him. Even if we say that He is omnipotent or omniscient, the sole fact of preaching a distinctive godly feature is heretical. Consequently, according to this current in theology, God is nothing but ineffable. As we can deduce, the word *negative* does not entail a hierarchical value. We may resort to a similar procedure to understand the ontology characteristic of the causal hiatusness (*hiancia*) of the unconscious. The unconscious is neither the instincts, nor certain feelings. Nonetheless, there is a particular definition that Lacan will use with strict orthodoxy, respecting the Freudian spirit: *Kern unseres Wesens*, that is, "the core of our being, consisting of unconscious wishful impulses," as *La interpretación de los sueños* (*The Interpretation of Dreams*) teaches us.[6]

---

6. *O. C.*, *op. cit.*, vol. 5, p. 593. [p. 603, "*Mociones de deseos inconscientes*" in the Spanish edition.]

In Freud's definition the question of being appears under a deceiving positive ontology, for this author attributes a feature to being. Yet a new paradox emerges, namely, such attribution determines a being in lack. If there is desire, it is a desire for something that is not there and that one does not have. Desire means lack. If this is true, we may infer that through such a lack, pre-ontology leads us to specify that what emerges in the hiatusness (*hiancia*) is desire. In sum, desire consists in a structure of lack or, rather—according to another concept that appears often in the *Ecrits*—in the "lack in being":

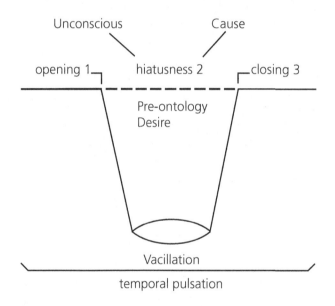

The being of the unconscious is not a positivized being, it is rather a lacking being. This circumstance must be articulated with the fact that the speaking being is a being who is confronted from the start—as Freud pointed out in the *Proyecto de una psicología para neurólogos* (*Project for a Scientific Psychology*)—with a defenselessness that is not simply related to a biological matter. There is a key phrase in the *Project* that says that such a state of defenselessness, of psychic and motor helplessness, "is the *primal source* of all *moral motives*."[7] As you can see, it is a strong and weighty definition, which elaborates on the being's initial condition

---

7. *O. C.*, *op. cit.*, vol. 1, p. 363; author's emphasis [p. 318].

and its subsequent consequences. Helplessness leads us inevitably to remain tied to the need to abide by a morality under penalty of returning to
the state of helplessness.

To be born in lack conditions the lacking structure to systematically remain in this circumstance all the time; for instance, what the
current ego lacks to reach the ideal must persist in order to avoid suc-
cumbing to mania. We can see how such a view is not as childishly
optimistic as others we might encounter. Yet only psychoanalysis takes
into account the limitation of the speaking being who, due to such a
helplessness, speaks, asks for help, is dependent. And by speaking, he
builds culture. In the schema, therefore, we must include the structure
of the lack:

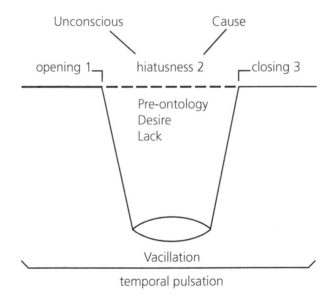

To clarify the notion of the structure of the lack, of its irruption,
Lacan resorts to a pun. You will remember *Grundbegriff*, the fundamental concept, as we explained it in our first meeting. By means of a sort of
productive theoretical joke, Lacan refers to an *Unbegriff*, literally, a
nonconcept. He then explains that what we are dealing with in the causal
hiatusness (*hiancia*), in this gap characteristic of the unconscious, is not
that much the nonconcept, the lack of a concept, but the concept of lack,

of that which is lacking (*lo faltante*), of what is not there. The *Unbegriff* is therefore what accounts for the concept of lack (and it is also a translinguistic pun, since *Un* in French sounds like "one"), that is, that which allows for the formulation of the pre-ontological condition of the unconscious. It is then "*Begriff* of the original *Un*, namely, the cut."[8]

This demonstrates once again the task of epistemological cleansing to which Lacan devoted a significant part of this seminar. He gradually clears the way of seemingly taken for granted situations like the ones that open up in the face of questions such as, what is the unconscious? In this case, Lacan very cunningly avoids giving an answer that resorts to positive ontology by affirming that the nucleus of this being in lack is the act of desiring. Since desire, in turn, entails an act—because it is not an instance liable of being gagged (*amordazable*)—there is nothing subconscious but an efficient action, that is, the action of that which bursts in at the moment of the gap. Desire, on the other hand, entails a finding:

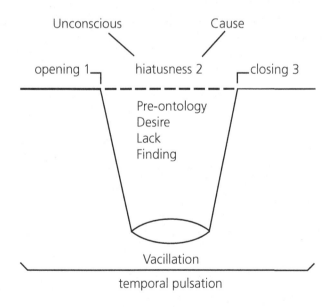

        8. J. Lacan, *Los cuatro conceptos* . . . , *op. cit.*, p. 54; author's emphasis [p. 43 of the English translation].

This is another specifically Freudian concept. We may find it in the third of the *Three Essays on the Theory of Sexuality*—"*Metamorfosis de la pubertad*" ("The Transformations of Puberty")—under the title "*El hallazgo de objeto*" ("The Finding of an Object").[9] The author states there that every encounter with an object is nothing but a reencounter with something (which is or is not considered) lost, and which one believes to have recovered at the time of the finding. In the same way, the found desire immediately goes on to inhabit the loss due to the closing of the unconscious. What is at stake here, homologically, is the recovery of some truth of the subject's at the time prior to the closing.

Lacan has always maintained that his motto, his task, and his determination have been to bring about the awakening of the speaking beings. Now, it is clear that what precedes the awakening is the state of sleep—obviously, the state of sleep we are in when we are awake, for we live in a state bordering collective sleep in which the truths characteristic of each of us remain lethargic. Could we say that it is at the time of the hiatusness (*hiancia*) when we meet the Lacanian goal of awakening? And that here, at the time of the closing, the awakening vanishes to give rise to a new sleep?

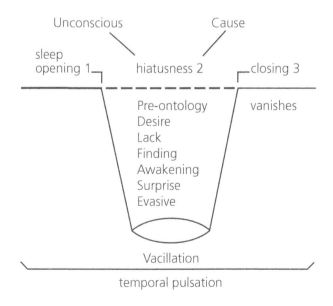

---

9. S. Freud, *O. C.*, *op. cit.*, vol. 7, pp. 222–230 [pp. 222–230].

When one is physiologically asleep, one has better access to the Real of desire than when one is awake. Let us recall in this regard that phrase about the dreams as the royal road to the unconscious.

There are still two more points to add concerning the hiatusness (*hiancia*). One we already noted before, namely, the unexpected, the surprising character of the irruption. The other refers to the evasive nature of the status of the unconscious:

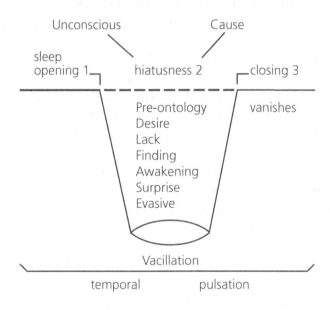

We are not speaking here, of course, of an evasive subject in the phobic sense. The structure of the unconscious is in itself evasive. In this state of pulsation (we must attend to these Lacanian slippages, that is, pulsation, eyelid vibration, syncopation, since they all allude to a rhythmic condition), the unconscious springs up, and we need at least three stages to be able to identify its origin and pertinence.

As a corollary to something as crucial as the pre-ontological, Lacan surprises us with an aphorism: "The status of the unconscious is ethical, not ontic."[10] To explain this statement, he points out that one might

———————————

10. J. Lacan, *Los cuatro conceptos* . . . , *op. cit.*, p. 45 [p. 33 of the English translation].

think that it refers to the thirst for truth that animated the Freudian course, that is, Freud's need to pursue his research and publish his findings regardless of medical and/or social conventionalisms and taboos. This is an alternative to understand the ethical dimension, but it is not what interested Lacan, because in Lacan's view this goal was not about investigating the truth, but the certainty. The topic of truth is key in the whole course of Lacanian teaching. In "The Freudian Thing, or the Meaning of the Return to Freud in Psychoanalysis," there appears an already famous prosopopoeia: "I, truth, will speak."[11] In principle, certainly, truth itself cannot speak. The evil-minded, therefore, thought that by means of this resource the author took upon himself the right to speak in the name of truth. That was not the case; Lacan wanted to convey that the only thing truth can do is speak, that what we may attain of truth can be reached through speech (*habla*), into whose bosom truth slips.

Truth is said, but it is not fully said. This was a point I partially highlighted in our previous meeting. We should now dwell on it again. In order for something to be said, something else must inevitably remain unsaid. This is where the register of the Real appears. Truth is real because it cannot be fully said. As Lacan used to point out—and is frequently repeated—the Real is the impossible. When this category emerges we should ask ourselves in each case, impossible in what sense? For instance, impossible to say the whole of it. In our last meeting we brought up the well-known juridical sophism that goes, "Do you swear to say the whole truth?" Those who answer yes, even if they do so in their best faith, wager on the misrecognition (*desconocimiento*) of the possible truth.

Why is it that we can only half-say the truth, we can only say it in part, with no other alternative? Freud makes this topic clear in terms of primal repression, namely, that which is impossible to ever become conscious, since it is an impossibility that lies not in a deficiency of psychoanalysis or of the analyst, but in that which ensures the possibil-

---

11. J. Lacan, "*La cosa freudiana o sentido del retorno a Freud en psicoanálisis,*" *Escritos I, op. cit.*, pp. 152ff. ["The Freudian Thing, or the Meaning of the Return to Freud in Psychoanalysis," in *Ecrits: A Selection, op. cit*, p. 121ff.]

ity of existence of the psychic apparatus, that which allows for the separation of its systems. Primal repression in Freud is the sine qua non requirement for the constitution of the psychic apparatus.

In the case of Lacan, this particular ethics of the unconscious is formulated in what we might call truth in the certainty manifested as doubt. Lacan points out that Freud introduced the substantive nature of doubt in *The Interpretation of Dreams*, when he stated that doubt constitutes an unsurpassable indicator to grasp a certainty born by the subject. When someone doubts, something resistential sets off in its path. Doubt, therefore, does not indicate what has been scarcely affirmed, what can be discarded. On the contrary, it should be privileged. Lacan will say that it is as if Freud had introduced the colophon of doubt. This reference takes us to Chapter 7 of *The Interpretation of Dreams*, in the section titled *"El olvido en los sueños"* ("The Forgetting of Dreams"),[12] where he shows the way in which one attempts to grasp the subject's certainty. We should reiterate here that certainties are those in which the dreaming person doubts, or where he modifies traces of his dream in a second account of it. The Freudian endeavor is thus revealed as the search for the certainty where the truth of the subject, expressed tentatively, resides.

The status of the unconscious is neither that of being or of a positive ontology, nor that of predetermined contents that fall into the bottom of an alleged double sack. We are dealing then with that which pertains to the order of truth, the regulating order, par excellence, of psychoanalytic practice. Insofar as they both converge in the hiatusness (*hiancia*), between the unconscious and the cause, something will gradually emerge of which we have spoken in passing on various occasions, namely, object *a*. All these issues would require a much larger exposition than the one we may develop in ten meetings. I will confine myself to presenting them in an introductory way. Such an exposition may thus operate as the cause of desire, leading you to look up the texts I would not attempt to replace. Consequently, we provisionally end here our conceptualization of the unconscious.

---

12. S. Freud, *O. C.*, *op. cit.*, vol. 5, pp. 507–526 [pp. 512–532].

We go on to a thrilling account, especially because Lacan elevated the concept we will discuss to the level of a fundamental concept. We will talk about repetition. At first sight, the inclusion of repetition along with concepts that are unequivocally central, namely, the unconscious, the drive, and the transference, may seem surprising. Lacan introduces this problem seeking to discriminate repetition from transference—a frequent mistake made by what we have called here the "other psychoanalysis" is to reduce transference to repetition. Faced with this problem, Lacan takes a different path by means of a discursive strategy both classic and congruent, namely, he starts with an epistemological critique of this traditional conception.

Lacan relies on two of Freud's fundamental texts: "Recuerdo, repetición y elaboración [perlaboración]"[13] ("Remembering, Repeating, and Working-Through"), and *Más allá del principio del placer* (*Beyond the Pleasure Principle*).[14] As to the first one, we should reiterate that Lacan translates *Durcharbeitung* (working-through, *perlaboración*) as the work of the transference. As we have already seen, the work of the transference is what takes place in analysis, and it's not just the moment of seeing—of insight[15]—but also the stage of understanding, which often occurs a posteriori of the time to conclude. The work of the transference will allow for what emerges in analysis not to remain as a mere instant of opening and closing of the unconscious, but as an impulse tending to modify the analysant's subjective position. Lacan articulates "Remembering, Repetition, and Working-Through" with *Beyond the Pleasure Principle*, where Freud introduces the death drive along with the repetition compulsion. I, on my part, will add "The Uncanny" to this list,[16] which allows us to glimpse in Freud's work what Lacan will account for years later.

---

13. The Spanish word *perlaboración* corresponds to the French *perlaboration*, the French translation of *Durcharbeitung*, in English, working-through. The traditional Spanish translation is *elaboración*. (Translator's note)

14. *O. C.*, *op. cit.*, vol. 18, pp. 3–62 [pp. 7–64].

15. In English in the original. (Translator's note)

16. *O. C.*, *op. cit.*, vol. 17, p. 215 [p. 219].

Lacan's approach to *Beyond the Pleasure Principle* focuses particularly on Chapter 5. I believe that in order to complete Lacan's account, we need to process also the concept of compulsion of destiny that appears at the end of Chapter 3. These are the defining passages that will enable us to grasp Lacan's views on repetition. First, he establishes a distinction between return and repetition:

Return | Repetition

Let us resort to the Freudian tradition. Where do we find the word *return* in Freud? The answer is obvious: the return of the repressed. If we do the same for the notion of repetition, we encounter it as the repetition compulsion:

Return	Repetition
(of the repressed)	(compulsion)

We can deduce here the determining difference Lacan wants to establish. With the notion of return, Lacan tells us, we are dealing with the open or shut nature of the circuits. In resorting to such an explanation, he seems to be implicitly drawing elements from graph theory, which attempts to give expression to certain processes through diagrams. We may illustrate this method by drawing a simple union of three vertices by means of two lines, and indicating a direction:

There is a trajectory, a direction here. The vertices join in a certain way and not other, determining the respective lines as given in a certain order. It is an open circuit, since the return that defines the closed nature of a circuit has not been drawn. A circuit in a strict sense is closed, for instance, if I add a line that instigates return:

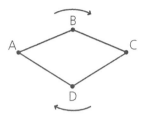

From this example we might posit repetition as a return structure, in the sense that a sort of reproduction would be in evidence. This is precisely the point where we may find the mistake made by the other psychoanalysis, which conceives of repetition as reproduction. In this way, when transference is interpreted as the exact reproduction of a past that spills onto a present, the idea of a closed circuit is thematized. Return bears a reproductive nature, which leads us to think about psychoanalytic clinical practice fundamentally in terms of a rememoration:

Return	Repetition
(of the repressed)	(compulsion)
Reproductive	
Rememoration	

This interpretation would seem congruent with Freud's title—"Remembering, Repeating, and the Work of the Transference." The emphasis on rememoration evokes the pioneer years of psychoanalysis, those that Hollywood has exploited so fruitfully. The memory appears, catharsis takes place, and the cure befalls. I wish it worked that way, but that only happens in the movies. Even though life tends to imitate art, there are some limits. Hardly will psychoanalysis consist of something as simple as those rememorations with an affective discharge, crying, and so on.

In actuality, this is no more than an imaginary way to pretend to account for analytic clinical practice based on the discovery of some memory that will presumably allow for the restitution of a subject's mnemic continuity. Whether we want to or not, when we allude to the mnemic we are referring to the dimension of the past. Repetition itself connotes a reference to the past, for it seems as though what was repeated were something that took place at a certain place and time. From there to thinking that the analytic endeavor will lead to a long-gone past there is but one step. Lacan will surprise us by establishing a difference between rememoration and repetition resorting to Kierkegaard's cogitations:

Return (of the repressed) Reproductive Rememoration	Repetition (compulsion)	→ Kierkegaard

There is a book by Sören Kierkegaard titled *Repetition*. It is scarcely an academic text, for it is not an arid philosophic exposition but a dialogic, epistolary discourse. Lacan relies on this text to point to the Danish philosopher as a conceptual precursor on the topic of repetition. When Freud brings up this topic, he does no more than enact the discursive guidelines of "the most acute of the questioners of the soul before him."[17]

If repetition were mere rememoration, how is it possible that Freud will warn us that nothing may be conjured in absentia or *in effigie*[18] (in absence or in a statuary mode)? It is not the effigy that may bear testimony of what takes place in repetition, although it may in rememoration, for there the transference relation with the analyst doesn't matter. What is decisive there is the discovery of a memory that seems to be in absentia, and not a repetition in act. In this sense, the Freudian caveat refers precisely to the dynamics of the transference. At the same time, it accounts for the fact that the latter is the primordial milestone through which psychoanalysis circulates. Let us recall that Lacan, in one of his rare definitions, will refer to the transference as "the enactment of the reality of the unconscious." A reality that is, furthermore, sexual, as we pointed out in our first class. In our practice, we can by no means do without the reality of the unconscious, which is enacted in the psychoanalytic relation. Why? Because what is at stake is a dimension related to the ethics of the psychoanalyst.

---

17. J. Lacan, *Los cuatro conceptos . . .* (*The Four Concepts . . .*), *op. cit.*, p. 45 [pp. 60–61 of the English translation].

18. S. Freud, *"La dinámica de la transferencia"* ("The Dynamics of Transference"), *O. C.*, *op. cit.*, vol. 12, p. 105 [p. 108].

In this way, the conceptualization of the transference an analyst develops will determine how he will direct the cure. Yet on the other hand, the mode of this steering will lead to a certain concept of transference. Finally, the analyst will sustain this or that concept depending on what stems constantly from his analysants' cure. We can see here that, beyond empiricism and nominalism, the issue pivots around the analyst's desire, since transference consists neither in what happens when two people start talking about something absent—in absentia—nor what happens when they try to carry out a reproduction—*in effigie*—or a copy of something original and past. We can see this clearly in Freud's text—when remembrance is blocked, what takes place is a repetition in act.

Lacan is concerned precisely with the word *act*. He says about it something categorical, namely, that if there is an act, it means that there exists at least a brush with a tip of the Real via the signifier. This means that the subject, when traversing an act, will not come out the way he went in. The act consists in an experience of mutation of his subjective position. If there is no act, analysis is reduced to an experience of passing the time (*pasatista*), as it usually occurs during periods of stagnation when "nothing happens." In a certain stretch, indeed, what eventually may happen does not "happen." We have already noted that an analysis does not bear testimony of a continuous progress but it encompasses back-and-forth movements that are utterly inevitable. When a bastion, an important fortress of the analysant's is about to fall, Freud would say, in that very occasion resistance increases. We might say that neurosis resists through the maintenance of the symptom, since the latter constitutes a fulfillment, however partial, of desires. That is why it tends to foster resistance. If we were physicians, we would say maybe in a banally clinical way, this patient is increasingly worse. But this is not what's nodal for us, of course.

In the same way as he refers to Kierkegaard, Lacan also quotes another philosopher whose work he has read thoroughly and profitably—Aristotle:

Faced with such sources, one might ask again where's the clinical practice, for this seems to be a philosophical psychoanalysis. What do philosophers' quotes and ideas have to do with psychoanalysis? We should invite those who hold this view to read Freud's texts in order to see that—as Paul Laurent Assoun has pointed out in his book *Freud, la filosofía y los filósofos* (*Freud, Philosophy, and Philosophers*)[19]—when the father of psychoanalysis casts out a great conception, when he "twists" theory and suddenly rearranges it, he always tries to base what he says on a *Vorgänger*—a precursor, a predecessor. It is as if he were telling us: I haven't thought of it but a certain personage precedes me, backing me up. In general, these precursors are philosophers. If one believed that the philosopher is an individual who spends his time sitting at his desk lucubrating strange theories, then such an activity would be utterly divorced from analytic clinical practice. Lacan, instead, offers a very interesting conception about the relation between philosophy and psychoanalysis. He claims that our endeavor does not consist in being influenced by philosophy or philosophers, but in retrieving from that field what belongs to psychoanalysis. This does not mean to psychoanalyze the philosophers' conceptions, but to incorporate them so that they fertilize our discipline. Such a procedure involves retransforming the philosophical problem in order to change it into a congruent question about the status of the subject.

Lacan's drift (*deriva*) through the notions of countless philosophers (his erudition was truly overwhelming) has as its goal profiting from them and using them fruitfully. It is not confined to picking up certain conceptions in a juxtaposing mode. For instance (and this is what we were talking about), when he discusses repetition, Lacan also resorts to Aristotle. He takes Chapters 3, 4, 5, and 6 of the second book of *Physics*[20]—notice how extremely unusual is the choice of text—where the notion that will act as hinge between unconscious and repetition may be found, that is, the cause, once again:

---

19. P. L. Assoun, *Freud, la filosofía y los filósofos*, F. Alves, Rio de Janeiro, 1978, pp. 130ff. [I haven't been able to find an English edition.]

20. Aristotle, *Física, Obras*, Aguilar, Madrid, 1973, pp. 589–895. [*Aristotle's Physics*, Daniel W. Graham, ed. Oxford University Press, 1999.]

As we have already pointed out, Lacan's discussion on the cause concerns, in principle, a signifying structure. When we look up the chapters of *Physics* quoted above, we run into the problem of causes, in plural. The summary, the explanation of these passages can be found in any philosophy manual, where causes are usually classified as efficient, formal, material, and final. I won't dwell on them other than to highlight what Lacan points out. He alludes to two other causes that are not usually considered at the same level of the others. These are precisely the ones that give title to Chapter 5 of Seminar 11. The first one, remember, is the *Tuché*, from the Greek τύχη.

Tuché was the goddess of fortune, the Greek correlate of the Latin *fatum*, fate. It is, precisely, a representation of chance with which the "already written" of our lives is confronted. Yet it is a peculiar kind of chance, since from a psychoanalytic perspective, it takes the place of the cause. Indeed, when the seminar mentions *Tuché*, it refers to the existence of an accidental order that functions as cause for the speaking being. Furthermore, the seminar's author asks himself how to find it. It is precisely about this: *Tuché* refers to an encounter, but a failed encounter. This does not mean a bad, an unsuccessful encounter, since through it the truth of a subject has been half-said. Such an encounter is then, in a homologous way to the parapraxis,[21] a successful act. This missed encounter (*desencuentro*)—a failed encounter with the Real, Lacan will say—is what marks the action of *Tuché*. The latter constitutes then the conceptual resource to account for repetition.

To illustrate what I just explained, we may appeal to the concept of compulsion of destiny as it appears in Chapter 3 of *Beyond the Pleasure Principle*. How to conceive of the case of the poor woman who saw her three husbands fall ill, having to take care of them and then see them die? Because it is certainly acceptable to think of repetition as based on a certain personal trait that is seen as the cause of that which is repeated.

---

21. See note 47, Chapter 2. (Translator's note)

Yet in this case, is it viable to hazard that in her choice of husbands this woman sought the fate of a suffering nurse and widow? We find, incredulous, that Freud ratifies that this case is also about repetition. She has repeated the same circumstance three times. This is a repetition that occurs as if by chance, which is far from being the reiteration of a certain behavior.

There is another example of unexpected repetition in "*Lo siniestro*" ("The Uncanny"), which had Freud himself as its subject. It concerns something that happened to him when he was wandering about in a small Italian town he had never before visited. Freud suddenly found himself in a side street where ladies of dubious reputation were waiting with their heads out their windows. He tried to get away from the place, turning the first corner, and when he thought he was quite far away, he ended in the same place. Alarmed by this circumstance, he turned in the opposite direction. After turning around quite a few times and making several detours, he only managed to return to the same place.[22] He repeated as if by chance.

An everyday example that may happen to any of us is the following: I take a bus, I look at my ticket number, and it ends in a 7.[23] It is a number like any other. Yet I get on another bus and I receive another ticket ending in a 7; the fact is already quite suggestive. If the same thing happens to me again on the same day, we could assume a strange force that is determining repetition. What could have happened here but chance as a cause? Still, we should ask ourselves, cause of what? It hasn't certainly been chance qua the goddess of fortune that originated the three almost consecutive appearances of number 7. Neither was chance the cause of my consternation. Which chance are we talking about then?

Let us move on to another example. A woman's parents die in a highway accident. Ten years later, she has a boyfriend who is driving on the highway and dies in another accident. There appears again the instance of *Tuché*, the goddess of fortune—of bad fortune, in this case—who brings about the death of this woman's parents and boyfriend in

---

22. S. Freud, *O. C.*, *op. cit.*, pp. 236–237 [p. 237].

23. At the time of Harari's lectures bus conductors in Argentina sold tickets with a serial number on them. (Translator's note)

traffic accidents. Chance as cause is *Tuché*. Nonetheless, it is not that which had parents and boyfriend die through a hidden design. Neither was there an omnipotent desire on the part of the woman. Cause relates to the fact that in that moment of the repetition of the accident, she is "taken" by that circumstance. Her question will be, why is this happening to me? Events such as this one must have probably brought about the creation of a goddess like *Tuché*, or like Nemesis, the goddess of revenge or, sometimes, of justice.

Lacan's clever, smart articulation of repetition as if by chance indicates that it does not consist in a reproduction of stable traits, of signs of behavior, of ways of thinking, or of worldviews; at stake are rather surprising, disconcerting, uncannyfying (*siniestrizantes*) circumstances. These events are in the nature, doubtlessly, of a trampling upon the subject, even though what charges into him in this case is not a signifying constellation that returns from the repressed, but an encounter. There is something that returns from the Real, that returns always to the same place in terms of a failed encounter, disturbing the subjective status and opening the hiatusness (*hiancia*) through which the question bursts in: Why does this fatality happen precisely to me? We can see in such a reference (of a paranoid mood) the "presence" of *Tuché*, the dimension where a nucleus of the Real is present.

To circumscribe the conceptualization of *Tuché* we must mention its partner, *Automaton*. The latter overlays the action of *Tuché* from the realm of automatism, in terms of a sort of calculation of probabilities on the reproductive-nonreproductive possibility. There exists, therefore, a margin of indetermination characteristic of that which pertains to this order. The *Automaton* helps in the stipulation of the imaginary-symbolic "sleep" that will suddenly suffer a violent commotion due to the nucleus of the Real operating in repetition (in act). It is repetition with its impact—with the failed encounter it entails—which decisively confronts the subject with the experience of the Real. Psychoanalysis, understood as practice of the Real, deals with such an experience in a defining way.

Our work is generally considered as if it were only a practice of the Symbolic, a mode of translation of what the analysant says, without taking into account that this speech certainly comprises specific, unavoidable encounters with the Real. The concept of encounter refers us back to Lacan, who emphasized its subverting quality and its consequent use for the direction of the analytic cure.

There were those who understood repetition differently. Daniel Lagache, for instance, considered that there is a repetition of need—a biologically obvious circumstance—and by way of a pun, he pointed out that there is, correlatively, a need for repetition.[24] The problem here lies in the introduction of the word *need*. When we talk about causal hiatusness (*hiancia*) we do so on the basis of desire, not of need. Desire wanders, is not linked to a specific object. Need, on the contrary, only comes into effect when fixed to its object, as is the case, for instance, with the need for food. Food will vary, but one must eat something nutritious because not everything is edible. Anything, however, might be desirable.

The hiatus between need and desire is sufficiently marked for us to notice that they don't belong to the same order. To talk about the need for repetition can't go beyond the need to make a pun work. At our level of analysis, the consideration of the likelihood of a repetition of the need connotes a reductive, biologizing conception. Return takes place, but— and here lies the decisive difference with the notion of repetition as if by chance—it is regulated according to a cycle, that is, it is predictable. What is distinctive about this chance, on the other hand, is its condition of unpredictability, the supposed arbitrariness that marks the course of the repeated.

With the various examples he offers in his teaching, Lacan shows that repetition demands the new, which seems a paradoxical affirmation. It isn't so, however, if we consider the fact that there is no repetition without difference. This is a very important fact, because Freud's example that we summarized above indicates the tendentious partiality of a certain kind of reading (of a certain ideology, I would say) focused on a hypothetical "fear of change" as the cause of repetition. The example, as we can see, emphasizes that the only thing repetition does not want is to maintain a situation statically consolidated, without escape. We should point out the presence of the demand for change, for difference, in the

---

24. D. Lagache, *La teoría de la transferencia*, Nueva Visión, Buenos Aires, 1975, pp. 121ff [I have not been able to find an English translation.]

example from "The Uncanny." The situation there is almost claustropho-bogenic, a confinement from which Freud could not come out even though he tried. It was such a confinement that produced anxiety. We must therefore be quite cautious about putting the fear of change on a pedestal as, presumably, the most terrible thing for the speaking being.

QUESTIONS AND ANSWERS

Q: Regarding the topic of the truth that can only be half-said, I don't understand that very well, if we refer to "The Agency of the Letter," where Lacan speaks about the subject who thinks he can say the truth between the lines, despite censorship. In that text Lacan situates in the place of truth the signified that is never reached, since it is separated from the signifier by an insurmountable bar. He says there that truth cannot be said; it would seem that the half-said would be a sort of belief. If we see the differentiations between the subject of the statement and the sub-ject of the utterance, or between the subject of the unconscious and the subject of certainty, it isn't clear how this articulates with the alleged half-said of truth.

A: First, it is not that somebody decides to half-say the truth; we are speaking of a nonwilled emergence. The emergence of truth occurs through a causal hiatusness (*hiancia*). Second, the apparent "truth" of the signifier is a different thing, because what summons us here is the truth of the subject of the unconscious, and the latter is detected in, and by, the colophon of doubt.

Q: But when Lacan points out that it is possible to say the truth between the lines, it would seem that in such a belief there is a certain aspira-tion, the assumption that truth is being produced.

A: I will try to answer through a brief detour. For that purpose, I will start with the use of the Borromean knot to process certain Lacanian con-cepts. Well, we can certainly find a series of accounts within his teach-ings that can be accurately dated. However, I am not an evolutionist, for we cannot demonstrate that there has been a forced progress in his theory thanks to which, while he developed new conceptions, he would abandon others for deeming them obsolete. I emphasize this because there is a certain facile trend these days that considers that some of Lacan's texts have expired, have been surpassed by later developments. To get to the point: Regardless of its date of publication (1957), "The Agency of the Letter"[25] is not obsolete in any way. I am convinced at present that the knots Lacan suggests in his latest teachings structurally allow us to clarify certain issues in his earlier texts. For instance, in the Borromean knot—in flattening it—we may locate some conceptualizations that might at first have seemed contradictory or confusing:

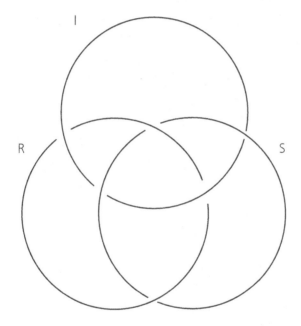

It is true that Lacan refers to the relation of the signifying chain with its products, its effects, with different terms. He will talk about meaning, on the one hand, and alongside it, about signifierness. Yet he will also talk about effects of meaning. In some passages, he recommends to break with the imaginary sense—that would correspond to the signified—in

---

25. J. Lacan, "*La instancia de la letra en el* [lo] *inconsciente o la razón desde Freud*" *Escritos I, op. cit.,* pp. 179–213. ["The Agency of the Letter in the Unconscious or Reason since Freud," in *Ecrits: A Selection, op. cit.,* pp. 146–178.]

order to reach the effect of meaning. On a different occasion he will point out that what interests us is signifierness, that is, the singularization founded on a subject's desire, as opposed to the lexical signification, that is, that of the dictionary. If we open the field of the problem in a synchronic mode, which can be also applied of course to Freud's work, there are no obsolete opinions that yield their place to modern conceptions. If we were consistent with our affirmation that there is no progress, we could place the everyday sense, the *signified*, in the region of the Borromean knot that links the Imaginary and the Symbolic. As to the *effect of meaning*, which goes beyond the lexical saying—for example, when an interpretation provokes the emergence of an unexpected Real— we can situate it between the Imaginary and the Real. Finally, the reason to place *signifierness* in the region that articulates the Symbolic and the Real is that it accounts for a certain singularity:

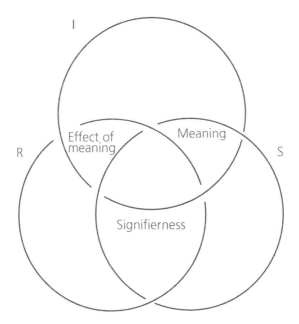

Concerning signifierness, we should note that it is a term Lacan postulates in order to have an alternative to sense or meaning, to the extent that the latter is that which belongs to a class (in the logical sense). On the other hand, since we have given ourselves permission to use the knot, we can apply it to apprehend another work that has been mentioned, where Lacan produces the juncture of remembering, repetition, and the work of the transference. As we have tried to demonstrate, these terms are related, they are placed one after the other for a reason, according to an articulating mode of relation. The positions in the knot would be the following:

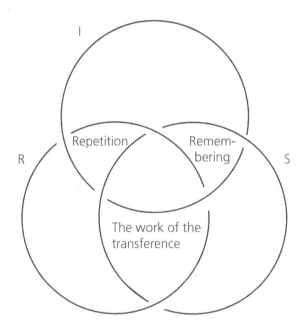

Now, this detour takes us back to our point of departure—the question that was asked, namely, the truth that cannot be but half-said. We should think how we could articulate it in the knot, since the latter is a highly useful alternative from a methodological point of view. It prevents us from wasting concepts for hastily considering them contradictory, or worse, antiquated. Many of these presumably antiquated conceptions are actually veracious and fertile. At the same time, they even make it possible to endure the apparent contradictions often present in Lacan's work. What we can achieve is the overcoming of the confusion among the various registers. The Borromean knot is, as Lacan reminded us, scripturally real. It is advisable to reflect on the psychoanalytic problem from its perspective, and in it. In this way, we will elude categorical and disqualifying judgments by taking the issues through diverse and valid binds.

If Lacan affirms in a certain text that there is no metalanguage, and in a different passage we read that in some cases there is a metalanguage, then we might think that we are facing a contradiction or a change of mind. Yet there is another possibility. From which perspective is Lacan stating that there is no metalanguage? Where is it that there is no special language that will speak as Other about the Other, about the shared language? Lacan will defend this last affirmation insofar as it is a statement that says about the Real (*que dice de lo Real*). There is no metalanguage there. Nonetheless, in the register of the Imaginary, metalanguage is indeed possible.

We must keep the various registers in mind all the time in order to realize that we are dealing neither with contradictory statements nor with statements that supersede each other. The question is to place them in relation to each particular register. For instance, there is a plane where repetition and transference blend, namely, that of the Imaginary. That is precisely why there exists a symbolic transference that is essential for us to discriminate from imaginary transference. If we don't transcend the imaginary dimension, if we see both concepts as synonymous, we equate transference with repetition, understanding the latter as the reproduction of the same.

To suggest that we consider the registers by means of the knots is not a twisted postulation. It gives us the possibility to overcome, to transcend the register of the Imaginary, in which the clinical experience often gives us occasion to get into a mess. The presentation of the knots is an invitation to work on certain concepts within that frame. I think that many of the alleged incompatibilities forged in the light of clinical experience may be elucidated by means of these conceptions.

4

Trauma or Stages? Repetition and Scopicity

Today we continue with the function of repetition that we started unfolding last class. We start with a short recapitulation in order to re-situate the problem we have been studying.

First, it is worth remembering that we posited this question in terms of a novel concept Lacan introduced, that is, the notion of the encounter. We should point out that it is an unplanned encounter, not a date that people who plan to see each other face-to-face have set up. It is neither regulated nor foreseen. The encounter Lacan tells us about is given as if by chance. In the last analysis, it consists in an encounter with the Real. In our past meeting, we worked on some examples from Freud's work and on certain everyday experiences that might be located within this type of nondeliberate, unpredictable encounter. The fundamental concept of repetition, then, accounts for chance as cause. It seems to me that we must note, beyond any idealism, that such a chance concerns us as a cause of the production of the psyche and not as an efficient cause of the occurrence of certain happenings in the order of things, of the world, or of objects. It is cause insofar as it refers to a particular determination of the psychic. Well, we have discriminated a series of concepts relatively akin to repetition that we will continue to recall today.

I use the order of memories on purpose, for it is one that haunts our conceptualization. We have also alluded to the function of return, and we placed it in a relation of disjunction (which we agreed to write as V) with respect to repetition. We pointed out that return is basically the return of the repressed, which interests us enormously from the point of view of clinical practice, because it manifests itself under a form we call symptom:

$$\text{Return} \quad \lor \quad \text{Repetition}$$
$$\text{(of the repressed)}$$
$$\text{Symptom}$$

Return indicates that a dimension of similarity is at play. That is why a confusion between return and repetition may easily arise. It would seem as though the realm of similarity, of analogy, unified both domains. Faced with this fact, Lacan teaches us that when we speak about repetition we are not referring to a Platonic reminiscence. This is a typical Lacanian mode, that is, to surprise us suddenly with a philosophical interpolation. As we have already detailed, these quotes are not the exclusive patrimony of philosophy, but they include notions from the *psy* field that are also influenced by the same kind of conception.

For instance, we could say that when we talk about Platonic reminiscences we allude to a series of ideal prototypes that exist in every subject regardless of the *accidental* experiences that participate in his life and history. In this way, each experience, or lived experience (*vivencia*), refers to a definite archetype. Consequently, a universe would exist (in Plato it is the famous *topos uranos*, the world of ideas) of which what takes place in our everyday life would be but a sort of attenuated reflection, or a shadow. That which is true, which is indeed determining, is located in that other, clearly privileged, world. If each occurrence, each of my happenings, refers to that transcendence, we are looking at a way of thinking that is not just Platonic, but Platonic-Jungian. Indeed, according to Carl Jung, there are certain archetypes in which each of our experiences is solved, and to which it is reduced. In sum, we are in the presence of one of the conceptions that are utterly discordant with the Freudian endeavor.

Another diverging point between Freud and Jung is the latter's desexualization of the libido—a very strange move, for the libido is sexual by definition. It is one of the factors that led him to abandon psychoanalysis. He would later baptize his doctrine with the term *analytic* or *complex psychology*. In attempting to "solve" (so to speak) a subject's problems by means of reminiscences, the Jungian approach loses the feature of singularity as it pours the latter into a preconstituted and generalizing mold. Such a set of ideas is quite far from a concept like repetition, which asks for difference, which is the repetition of the different. Let us highlight what was common to both return and repetition and unified them (exclusively) in other conceptions, and what was different, according to the Lacanian proposal:

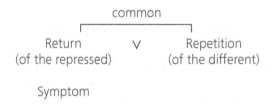

The common trait is subverted by the affirmation that repetition acts in favor of the different. We must keep in mind that what Lacan affirms in this seminar acknowledges Kierkegaard's *Repetition* as its antecedent. There, repetition is opposed to the procedural mode of remembering:

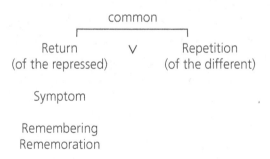

If the direction of the cure aims at rescuing it from a certain exclusive, traumatic lived experience (*vivencia*), then remembering will be the focus of the analytic endeavor. We might say that such remembering gives rise to an analytic practice based on rememoration. If we suggest an oppositive order, we must note that repetition is not return, for the latter denotes a return "from the inside." It is actually wrong to express it this way—it might be the result of an excessive didactic zeal—but I do so in order to allow us to place repetition differentially with regard to the order of the symptom, which Freud once designated as "internal foreign territory."[1] The symptom is foreign because the subject, in his way of recounting it, reveals it as something that doesn't belong to him because it did not form out of his will. And yet, whose is it, if not his? This fact reveals the action of what Lacan calls the discourse of the Other, the locus of the signifiers, that tramples on the subject via the symptom. The symptom "is" his, it is inner, but it does not belong to him. Let us endure the ambiguity, for it is the only way to render it intelligible.

Doubtlessly, in the symptom there is no reference to anything that might have happened as a haphazard repetition in the act that may be located from the Real. Here we run into a crucial characteristic that will enable us to discriminate return from repetition. Return gives rise to a "novel" creation, the symptom, in which the repressed is said, homogeneously, in a disguised way. On the other hand, there is repetition, which, as we could grasp in the example of the bus tickets, returns heterogeneously from the Real, from another place, different from the interiority affirmed-negated by the symptom. The brush of the Real is also made evident, presents itself, to those practicing analysts who are victims of the confusion between repetition and rememoration, a confusion laden with clinical implications. One may thus decide to engage in a work of rememoration with an analysant. In principle, it shouldn't be a problem, but sooner or later a ceiling will be reached to this work given by the register of the Real. We will stop here briefly to make some comments on this dimension to which we have referred earlier. It is worth

---

1. S. Freud "*31 conferencia. La descomposición de la personalidad psíquica,*" *Nuevas conferencias de introducción al psicoanálisis* (XXXI Lecture. "The Dissection of the Psychical Personality," in *New Introductory Lectures on Psycho-analysis*), O. C., *op. cit.*, vol. 22, p. 53 [p. 57].

noting a sort of joke implied in the determination to call "Real" a circumstance that is rather part of what is conventionally, lexically known as unreal.

Anybody could understand the Real if it were something similar to the Freudian reality principle. Lacan, instead, disconcerts us when he insists that the Real is the way of subverting reality. The latter bears a shared collective code, which leads us to affirm that it is to a large extent predictable. It entails an order of reiterated routine where occurrences may be predicted according to a certain command of the prevailing codes. The latter even regulate the tolerable margins of change, of slippage. Irruptions such as repetition in act tear this blanket that reality constitutes for us—they create a hiatusness (*hiancia*). It is there that the subject comes into contact with the Real, which displays features that are usually attributed to the unreal[2] as it makes the subject "faint," it dumbfounds him, makes him vacillate; in sum, it unbalances him.

In such circumscribed experiences there appears a pulsation homologous to the unconscious's hiatusness (*hiancia*). The Real bursts in, makes contact, and, suddenly, a closing is produced, propelled by the structuring of reality. One does not live in the Real. One has only punctual experiences of such a register. We live in reality, but the Real is disjointed from it. Reality is structured in the plane of similarity characteristic of the Imaginary, and with codes typical of the Symbolic. Psychoanalysis searches for the privileged reference of the subject's contact with the Real, trying to steer the cure toward that goal as well. As we can see, such a goal has an intention different from mere rememoration. This is not about reconstituting personal history and accumulating new symbols to constitute a clear view of one's own life. If that were what psychoanalysis is about, we would stay trapped in the Symbolic and the Imaginary. There would be no room for these experiences that disturb the status of the subject insofar as they imply a form of subversion. We have already approximated (*hemos aproximado*) these encounters—that repetition is about—when we referred to the Aristotelian category of the *Tuché*:

---

2. Chapter 9 includes Lacan's definition of the "unreal."

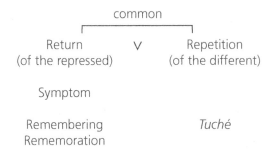

Regarding this notion, we didn't mention last class that there is a Freudian quotation that also refers to it in the text "*La dinámica de la transferencia*" ("The Dynamics of Transference") that we cited before. In one of the footnotes,[3] Freud reflects upon the matter of causes, and establishes a division between causes that belong in the order of the constitutional and inherited, and those he calls accidental. He affirms that so much has already been written about the inherited and the constitutive biological, that if psychoanalysis wants to contribute with something new, it must do so in the plane of the happening, of the accidental. Freud also points out that the two series of determinations—the constitutional and the accidental—condition each other differentially in each subject. One series will predominate in some, and in others, the remaining one. This is where he quotes the two Greek terms that are the precursors of each series, *Daimon* and *Tuché*, respectively. In the most recent Spanish version of his work, these words are translated as disposition (*disposición*) and chance (*azar*).

In my view, the choice of "disposition" as equivalent of *Daimon* is not the right one. Even though it has different meanings that can be traced in its various elaborations within Greek thought, we should highlight, as we believe does Freud, the sense of personal "demon" that is inherent in the term *Daimon*. In Greece, from Socrates on, *Daimon* will be the demon in charge of preserving the subject's balance, warning him about dangers and impulses. Previous conceptions had considered it the form of irruption of the unconscious, that is, what appears unexpectedly from the inside as uncontrollable and ungovernable, determining

---

3. S. Freud, "La dinámica . . . ," *op. cit.*, p. 97 [p. 99].

irrational behaviors. The Socratic *Daimon*, instead, seems to be located on the side of reason.

Insofar as it is singular, *Daimon* refers neither to hereditary constitution nor to that which is inherent to the species; thence my disagreement with the choice of disposition as its Spanish equivalent, since doesn't the latter bring the doctrine of reminiscence back to light? In sum, Freud had already considered *Daimon* and *Tuché*, albeit in a footnote. Lacan's reference to Freud's text, by the way, shows how thoroughly he has read the work of the creator of psychoanalysis to be able to account for the implications of this tiny allusion. His task there was to unveil the meaning of what Freud expressed. We should recall the Lacanian dictum, namely, "Beware of understanding." The speed of comprehension leaves us fascinated with reality without questioning in our reading what lies there, "ready" to be processed, even if in this occasion Lacan does not refer us explicitly to the Freudian quote we just considered. (There is another precedent that refers to *Tuché* in *Análisis terminable e interminable* [*Analysis Terminable and Interminable*], where Freud recalls that the Presocratic Empedocles was concerned with the action of *Tuché*, chance, in everyday life.[4])

To end this brief recapitulation—where we have also moved forward, it's true—we point out that *Tuché* indicates an encounter with the Real, a circumstance that is hidden in, and by, that order called *Automaton*, which refers to the network of signifiers:

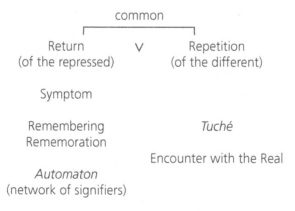

common

Return   ∨   Repetition
(of the repressed)   (of the different)

Symptom

Remembering   *Tuché*
Rememoration
         Encounter with the Real

Automaton
(network of signifiers)

---

4. S. Freud, *Análisis terminable e interminable* (Analysis Terminable and Interminable) *O. C., op. cit.*, vol. 23, p. 247 [p. 245].

The term *network of signifiers* summons an order where there is a place for approximate foresight, for automatism. Concerning the signifier (*lo significante*), we are particularly interested in this reticular nature, in the manner of a certain distribution in a tissue. Lacan goes as far as to say that "beyond" this network lies the Real. This is an audacious, risky statement, for it invites us to think of a hidden nucleus around which something gestates that envelops it. Yet in addition, in an ontological sense, the allusion to a "beyond" is due to the conviction of the need to transcend appearances, to try to remove them.

The following elaborations on the gaze that we will carry out, along with the seminar, are very much tied to such a project—to transcend appearances—that, on the other hand, constitutes a traditional topic in the field of philosophy. The risk lies in the fact that this project may slip into the conception of the thing-in-itself, in the Kantian manner. Immanuel Kant claimed that behind all phenomena there exists an inapprehensible thing-in-itself that can neither be grasped nor known. Such a way of understanding being and appearance is not precisely that of Lacan, who takes into account a different issue when he very acutely retrieves that thrashed psychoanalytic category known as trauma. The term *trauma* has long moved to the (degraded and consecrated) order of being transformed into an insignificant word for everyday use. The seminar slides it away from that place, including it in the plane of repetition:

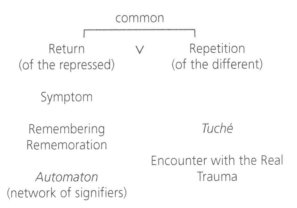

We all have an approximate idea of what trauma is—a circumstance that has disturbed a subject's balance and that has appeared suddenly as something fracturing, disturbing, and unbalancing. As we can see, this characterization comes closer to the idea of the Real. In the state he's left—and this is what is particularly striking—the subject not only cannot assimilate the trauma, but keeps repeating it, for example, in the oneiric plane. He dreams once and again with the same traumatic situation, or even retells it uncontrollably at every opportunity. A very elementary instance of this fact is what may happen after a car accident that leaves the victims more or less unharmed. A compulsion immediately emerges to tell what happened, even though it could be considered an event not very pleasant to presentify. Yet the victims retell it everywhere, and on top of that, since this is not a matter that belongs simply in the waking state, they dream it almost exactly as it happened.

Another example present in everyday life is that of gossip, this discourse that is organized around a comment such as, "I'll tell you, but don't tell anybody." After this warning, and once the piece of gossip itself has been told, another comment emerges: "You're kidding me!" proffered by the listener. Since the "Don't tell it" is actually a "Tell it," as Freud has taught us, through negation, the receptor reproduces the tale for another person. We are facing here a traumatic microsituation that is indicated by all those "You're kidding me!" and "You don't say!"—those reactions of surprise, of upset of the ego's balance, where the immediate retelling of the tale on the part of the interlocutor entails a way to establish a signifying chain that soothes the trauma.[5]

We shouldn't stay with a quasi-medical reading of trauma, in the manner of traumatology, as the term itself invites us to do. In the Freudian sense, the trauma also consists in an eventual fracture, in this case, of a subject's balance. What is clearly different from the medical concept is that the trauma psychoanalytically conceived requires at least two scenes that are connected to each other, as Freud noted already in the "*Proyecto de una psicología para neurólogos*" (*Project for a Scientific Psychology*).[6] It does not respond to the impact of a single, punctual scene, in accord with a linear causality. It is structured, conversely, on

---

5. This analysis is evidently isolating the variable we want to highlight, but we should note the causal complexity that we are deliberately omitting.

6. *O. C., op. cit.*, vol. 1, pp. 400–404 [pp. 352–356].

the articulation of a first scene with a second one, which determines the effectiveness of the former. If only the first one took place, there would be no consequences. With the second scene, the first one can trigger an effect. We can write this process by way of a classic matheme of Lacan's:

$$S_1 \longrightarrow S_2$$

This matheme admits multiple readings; in this case, it represents an S_2 that returns upon S_1, which, in turn, refers to it. Second scene upon first scene. It is there, and only there, that the unbalancing circumstance occurs. Faced with this matheme, readers will commonly understand it in terms of the second scene "resignifying" the first one. In actuality, there is no resignification, since any sense that is produced only precipitates, decants, in the second occasion. If we affirmed the opposite, we would be falling into a similar confusion as that present in the vulgar meaning of the term, according to which it is a second meaning that is added, superimposed on the original one. According to the Freudian demonstration, the etiology is only effective at the time of the binding of, and with, the second traumatic scene.

It is not that the second scene resignifies the first, but that an effect of (to use a more precise term) signifierness decants between them. Signified, instead, is a notion that allows for an easy and tempting slippage into the dictionary's meaning. With the notion of signifierness we retrieve the slant of the unary, of what is part of the subject's present, which becomes evident, among other aspects, in the processed reading of—on—symptoms. If we do not attend to this, we will generate abstractions that are light-years away from the specific analysant.

In sum, we can only know that "this was virtually there" when faced with the produced effect. As we mentioned in past meetings, psychoanalysis's epistemology entails an epistemology of effects. Only once the effect has been produced can we trace the productive condition, namely, the cause. A different procedure that will overlook this datum and will take into account only single scenes will be close to pure imagery, science fiction out of context and occasion. For instance, if a certain analysant's mother had not died when he was 5 years old, what would have happened? Maybe he would be a different person today, or wouldn't he? Yet these are all speculations. As we can see, such an order of foresight is not the one that may be required for the psychoanalytic episteme (to use Foucault's term), which requires occurred events.

The epistemological requirement of effects also operates in the case of repression. It is common to talk about successful repressions, but how can we learn about them? If that of which we may have something to say is the repression where what has been repressed returns, the one that produces an effect is then the failed repression. If we don't take this into account, we may fall into a substantialist conception that presupposes a certain inner essence of something that may or may not generate effects. It is a truly dangerous clinical trap.

Years ago, a certain current within Freudo-Marxism believed that there existed within the subject a dimension that these thinkers called "the social." They had coined quite a peculiar definition of this dimension, since its assumption entailed a degree of political commitment that wasn't any political commitment whatsoever, but one oriented in a particular direction, namely, that of Marxism. Now, since the analysants did not often show such a commitment, this current's move was to appeal to the theoretical resource of a repression so subjugating and effective that it had left no trace on the surface. It is valid to assume that the analyst's consequent endeavor in cases such as this is to engage in the task of suggestion. If one affirms that something is so well repressed that it does not manifest itself in the least, it is impossible not to carry out a suggestive induction on the analysant that is disguised as "maximum" therapy. Conceptions such as this one have played havoc with psychoanalysis. Such was the behavior of those who, in the name of an extremely unusual "left-wing psychoanalysis" [sic], produced legions of slaves to their "de-repressive" injunctions.[7]

The repression of which we may have something to say is then the failed one, the one that gives rise to a sprout (*retoño*), in Freud's terms, because it "speaks." There is something in that sprout that wants to be

---

7. R. Harari, "*Psicoanálisis, ¿ciencia o ideología?*" ("Psychoanalysis, Science or Ideology?"), in Varios *Psicoanálisis, ¿adaptación o cambio? (Psychoanalysis, Adjustment or Change?)*, Rodolfo Alonso, Buenos Aires, 1972, pp. 85–133.

said, something that bothers, that asks for interpretations. As for the trauma, we should add something more. Popular culture partly crushed this theoretical concept. One might even say that it bastardized this concept, understanding it in a unilinear dimension, according to which it is said that somebody "was traumatized" in this or that opportunity. As we have said before, in psychoanalysis there is no viable trauma without the intervention of at least two scenes, and that is why we may articulate trauma with repetition. Traumatic scenes may be as simple as that of the bus tickets. As innocent as it seems, the repetition of the same ending digit in the ticket numbers precipitates a traumatic situation because it may be construed as something inassimilable.

We may extract from this experience a key parameter, that is, this inassimilable is a Real, which, as such—no matter how many signifiers are ready to capture it—cannot be integrated to the chain. Freud expressed this fact in energetic terms. Notwithstanding the repeated attempt to bind the energetic excess that brought about the trauma,[8] there is no way to succeed in incorporating it into the system. The energy remains, therefore, in an unbound state. If we transfer these references into the Lacanian field, we may postulate—let us reiterate this—that this encounter with the Real, this repetition that occurred as if haphazardly, marked a trauma inassimilable insofar as it cannot be ensnared by the signifiers, which are unable to account for its condition. In this way, a remnant of the real stays resistant, untamable to all assimilation, to all signification.

There exists an interesting debate in relation to this point between Jacques Lacan and Françoise Dolto. This debate emerged before the need to posit a criterion in reference to a certain matter, a certain branch quite dear to psychological research, namely, developmental psychology. Whether we want it or not, as long as we take the risk of leaving accident aside, any notion of stages will refer, in one way or another, to the problem of heredity, to something that recurs. We can note here that if,

---

8. Lacan will assert that the understanding of the trauma as referred to the "too much" is acceptable in the case of obsessive neurosis, but that the "too little" is what constitutes the characteristic trait of hysteria (*Los cuatro conceptos . . .*, *op. cit.*, p. 80) [pp. 69–70].

as Freud recommends, we should emphasize *Tuché* rather than *Daimon*, the notion of stages (of intelligence, of the evolution of the libido, and all the others that abound) does not reconcile with the psychoanalytic goal of highlighting what is repeated accidentally. The thought of a psychoanalytic developmental psychology entails, therefore, a true impasse, since both endeavors are not precisely allied in the stipulation of their respective goals. Whereas one aspires to establish developmental cross sections, the other is interested in the value of singularity, that is, in what is not common to all children of a certain age. The cross section, the datum, and the mode of approach are absolutely different in what concerns the distinctiveness of the subjects. In the face of such difference, Dolto pointed out that it was certainly difficult for her to apprehend what occurred to children in this nongeneral way, with respect to intelligence and to what is at stake in the fantasmatics of castration. Lacan, with his eminently Freudian episteme, answered that it is necessary to observe the peculiar articulation produced when psychoanalysis refers to the stages "which go to form the libido"[9] outside any natural pseudo-maturation.

Let us think, for example, of the classic division into three stages, that is, oral, anal, and a third one, suggestively called phallic, where castration anxiety pivots, establishing along with the seminar that such an anxiety perforates, traverses, all stages. Does this mean that it simply retroacts, or that it actually determines the so-called stages? We can situate ourselves in an empiricist position and think that there exists in the oral stage a problem with the moment of weaning. The infant will be marked by this fact that entails a loss equivalent to castration. As to the anal stage, a similar determination takes place due to an everyday action such as defecation. Yet, what should we say about castration? Where is the event that took place as the corporal datum of the order of the experience of the cut and the loss?

Castration in the psychoanalytic sense does not allude to a cut of the penis—to an emasculation. It refers to a symbolic circumstance. Suddenly, it seems that the homogeneity of the criterion maintained for both the oral and the anal stages does not satisfy once we reach the phallic

---

9. J. Lacan, *Los cuatro conceptos* . . . , *op. cit.*, p. 74 [64].

stage. There is no linear, terse continuity between the alleged maturational stages. We are faced with something that questions a constant and progressive order. There is a symbolic castration that is not given in the precise sphere indicated by a part of the body that is lost or separated, but in the sphere of an organ that "falls," that suffers detumescence. This sole fact leads us to think that stages in psychoanalysis are quite different from the conception that those who look at them from the perspective of developmental psychology want to have of them, since, from a psychoanalytic perspective, stages are actually organized around singularized bad encounters. I think that we must highlight this fact once and again, as we are actually doing, in order to circumscribe points of convergence and divergence.

This last comment came up when glossing Chapter 5 of Seminar 11, where the matter of the "failed" (des), of the bad encounter plays a central role.[10] The dustuchia, the failed encounter, ruled by the Tuché, which will impose its mark, emphasizes the extent of its significance when Lacan broaches the next topic, for in Chapter 6 of the seminar we face, indeed, the beginning of one of the facets of Lacanian teaching for which I must confess a particular weakness and predilection. With remarkable brilliance and originality, Lacan will articulate repetition with what he will call "The Schizia between the Eye and the Gaze."[11] Schizia is understood here as the split, the cut of the subject, introduced prior to any mention of the eye or the gaze. This split (among others) becomes evident through the cited dimension of dustuchia, of failed encounter of the subject with the Real, where, as we have pointed out repeatedly, the former is dumbfounded, perplexed, disconcerted, that is, in a state of schizia. It is not, as we know, an absolute and permanent unbalance, yet the effects of this (repeated) "blow" whereby the Imaginary and the Symbolic have been momentarily injured by the encounter with the Real

---

10. A literal translation is not possible here because the author plays with the Spanish word desencuentro, in English, failed or missed encounter, scanning it in the Lacanian manner. (Translator's note)

11. Sheridan translates here "The Split between the Eye and the Gaze," but such a translation narrows the sense of the term, and would detach the English version of Harari's book from the original. That is why I have chosen not to follow Sheridan in this particular case. (Translator's note)

are noticeable. This schizia of the subject is put in writing as soon as Lacan presents the notation $.

In this writing we read, among other things, the subject's schizia; the subject, as split. The bar is not a crossing out—I point this out due to the common allusion to a "crossed-out subject." We talk about a split or, in any case, a barred subject. Why? Because the bar is none other than the transformation into an oblique bar, or a vertical bar, of that same bar that in the dawn of his teachings Lacan had drawn horizontally when he wrote signifier over signified, separated precisely by a bar resistant to signification[12]:

$$\frac{S}{s}$$

When applied to the subject, the bar[13] denotes a split that alludes, among other references, to the subject of the unconscious, split—insofar as an effect of the signifier—between what he says and what he knows. On the other hand, what "The Schizia between the Eye and the Gaze" deals with is the action of *Tuché* as it is played out in a particular field designated as scopic. By the way, I will allow myself a brief digression on all these novel words. In them and by them we can verify the construction of a theory—we notice the existence of a production. Once each term is introduced, it requires its own time and place to be explained. This circumstance makes us realize that we are not in the realm of all that post-Freudian psychoanalysis that, blindly echolalic, concerns itself merely with reproduction, without the emergence of repetition, to resort to Lacanian terms. If one wishes to produce, one must repeat, instead of remaining in the realm of rememoration, of reminiscence. A great part of post-Freudianism dilutes, insipidly, in the simple rememorating

---

12. J. Lacan, "The Agency of the Letter . . . ," *op. cit.*, pp. 149–150.

13. The impropriety of the "crossing out" is reinforced in seminar 10 (*op. cit.*) when Lacan remarks on the appropriateness of delimiting an experience of the bar (class of November 14, 1962). To elaborate further, this is also the case when he writes in "The Direction of the Treatment and the Principle of Its Power": "(Which is symbolized by the oblique bar of noble bastardy that I attach to the S of the subject in order to indicate that it is that subject, thus $.)" (*Ecrits: A Selection*, pp. 269–270).

citation of Freud's text. If we process a slight gliding, these trends tear their hair out in the face of the commission of alleged heresies. With Lacan, on the other hand, the novel terms, characteristic of his creative, repeating boldness, must be made explicit once and again, step by step. Scopic (from *skopos*, to see), however, is not a novel term for psychoanalysis; Freud himself had worked on the pair *voyeurism*-exhibitionism in *Instincts and Their Vicissitudes*. The definition of scopic, however, belongs to Lacan's production. It will thus be one of the items of the drive quartet (*cuarteto pulsional*) that we will develop next.

Having postulated that the drive constitutes one of the four fundamental concepts of psychoanalysis, Chapter 6 of the seminar submits this concept to a list where the scopic constitutes an integrative element. Freud had discussed the oral and the anal drives, something that is quite well known, almost a matter of general knowledge:

Drive
– oral
– anal

In his itinerary, Lacan will contemplate another two:

Drive
– oral
– anal
– scopic
– invocatory

Each of these drives recognizes a specific object that we designated as object *a* at the beginning of this course. To what we said then, we will add only two notes. It is a privileged object of which the subject, in an act of self-mutilation, separates in order to constitute himself, leaving something of himself aside. As we explained before, setting aside (indicative) visual empiricism allows us to include the axis phallus-castration in this characterization. Self-mutilation entails the falling off, the separation, the detachment of a part of the body. In this fall—this loss—a lack is evoked. For the moment, object *a*, insofar as it is the object of the drive, must fulfill, invest, and embody this condition. During the oral stage, what the Kleinian current posits does not take place. This current explains the oral stage through the presence or absence of milk (of food). In actuality, it is the breast that plays the role of object a:

Drive a
– oral   – breast
– anal
– scopic
– invocatory

In the face of the Lacanian proposition, it is a valid question to ask where Melanie Klein's notions of the good and the bad breast are left. We can show that in the Kleinian concepts a metonymy takes place whereby, while what is named is the container, the reasoning is developed in terms of the thing contained.[14] What Kleinianism is concerned with is the existence or nonexistence of food. The situation is not defined through the relation with the breast but in biologizing terms, that is, according to the periodicity of appetite and the possibility to satiate it.

Regarding the anal drive, object a presents itself to us cuttingly (*recortadamente*) precise—a part of the body of which the subject separates when constituting himself. It is obviously the feces:

Drive a
– oral   – breast
– anal   – feces
– scopic
– invocatory

In the case of the scopic drive—conceived along the dimension embraced by the seminar—it is not so clear, because the specific object a is that which succeeds best at hiding its condition with respect to castration,

---

14. M. Fabio Quintiliano, *Instituciones oratorias*, Hernando, Madrid, 1942, vol. 2, pp. 78ff. [*Quintilian As Educator: Selections from the Institutio Oratoria of M. F. Quintilianus*, Twayne, New York, 1975.]

to the central lack of desire. It is the one that appears most overshadowed, least transparent. It is, of course, the gaze:

Drive	a
– oral	– breast
– anal	– feces
– scopic	– gaze
– invocatory	

If we apply to the gaze the two concepts we have been working on, we must also consider it as something that was separated from the body and was lost, detached. It is not the gaze in the sense of seeing with the eye. When we postulate it as a detachment, we are forced to an unexpected conclusion, namely, that the gaze as object a is outside. The gaze is something different from simple seeing. It is in this sense that we can appreciate the meaning of the title "The Schizia Between the Eye and the Gaze." Such a gaze is not a function of the eye, for it is in the world, which is—and here I quote Lacan literally—"*omnivoyeur.*"[15] I see from a certain point, but I am being seen from everywhere. As to the invocatory drive, Lacan considers it from the perspective of the vocal, phonic dimension at play. Here the object a will be the voice:

Drive	a
– oral	– breast
– anal	– feces
– scopic	– gaze
– invocatory	– voice

To represent the central lack to which this object refers, we must keep in mind that it is not the act of speaking that defines it as object a. For the moment, the voice constitutes a trait that must mark the signifying absence, and in this sense, it has a privileged reference in the case

---

15. The transcription of the original reads here *omnivoyant* (all-seer), which we believe takes away from it the perverse nature that the term *voyeur* carries in the psychoanalytic lexicon.

of the scream. The latter constitutes a valuable example insofar as voice without a signifier, that is, insofar as it does not produce signification in a "direct" way. The scream bears testimony of the "fillist" (*llenista*) weight of object *a*. In a text I mentioned to you elliptically in our second class, I analyzed another exemplary case of the invocatory drive that was triggered when a twist took place in the transference of a female analysant.[16] This case was articulated with the appearance during her sessions of a muteness I designated as a-phonia. The prefix *a* refers to the object *a*, and a-phonia is, of course, the lack of voice. The analysant had literally "lost her voice," which had detached, thus accounting for the void of the object. This example constitutes then the flip side of the "fillism" of the scream. The lack of voice "speaks"—mutely—about the voice as lack.

Besides its object *a*, each drive bears its respective erogenous zone, that is, that which engenders eros. Some psychoanalysts, such as Serge Leclaire (old Lacanian, now "formerly"), posited that the entirety of the breast-fed baby's skin operated as a field susceptible of being carved by maternal desire. The mother's finger, metaphorized Leclaire, writes and seals this open and offered tegument. In principle, this formulation sounds convincing, at least poetically. Yet Lacan will offer a brilliant conceptualization as to why there are privileged zones with erogenous qualities, instead of considering that the whole epidermic surface possesses them. In these zones, Lacan will tell us, the structure of the hiatusness (*hiancia*) insists. The opening and closing mark the prevalent presence of certain orifices, in which the experience of the unconscious and the erogenous zone share the condition of possessing a hiatus (*condición hiante*).

These are border structures that open and close. If we refer to the oral drive, for instance, the mouth possesses such a pulsating capacity. The same can be said of the anal drive, in which the corresponding sphincter also evokes the hiatusness (*hiancia*). As to the scopic drive, the eye will be the correlative erogenous zone, for it can also open and close. In the case of the invocatory drive there occurs an exception (which

---

16. R. Harari, "El desengaño . . ." ("Disillusion . . ."), *op. cit.*

leads us to think about it in a similar way to our considerations on castration, since it produces an effect of signifierness with respect to the whole series), for its erogenous zone—the ear—remains constantly open. It cannot close physically, but the hiatusness (*hiancia*) makes itself present nonetheless, because the anatomic blockage is not needed for the ear to close when the person does not want to hear due to the symbolic slant. The resulting table of the drives with their objects *a* and their respective erogenous zones is the following:

Drive	*a*	Erogenous Zone
– oral	– breast	– mouth
– anal	– feces	– anus
– scopic	– gaze	– eye
– invocatory	– voice	– ear

When we refer to the drive circuit[17] we will elaborate on the differentiation between drive and instinct in more detail—what is its goal, if you will, and in what sense is it a fundamental concept of psychoanalysis. Right now we are interested in the following:

Drive	*a*	Erogenous Zone
– oral	– breast	– mouth
– anal	– feces	– anus
– scopic	– gaze	– eye
– invocatory	– voice	– ear

We identify the scopic drive as the one that settles in the schizia between the eye and the gaze, where the latter appears as object *a*.

In the same way that we thought (with Lévi-Strauss's help) of an order that preexists the subject in relation with totemism (in our second class), we may notice here, in a homologous way, that the gaze preexists the insertion of the subject in the world. The subject is seen before he is able to see. This situation may even have an empirical correlate in our everyday imaginary, namely, I only see from a certain perspective, but I'm seen

---

17. Cf. Chapter 8.

from everywhere. The world appears in its quality of *omnivoyeur*.[18] Continuing with his citations—in this case from the essay tradition—Lacan quotes Diderot. Not the Diderot of the *Encyclopedia* but the one who became the satirical editor of the *Carta sobre los ciegos para uso de los que ven* (*Letter on the Blind for the Benefit of Those Who See*),[19] a text I recommend to you, for in its reading you will be able to enjoy a highly clever mordacity as well as appreciate the density of the Lacanian reference. The allusion to Diderot serves Lacan to demonstrate that the signposting of space is indeed within the blind's reach. The directions on where to go—as if they were really able to see—are perfectly possible. The seminar asks, then, if the blind can organize a space in the same way as those who can see, what is the crucial difference between them?

The divergence will not depend on the ability to grasp geometral perspective, which is apprehensible and construable both by the blind and by those who are able to see. The research will then start from a different point to which Lacan will return on several occasions, namely, anamorphosis. The fact that Lacan resorts to this optical issue signals that the point of interest is the status of the subject and his conditions. With this framework in mind, Lacan will point out that sight is what renders possible for the subject to "see himself seeing himself."

This seeing oneself seeing oneself is precisely the trap where a large branch of psychology, introspectionist psychology (the one that adopts introspection as its method), succumbs. Psychoanalysis is not about introspection—the latter constitutes in fact a serious obstacle. Regarding vision, seeing oneself seeing oneself determines that every subject is condemned to the presumption of idealization. This is an intricate expression, but it refers to something relatively simple, that is, the fact that any subject, as a structural effect, is a victim of Bishop George Berkeley's temptation. Based on his systematics of subjective idealism, the latter once affirmed that if he didn't see something, it didn't exist. In the original Latin dictum, *Esse est percipii*, to be is to be perceived. I close my eyes

---

18. The author always leaves the French term untranslated. (Translator's note)

19. Diderot, *Carta sobre los ciegos para uso de los que ven*, La Piqueta, Madrid, 1978. ["Letter on the Blind for the Benefit of Those Who See." In *Thoughts on the Interpretation of Nature and Other Philosophical Works*, David Adams, ed., Clinamen Press, Manchester, 1999.]

and the world vanishes and, correlatively, it is my vision what generates the existence of things in the world.

Vision, therefore, constitutes the mode, the slant, through which Lacan attempts to account for the status of consciousness. Vision makes a subject who sees himself seeing himself believe not only that he is conscious, but also that he exists in the Cartesian sense, that is, "I think, therefore I am." The only think I can be certain of, according to Cartesian reasoning, is of the fact of thinking. It is the only indubitable certainty of the subject. The rest occurs with this thought as a starting point. The Lacanian expression is presumption of idealization, an expression that does not allude merely to a philosophical trend or to an idea of Berkeley's. Such a presumption is present in everyone and each of us.

The Freudian endeavor is oriented in the direction of leaving aside the dimension founded on the seeing oneself seeing oneself, which the seminar calls subject of representation, in order to establish its specific problem. Now, this does not configure a global criticism to what Descartes postulated. Lacan goes as far as to recall that if there hadn't been a Descartes, Freud would not have been possible. Why? Because Freud makes of the doubt the support, the buttress of his certainty but, of course, the doubt inserted into the narrative of the dream. If there is doubt, there is something to preserve, namely, an unconscious thought. And from there on both conceptions diverge again.

We will now organize some of these concepts and point out those that can be encompassed within a common denominator:

Seeing oneself seeing oneself

Subject of representation

Idealism

The seminar warns us very particularly about the risk of confusing psychoanalysis with a form of idealism—life is not a dream, far from it. On the contrary, what is at stake is the most privileged (and mutating) experience of contact with the Real ever achieved by the speaking being before the arrival of psychoanalysis, and this is only viable if we place ourselves on the other end of an idealist perspective that pretends to connect with an alleged inner world. This type of metaphor is highly dangerous. We should include here some clinical references in order to counteract a certain assertive tendency in what I stated above.

A broad range of concepts that are said in passing, such as *inner world, inner object,* and so on, or expressions that appear in interpretations such as *below, inside of, behind, deep down,* and so on, convey, consciously or not, the idea that the subject in analysis connects with what lies deepest inside him. Nevertheless, Lacan insistently and congruently defines psychoanalysis as the practice of the Real, and not as a practice that connects the analysant with any inner homunculus. Freud himself had warned that in order for a psychic phenomenon to become conscious it must be grasped as if originated on the outside, that is, it must go through the field of perception.[20] It even happens that when one speaks, one hears oneself, and what has been said has the value of a perception coming from the outside. It is the case of the analysant who states, "I always had this *in mente,*[21] but now that I've said it to you, everything changed."

The fact of having been said provoked the fact of having been heard, without resorting to that deadly inner world that involves the dimension of the narcissic (*narcísico*) refuge implied in the idealizing presumption of seeing oneself seeing oneself. Within such an "interiorizing" order emerges then the postulation of a homogeneous space "evident" intuitively even for a blind person since, as it does not privilege a certain point, it supposes a bi-univocal correspondence between the points of the inner and the outer:

Seeing oneself seeing oneself

Subject of representation

Idealism

Homogeneous space

---

20. S. Freud, *El yo y el ello* [*eso*], *O. C.,* vol. 19, pp. 21–25. [*The Ego and The Id* (*it*), pp. 19–23.]

21. In Latin in the original. (Translator's note)

The seminar resorts to the experience of anamorphosis in order to try to undermine the illusion of a homogeneous space. The cover of the first Spanish edition of the seminar recalls such an effort for it reproduces *The Ambassadors*, a classic painting by Hans Holbein. This painting represents two personages equipped with the full *vanitas* of their time (as Lacan points out following Baltrusaitis).[22] A strange enlarged object appears in the foreground in front of them that evokes for Lacan the two-pound bread Dalí took pleasure in placing on the head of an old woman in his paintings. In actuality, what one should do once one encounters the painting is move backward toward the outside of the room. At a given moment, if one shifts one's gaze to the left, the alleged enlarged bread, the shape of a skull, comes into view.

What is the purpose of this little optical play? It may seem odd, but at the end of the fifteenth and during the sixteenth and seventeenth centuries, it was a seriously applied resource. This interest was due to the fact that because they require to be seen from a certain position (even from a little hole in the wall), anamorphic paintings allowed for the construction of a different picture of the world, different from the homogeneous, everyday, realistic one that the subject of representation intends. Lacan remarks on the commotion, the outlining of the status of the subject implied in the input delimited by anamorphosis, which, in sum, constitutes a special technique of distortion of perspective that entails the inverted use of its customariness (*habitualidad*).

Descartes' postulates (including his dioptrics) situated the subject in a certain place. Anamorphotic experiences, instead, presented something on the foreground that is out of the blind person's reach, as opposed to the classic dialectics dealing with perception. Even then the dimension of a space other, different from the everyday signposting that orients us, was being conceived. Another particular instance of the location of the subject emerges, different from the one signaled by geometral optics. It is in this order that we place anamorphosis, in disjunction with the homogeneous space we mentioned earlier. We may understand ide-

---

22. J. Baltrusaitis, *Anamorphoses*, Flammarion, Paris, 1984, pp. 90–112. [*Anamorphic Art*, tr. W. J. Strachan, Chadwick-Healy, Cambridge, England, 1977.]

alism in contrast with the experience of the Real, according, as we pointed out before, to the binding between the Real and the seeing oneself seeing oneself. As for the latter, we will place the world's gaze as *omnivoyeur* as disjointed and, finally, we will oppose to the subject a specific reference—the fact that the subject is conceived (*se gesta*) qua picture function. We will progressively clarify all these terms. In the two orders of disjunction we have mentioned it is possible to write, at the head of each series, vision in the first case, and the gaze in the second:

Vision	Gaze
Seeing oneself seeing oneself	Omnivoyeur
Subject of representation	Picture
Idealism	The experience of the real
Homogeneous space	Anamorphosis

What we are trying to briefly summarize here refers to one of the privileged ways in which Lacan detected the commotion tending to the thawing of the status of the subject. In other words, the ways in which such status was subverted by means of certain apparently innocent, or just curious, visive practices and investigations. Phenomena such as anamorphic painting were contextualized historically without forgetting the fact that they were tied to a certain collective experience that was eager to go farther than the sky—in a metaphorical sense.

The sky is what allows us to signpost space. If we relate it to a psychic experience under the form of geometral optics, nothing seems to escape this field of punctual replications. Circumstances such as anamorphosis, however, allow us to think of a space other, as we already mentioned. If we translate this into psychoanalytic practice, if one maintains that our task is to have the patient adjust to reality by correcting distortions, and hence orients the cure in that direction, it is clear that the whole chapter on anamorphosis in Seminar 11 will appear ridiculous, an erudite sophistication entirely expendable. If, on the contrary, we try to retrieve the distorting nature of anamorphosis (not that of perspectivist subjectivism), and we search not so much for the space of the sky but for the field of the subject, we will be able to grasp in what direction this particular reference is pointing.

Lacan was careful to clarify that in Holbein's painting, what he saw as a loaf of bread painted by Dalí, others might see as a different element. In this way, he pointed out the limits of the infatuation of which, for instance, projective tests make use. On the other hand, the "viable" place anamorphosis prescribes, without the "fantasizing" alternative, is a different thing. The research on the scopic carried out in Seminar 11 was stimulated by the recent apparition of a posthumous book by Maurice Merleau-Ponty, *Lo visible y lo invisible* (*The Visible and the Invisible*). That was, then, the avowed trigger that led Lacan to devote quite some time to rethink these topics. Maybe, without Merleau-Ponty's work, the developments we have analyzed again today would not exist.

5

Stain and Decoy: Transference I

After our last meeting, I realized that my exposition had been comparatively more difficult than in the previous sessions. It is partly due to the topic, and I am aware that this is a facile way of telling you that I overlooked that difficulty. The other reason is that I presented a subject and an approach that are clearly novel. Indeed, the problem of the scopic in Lacan shows remarkable originality. In any case, it is very likely that you will have asked yourselves with the best faith and eagerness to learn, what is the aim of these questions?

First, we must remember that the developments we discussed refer to classic themes in the field of philosophy that we have tried to outline and narrow down—not of philosophy as a specific discipline, but as a field that generates issues that psychoanalysis considers appropriate to import to its own conceptual perimeter. For instance, it is obvious that psychoanalysis runs into the problem of being and appearance. In other words, there exists a basic discrimination that every psychoanalyst must confront, for analysis teaches it from the beginning for didactic purposes. I am alluding to the discrimination between manifest and latent content. For now, this indicates the following: the subject is not what he appears to be, and what he *sees* is not what it is either. We may reformulate the last postulate by means of an aphoristic phrase coined by Lacan and stated in Seminar 11: "You never look at me from the place from which I see you." And then, conversely, "What I look at is never what I wish to see."[1] One way or another, a relation of asynchrony, that is, of lack of fit, of nonreciprocity is established. An effect of dissatisfaction, of noncompleteness is produced whereby one does not get what one sought. The scopic—and this is an important issue that must be highlighted—is not an example but the very basis of this circumstance.

Let us recapitulate part of what we developed in our last meeting. We accounted for the role of consciousness founded on the scopic, a consciousness that raises from the condition designated as seeing oneself seeing oneself, in sum, a reflection upon oneself where the scopic allows the gestation of a classic subject of representation (classic in philosophical inquiry, in the sense that the philosopher works with his representations). We must not forget a crucial item, namely, that to represent means traditionally to be founded on a similarity. If we think of representation, we put into play some kind of similitude, which implies the incontestable prevalence of the register of the Imaginary. What should we oppose to this subject of representation who, as it is to be expected, believes he possesses a perfect, specific replica of the world's things? If we take this to the field of painting, such an attitude will entail the belief that this activity consists in copying things present in space, that is, in the assumption of a presumably realistic position. We can understand here why Lacan retrieves a pictorial artifice such as anamorphosis, highly valued in past centuries. In the last analysis, this optical resource constitutes an inversion of the usual perspective. It disconcerts any kind of manifestness (*patencia*), of lived experience (*vivencia*), of naive realism. Consequently, anamorphosis offers a view of the subject very different from that which is characteristic of the subject of representation. Through it, then, what is lacking in the scopic field is restituted. To say it more precisely: in *The Ambassadors* Holbein puts into play the "nothinged" subject, consistent with the central lack of desire called castration and written as follows: $(-\varphi)$. Anamorphosis makes itself present. It offers, by means of images, the possibility that castration

---

1. On p. 103 of the English edition. (Translator's note)

may be enacted in the field of seeingness.[2] Let us remember that the subject of representation evades castration. This encounter and this evasion are conceived by means of an astonishing argumentation, namely, that of the blind's optics. As you must recall, Lacan posited this question using Diderot's text *Letter on the Blind for the Benefit of Those Who See* as support, and he stated that if the blind can find their bearings in space, it is because they diagram it according to the (virtual) stretching of a thread between determinate and corresponding points. They proceed by means of unitive representations:

The blind person is actually a metaphor. In fact, Lacan is speaking about anybody who will find his bearings in space through a punctual reproduction—from one point to another—in terms of what could also be called, in a more affected manner, a bi-univocal correspondence. In this relation, the designated and the represented points refer to each other. Lacan argues that one could establish threads that would join every point in space in the blind's universe one by one, so that such a universe could be signposted in its entirety:

and so on.

Lacan elucidates this consideration, already present in Diderot, as characteristic of geometral optics, and opposes to it the perspective of anamorphosis. Geometral optics places us in the presence of a subject tinged with the presumption of idealization, namely, the position of the one who says, "The world is built exclusively through me." According to the presumption of idealization, everything is created from the perception, the conception, paradigmatically characteristic of subjective idealism. Nevertheless, another aspect remains to be considered with

---

2. This is Sheridan's rendering of the French original word *voyure*. (Translator's note)

respect to this geometral optics construed according to straight lines. In terms of what interests us within an optical conceptualization, such lines indicate what in the most elementary physics is called reflection.

This phenomenon alludes to the propagation of the beam of light in a straight line, punctually, and under a bi-univocal correspondence, different from what occurs with refraction. If we consider the latter, the scene changes, since we must attend to sparkles and radiations from a point of light, instead of a linear correspondence. This could be graphed as follows:

The beam spreads gradually and obtains certain kinds of effects. Now, the initial point, the point of dissemination, is designated as point of light:

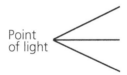

The plane toward which the beams emerging from the point of light are directed is that of the function we mentioned last meeting, that is, the subject as picture. We will see later on why Lacan adopts this simile, and how much it has to do with painting. For now, we will consider the point of light as the one that paints the picture in the retina of the subject qua picture, a picture that is thus left out. In the diagram we can see on one side the subject qua picture function, and on the other, also "outside," the point of light:

We can design another schema that will clarify this explication and that is included in the respective sections of Seminar 11. Lacan resorts to two triangles. One accounts for the set of ideas of geometral optics. The other summarizes the optics that corresponds to refracted light, involving the gaze as well as phenomena such as anamorphosis. The two schemata form a converging dichotomy that generates the differences Lacan wishes to highlight:

The first triangle corresponds to the "point of view"—geometral point—of the subject of representation:

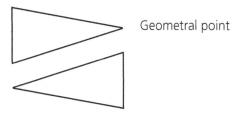

Geometral point

The upper diagram represents then the position of geometral optics, namely, a framing of space constituted thanks to the signposting of this space. Such is the method both of philosophy and of introspective psychology, that is, the psychology that, as does the philosopher, attributes to a subject his conscious representations. It won't hurt to repeat this: psychoanalysis does not devote itself to introspection; it only asks the analysant to speak. It does not order him to talk about his inner states, his states of mind, and so on. It focuses strictly on the implementation of an interlocutive dimension that is both founding and operating.

Insofar as it is a geometral point, the subject of representation apprehends the object through an image:

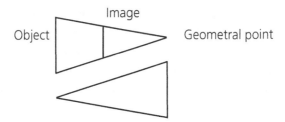

So far, we can understand these ideas very well because they coincide approximately with our imaginary or with the customary imagery. To say that the subject, in some way, possesses an image of the object is no news. Anybody understands it and, when faced with the question of being and appearance, has the spontaneous—phenomenological—experience that this is what it is about. Yet Lacan slides toward another (not obvious) demonstration, where he attends to the repetitive—the *tychic*—that is at play in the field of the scopic function. Lacan places circumstances in a different way by inverting perspective, and thus he develops the second diagram starting from the point of light:

Refraction, in turn, is indicated with its origin in that same vertex of the triangle:

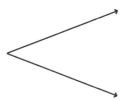

Now, in my view, the subject of representation is closely related to a theological conception. It is from the geometral point called God that the world of beings starts to gestate. Furthermore, if we invert the postulate symmetrically—that is, when we say that man created God in his image—we are dealing once again with *vanitas*, with the subject of geometral optics. In the non-"realistic" optics—characteristic of anamorphosis—the point of light will be located on the opposite side of the subject qua picture function. In the intermediate place, where we located the image in the former schema, in this case there will be a screen:

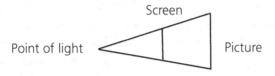

The screen renders the possibility of bi-univocal contact opaque. In the diagram of the subject of representation, the image and the object may be in discord, which constitutes a traditional problem that configures an *episteme*, a foundation characteristic of psychology. We should quote, for example, the well-known experiments of the *New Look*, namely, the fact that the perspective deformations occurred due to the peremptoriness demanded by various needs show (they say) how we perceive in a differential way. In my view, these experiences constitute a tautology, for they "demonstrate" what is known by the collective imaginary, by all of us, from the beginning, even if they expound it in a more affected way.

Returning to Lacan, he even points out the existence of a discord between the image and the object, but in a different sense. The point of light paints a picture in the subject. Even if it does it through a screen, the latter does not help; it is rather a disturbing element that renders opaque and disguises the possibility of concord. In this way, there is no bi-univocal relation, even though Lacan warns that albeit these conceptions seem to be similar in this respect, they are actually very different.

The inclusion of the screen allows the appreciation of the crucial importance of the decoy function in the lives of the speaking beings. Many and diverse texts examine this phenomenon, but Lacan refers to one in particular: *Medusa y compañía* by Roger Caillois.[3] In this book, the essayist mentions three issues tied to a function of the decoy such as

---

3. R. Caillois, *Méduse et Cie*, Gallimard, Paris, 1960, pp. 71–166. [*Mask of Medusa*, C. N. Potter, New York, 1964.]

it appears particularly among animals. Caillois analyzes this function especially among insects, where it operates in a way that the seminar postulates as being equivalent to the role of painting for the speaker. The matter at hand is mimicry, that is, the tendency to blend with the environment (with their respective habitat) typical of certain animals. It is usually believed that this phenomenon occurs strictly as an adaptive mechanism tied to survival. Nonetheless, if we set aside this preconceived idea, another angle appears. It is interesting to notice here the bias of the bi-univocal correspondence in its finalist, teleological branch, which considers that animals change color (*se mimetizan*) to attain a certain goal. Lacan points out that what animals obtain by exercising the mimetic function is to situate themselves in their environment in the same way the subject, the speaking being, situates himself in the picture. Animals settle in a multicolored place and paint themselves as part of what is designated as the stain in the picture. The stain will be located in the place of the screen, that is, of that which produces discord, showing that the picture does not bear a homogeneous condition, for something differential emerges there. The main dimensions of mimicry Caillois defines are the following:

$$
\text{Mimicry} \begin{bmatrix} 1.\ \text{Travesty} \\ 2.\ \text{Camouflage} \\ 3.\ \text{Intimidation} \end{bmatrix}
$$

These three varieties are thus named in *Medusa y compañía*. We may privilege one in particular that has a clear sexual connotation for the speaking being, namely, that of the travesty (*travesti*).[4]

We all know who is attributed the designation of transvestite (*travesti*)—subjects who dress in the clothes of the opposite sex as a way to appear to be what they are not. As you may note, the ideas of being and appearance are implicitly at play here. Even though it does not

---

4. Even though the word *travesti* in French means also "fancy dress," both in French and in Spanish the word corresponds to the English *transvestite*, which explains Harari's comment (following Lacan's in Seminar 11, *op. cit.*, p. 100). However, I have maintained Sheridan's translation here. (Translator's note)

pertain strictly to our topic, we should recall the difference between transvestites and transsexuals. The latter wish to change their sex and usually request surgery to ablate or transform their genitals. They want to undergo an operation and they sometimes succeed, changing sexes in terms of their biological body. Transvestites, instead, do not want to change sex at all, but rather wish (in the case of men) to embody the woman with a penis. They want to "show," to suggest that under that appearance there is a being different from the one on display.

This behavior refers to an image of completeness without a surgical purpose. It is probably the most prototypical example of the function of the mask, the decoy, the ornament or disguise. These are resources that allow the visive affirmation that one has or is something different from what one shows. The crucial place of the decoy in the capture of desire can thus be grasped. This circumstance is key for Lacan. He has undertaken a good part of the revision of the question of feminine sexuality based on the conception that may be summarized with a term introduced by the Kleinian psychoanalyst Joan Rivière in her classic text "La femineidad como máscara" ("Womanliness as a masquerade").[5] Since the publication of this essay, a concept (not a fundamental one, surely, but a concept in any case) was established, namely, that of the masquerade. It is certainly no mere coincidence that we usually designate certain feminine cosmetic procedures as facial masks. In the same order, it is a fairly common experience that when the same woman reappears sometime after her first appearance, due to a mutation in the masquerade, we may not recognize immediately the image of the first appearance. It is unlikely that this will happen with a man. It would seem that the woman has the possibility to mimic (*mimetizar*) that which she "lacks" through a constant variability.[6] The man, on the contrary, has (it seems)

---

5. J. Rivière, *op. cit.*, en VARIOS, Tusquets, Barcelona, 1979, pp. 11–24. [First pubished in the *International Journal of Psycho-Analysis*, republished in Atholl Hughes, ed. *Joan Rivière: Collected Papers 1920–1958*, pp. 90–101.]

6. Due to Lacan's observation that "she is without having it" (the Phallus). [J. Lacan, "El deseo y su interpretación," in *Las formaciones del inconsciente* (*The Formations of the Unconscious*), Nueva Visión, Buenos Aires, 1970, p. 173.] [The only translation published in English is "Desire and Interpretation of Desire in Hamlet," a fragment of seminar VI (*Desire and its Interpretation*), trans. J. Hulbert, in *Yale French Studies* 55/6, 1977, pp. 11–52.]

more to lose, and is therefore less prone to that order so ensnaringly (*atrapantemente*) feminine as is that of fashion. We mustn't believe that fashion is the simple work of some evil ideologues devoted to disturb the whole world in order to sell the products of consumer society. Even though this may constitute one level of analysis—whose appropriateness will have to be proved—we run the risk of falling into a dangerous revisionism. Such an argument forgets that in order to recycle itself, fashion must articulate with each person's desire. If this were not the case, we could not conceive such a proliferation of rapidly obsolete objects. In the last analysis, fashion makes evident a travesty condition, understanding the word *travesty* in a broad sense. Travesty refers to the condition of showing or wearing something different in order to hide the wearer. Why is it that this different thing may generate arousal? It will not be simply because of what the person is showing, but because this action evokes an order that is absent, that is located further away. In this sort of inquiry about a beyond, the arousing condition is generated.

Let us go back to the last two diagrams about the scopic. Lacan's next step consists in superimposing the triangles in order to account for all the implications revealed in this field. It is worth repeating that the latter is the one where the condition of the lack that founds desire— that is, castration—seems to be less noticed. The object *a* named as gaze is then what best eludes the condition of castration.

In the last diagram there emerges an important question: Is the initial concept in this case the point of light, or the gaze? In this respect, the seminar will make it clear to us that the gaze constitutes the manner in which one gets close to the light. In a broad sense, the gaze symbolizes the point of light (or light itself). In a text I wrote a while ago titled "El fetichismo de la torpeza" ("The Fetishism of Clumsiness"),[7] I tried to reflect upon other subjects who, in their own way, also account for the transvestite condition, namely, the fetishists. I asked why they sought as fetishes elements that shine, for instance, shoes, raincoats, condoms, and so on. The list is longer, abounding in elements that share, among

---

7. R. Harari, *Del corpus . . .* , *op. cit.*, pp. 71–81.

other qualities, the ability to reflect light. It is not the emission of its own light that matters in a fetish, but the fact that it can reflect it.

There it is precisely, as I see it, the question of the gaze. In fact, the fetish looks at me. This statement does not refer at all to an interpersonal, eye-to-eye relation. If there is a crucial cut we must produce at this point, it is the elimination of the belief that we are working on the pair *voyeurism*–exhibitionism. We cannot do so here because this pair requires the co-presence of two subjects in a certain situation (for instance, one who looks at the effect on the other's gaze brought about by the nudity of his penis; he watches how he is being watched). We are looking at a relation of parity, at reciprocity, at intersubjectivity.

On the contrary, understanding fetishism requires postulating a form of mediation. In this case, the mediator is an element where a—the—light reflects, which, without being the element's own light, generates an ensnarement of the gaze amidst moments of obvious fascination, as we hear in many analysants' narratives. As we advanced in our last meeting, Lacan points out that we will find the subject in a function similar to that of the painting that, he tells us, tames the gaze. Before the painting, the person contemplating it must lay down his own gaze as if it were a weapon. In the painting, insists Lacan, the painter's gaze makes itself present. This fact, of course, does not involve only portrait painting. If we considered only this case, we would fall into the trap of a specular conception—everything would be reduced to looking at the portrayed person's eyes. A still life, or even nonfigurative painting, posits the presence "out there" of the gaze that embodies the light.

If the subject can be situated in this picture function, it is because he is painted by the point of light. This is not demonstrated solely thanks to Lacan's discursive strategy with respect to the scopic. It is proved also by the existence of something congruent, homologous with the primacy of the order of the signifier upon the subject that we described in our first meetings, an episteme shared in difference. The order of the signifier preexists the subject's entry into it and, before anybody sees it, it exists in the world as *omnivoyeur*, sustaining the order of the gaze.

If we superimposed, as we said, the two triangular schemata, playing with what happens with the optical nerve, a chiasma occurs:

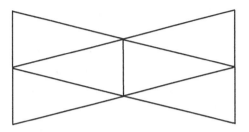

This interweaving will allow us to represent the announced integrity of what pertains to the scopic problem. The terms of the schema will be situated as follows:

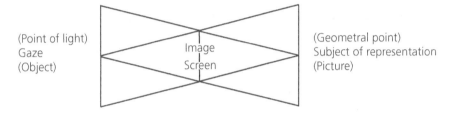

(Point of light)   Image   (Geometral point)
Gaze   Subject of representation
(Object)   Screen   (Picture)

(The inscriptions without parentheses reproduce the seminar's schema, and we added in parentheses those that complete it.)

In my view, the recourse Lacan employs in this opportunity shows his true wisdom. In terms of its episteme, his reasoning is very similar to that which he adopts when he states that affirming the want (*carencia*) of communication by means of language is not the issue, for the task consists in locating these problems in their appropriate terms. Obviously, language, as a code, serves the purposes of communication with all the traits linguists have painstakingly developed. What will be nodal for us, however, is the function of the signifier, which is not at the service of communication. That other function of language is the one that is revealed in misunderstandings, in *lapsus linguae*, in babbling, in polysemia, and so on. With this diagram of the scopic, something of the same tenor takes place. There isn't a Lacanian conception here that will cancel another one, because the former (I am referring to the subject of representation) isn't exactly wrong. It is simply the one that anybody, insofar as he is a speaking being, will continue to have, because it constitutes the customary way in which we live. The thesis presented by the seminar is that which we may access if we understand the status of the subject in a different way, disturbing it by means of psychoanalysis. In the first set of ideas lies the spontaneous nature of the lived experience (*vivencia*), the way of seeing that seems innate and constitutive. It accompanies every subject and it maintains the same point of view that defines language as communication. As to this schema of the scopic, one question will consequently be vision and, confronting it, the other question, that is, the gaze. In this way, we account for the schizia between the eye and the gaze.

In sum, I think that in the idea of the decoy as that which, without exhibitionism, offers something to be seen but at the same time suggests the not-seen, a homology is established with the schizia of the subject. The schizia implies what I explained before regarding the unconscious, that is, the hiatusness (*hiancia*). The latter functions as homological support—due to the topological slant—for the schizia that is specific to the terms of the scopic.

The matter of being and appearance constituted one of the customary misunderstandings where a large part of post-Freudian psychoanalysis failed before Lacan. This is the issue present in Seminar 11 that opens the field for the elucidation of the third fundamental concept, namely, the transference. Along with the seminar, we will start with one of the usual definitions of this peculiar phenomenon, regardless of its naive or banal condition. We could say, for example, that transference alludes to the global structure of the relations between the analysant and the analyst. It is a possible definition, but we must immediately add the caveat that we must be extremely careful, when examining this relationship, not to consider the affects, the thoughts—in sum, the statements of the analysant regarding the analyst—too literally.

The question of being and appearance presents itself. We must not believe that what the analysant says is tied to the situation to which it seems to refer, for it was conceived in a different place. The problem is that if I consider that what the analysant says originates somewhere else, the usual trap emerges that we already emphasized when working on the concept of repetition. What trap is this? The one that consists in thinking that the analysant repeats along with his analyst something that originated in a situation in the past. In this way, transference is subsumed and flattened by means of repetition. If they are pretty much the same thing, then in order to economize we should eliminate one of the two alleged fundamental concepts.

Yet what renders the situation complex is the fact that the analyst is indeed treated as if he were other. It is according to the way the analyst is treated that the classic discrimination between positive and negative transference was posited. The first one would be the one that facilitates the analytic work, affording the possibility for everything to develop without major setbacks. The negative transference, of course, would be the one that hinders the progress of the analyzing task. This division is usually displaced in its terms—positive transference is love, and negative transference is based not on hate (because one doesn't say that, Lacan comments humorously) but on ambivalence. In this regard, Lacan outlines another, more accurate characterization: positive transference occurs when one has "a soft spot" for the analyst, and negative transference—a very clever clinical observation—when the analysant doesn't lose track[8] of the analyst. In this last case, there occurs what the Kleinian school knows—in phenomenological terms—as control of the object. There are many ways to illustrate this attitude, but for the moment we will locate it in the lack of trust, in a certain paranoid tinge in the relationship whereby any "missing" information may entail a certain potential threat. Not to lose track of the analyst, having it in for him, is like wanting to "bleed him dry" (exprimirlo), so that every singularizing trait in his saying will die away, will fall. In everyday, common terms, the analysant doesn't leave the analyst alone. He is constantly alert, a state that accounts for his manner of permanently demanding explanations, or of raising questions about what has been said. We must not think that in the negative transference there are no love demands. We shouldn't constrain the detection of this fact to a mere vindication of the litigious sense of the term, for that would be quite naive.

---

8. In the French original and in the transcription it says here "on l'a à l'oeil." ["You have to keep an eye on him" in the English translation.] It is worth noting, then, how the eye (l'oeil) slides away from the scopic intellection toward the transference. Hence its preservation regarding the option chosen to translate the composite expression, and the clinical sense read into it.

Regardless of not fully convincing phenomenological descriptions, our goal is to introduce the fundamental concept of transference in the theoretical plane. In fact, none of us could be truly convinced by a presentation of transference as a global analysant–analyst relationship in which one must disbelieve the sayings of the former, or be satisfied with a classification as positive or negative. Since we are in the initial stages of this fundamental concept, there is another point to highlight. Some psychoanalysts such as Ida Macalpine[9] considered transference as created, engendered by the analytic situation. Lacan responds to this with what I believe is the experience of the least shrewd of mortals, namely, that there exist effects of transference in countless relationships, without the prerequisite of an analytic situation for them to develop.

Of course, analysis attempts to work on the effects of the transference, which signals a crucial distinction with psychotherapies in general, even those that are claimed to have an analytic slant—even if you never know where they cut.[10] Why? Because they always face an insoluble dilemma, that is, what part of the transference should be analyzed, and what part should not. It is something very similar to what happens in the therapies organized according to a certain stated goal. In both cases, an agreement is established with the patient whereby both pledge to treat therapeutically certain issues and not others. You will ask yourselves why I am particularly critical when I speak of these topics, yet, how can one say "with an analytic slant" when Freud himself noted,[11] a long time ago, that such a plan is equivalent to telling somebody, "I will get you pregnant so that you can deliver an arm"? If the process was set in motion, we can't say that what is sought is a certain fragment of the body and not the entire organism. This is not to dismiss the apologist of

---

9. I. Macalpine, "La evolución de la transferencia." In *Trabajo del psicoanálisis* (*Labor of Psychoanalysis*), vol. I, no. 3, 1982, pp. 329–350, and vol. 2, no. 4, 1982, pp. 93–106. ["The Development of Transference," in *Psychoanalytic Quarterly* 19 (1950).]

10. Harari plays with the meaning of "*psicoterapias de corte analítico* (psychotherapies with an analytic slant), and the verb *cortar*, to cut. (Translator's note)

11. S. Freud, "*Sobre la iniciación del tratamiento (Nuevos consejos sobre la técnica del psicoanálisis*, I)," *O. C., op. cit.*, vol. 12, pp. 131–132. ["On Beginning the Treatment (Further Recommendations on the Technique of Psychoanalysis)," p. 130.]

pregnancy. Something will emerge from it, but it will do so in such a way that one cannot foresee or plan. We don't know how it starts or how it ends, for it has its own rules. As to the transference, a similar phenomenon takes place. What does it mean to analyze the transference? What is analyzable? As you can see, we are faced here with highly pressing issues. It is particularly worth knowing the margin of concessions we may grant when somebody expects to articulate himself with the analyst's place. We should specify to what extent there are negotiable issues if a practice wishes to claim to be part of psychoanalysis. In this way, it is often quite easy to determine that the latter has been happily thrown away.

In this respect, I reckon that what we have just mentioned constitutes one of the nodular points in the analysis of the transference. The latter entails then certain indispensable elements or circumstances. Among other things, the action of what we have called (but not defined so far) transference may bring about spectacular cures, especially at the beginning of an analysis—the so-called transferential cures. In such cases, as opposed to the one who says, "I don't deal with that," the analyst asks himself, "How have I dealt with that without dealing with it?" This is the reflection that prevails if there has been a remission of a symptom, for instance, without having a detailed analysis of that symptom. What took place here is a phenomenon linked to the structure of the unconscious. Such a reticular structure, arranged like a language, renders the planning aspiration of psychotherapies impossible. Yes, because one may be taking a particular direction, may apparently be working on a certain aspect, and in fact one is affecting a different matter at the same time. Understanding the transference as these psychotherapies do is linked to the Solomonic idea of the child conceived in fragments to be chosen and/or in installments—for our experience indicates that we must think of conceiving of it, as we have already said, as a structured organism.

These transferential cures must be referred to the structure of the unconscious, and not simply to the action of a more or less veiled suggestive influence. This doesn't mean that somebody goes to his analyst believing he will be cured and that this sole fact produces results—a factor that must be considered, even though it is not the one to which we are referring here. I am talking about what occurs when the analysis is established and we may profit from the effects of the transference. It is usually said—with fairly good sense—that we must not interpret until the transference is established. It is a sufficiently sensible rule, but hard to abide, especially if one carries out preliminary interviews. Its implementation is difficult, for instance, when one is trying to verify the analysant's permeability to metaphor. In order to do so it is necessary to formulate interpretations, since they possess, precisely, an allusive structure. If they hadn't, they would be explanatory, pedagogical, universitycizing (*universitarizantes*),[12] in the sense that they would say nothing about the subject but simply confine themselves to generalities. Things do not tally with Ida Macalpine and her followers' conception of transference as a product of analysis. What is actually the case is that our practice has the commendable virtue of being equipped with the transference within its field. It was the merit of Freud's genius to have discovered it and generated the conditions to render it operational. Here begin, then, all the issues we are presenting concerning this fundamental concept. Now, does having the transference as an integral part of our operational field work in favor of us or against us? Does it help analysis or, conversely, does it disturb it? We are indeed penetrating here in the privacy of what takes place in psychoanalytic practice, beyond merely phenomenological discriminations.

The course Lacan will take in this regard in Seminar 11 appears in the very title of Chapter 10—*Presence of the Analyst*. This title glosses ironically (without mentioning the author) the ideas of Sacha Nacht's, one of the analysts in charge of the *Paris Psychoanalytic Institute* at the time of its split in 1953. Nacht, who published a book with that same title in 1967,[13] endorsed a curriculum for analytic training that received acid, critical comments from Lacan, included in his *Rome Report*.[14] This

---

12. The University discourse is one of the four discourses described by Lacan and mentioned by Harari in Chapter 1. (Translator's note)

13. S. Nacht *La presencia del psicoanalista*, Proteo, Buenos Aires, 1967. [I could not find an English edition.]

14. J. Lacan, "Función y campo . . . ," *op. cit.*, pp. 59–63. ["Function and Field . . . ," pp. 30–34.]

curriculum suggested that the science that encompassed the psychoanalyst's studies be called—pay attention to this—"human neurobiology." There is no need to highlight the medicalization at play, or the way in which everything related to disciplines connected to the analysis of the effects of the signifier was violently omitted. It was a training curriculum for physicians that followed that anti-Freudian misunderstanding that consists in assuming that psychoanalysis is a branch of medicine.

Just in case, we should make clear that psychology does not include psychoanalysis as a discipline of the signifier either. In a letter addressed to Pfister in 1928, Freud recalled that he had written two texts that were recent back then. The first one was *El análisis profano o ¿Pueden los legos ejercer el análisis? (The Question of Lay Analysis)*, published in 1926. A year later he published *El porvenir de una ilusión (The Future of an Illusion)*. Through these texts, Freud tried to show that both physicians and priests form a privileged set among those from whom psychoanalysis must be protected. In any case, he says, we should think of another professional group who might be called "profane soul shepherds."[15] In this way, Freud notes the epistemic cut involved in the advent of the field of psychoanalysis.

The fact is—and here I am referring to my own experience—that one must unlearn what one has learned, having come from medicine or from psychology. In exchange for this, one must try to acquire a mode of thinking within the psychoanalytic order. If the physician objectifies the organs, the psychologist objectifies the ego. This is a crucial topic, for it constitutes the decisive obstacle, the buttress of the post-Freudian psychoanalysis against which Lacan offers resistance. Ego psychology—and more specifically, American ego psychology—has developed quite popular a conception in relation to transference. It asserts that in the transference the analyst attempts to establish a therapeutic alliance with the healthy aspect of the patient's ego, so that the latter will be able to

---

15. S. Freud, "Carta a O. Pfister del 25/11/28," in S. Freud–O. Pfister, *Correspondencia 1909–1939*, Fondo de Cultura Económica, México, 1966, pp. 120–121. [*Psychoanalysis and Faith: The Letters of Sigmund Freud and O. Pfister*, H. Meng and E. L. Freud, eds., E. Mosbacher, Trans., Basic Books, 1963.]

confront, in coalescence with the healthy par excellence that the analyst embodies, the madness of the other part of the patient.

The seminar makes a very accurate comment. It is here, the seminar affirms, where the schizia of the subject in one of its manifestations may be identified. That with which the ego psychologists want to forge an alliance, what they judge as the healthy part of the analysant, is precisely where they should recognize his illness. It is, in the last analysis, what constitutes a hindrance, due to the specular dimension that characterizes this fascinating deadlock between two allegedly healthy and equal parts. Lacan sometimes comments ironically on this behavior based on an assumption. He claims that we could place this attitude under the tenet, where the it of the analysant was, the ego of the analyst should be; in other words, the subject should be "grabbed" up to the limits of his nothingization. Why? Because among other things—and especially at the beginning of the analysis—an effect of transference consists in the analyst being placed in the locus of idealization.

Among a variety of manifestations, this idealization is usually represented in terms of health, of manifold potency, and of access to the more or less beatific happiness the analyst is supposed to possess. It is clear that all of this is tied to a dimension of love. This is the determining point through which we may approach the question of the transference from a different plane. Prior to this, Lacan accurately punctuates Nacht's proposal. He points out that the latter's development takes transference in a sense that could almost be considered, in his view, as Christian. The Nachtian presence of the analyst implies that the analyst's "appearance" subsides, shrinks, so that the analysant—especially at the end of the process—may get closer to the analyst as presence and appreciate him as he "really" is. This, of course, involves forgetting completely what we had commented earlier, that is, "You never look at me from the place from which I see you," and "What I look at is never what I wish to see." In other words, it involves the dismissal of the dimension of the failed encounter.

In this sort of good marriage established at the end of the analysis (Nacht assumes), the function presence of the analyst emerges. As he does often, Lacan retrieves the term only to better subvert it. He will ask, what does "presence of the analyst" mean? And he will answer: it is that which allows the unconscious to display its effects. Let us recall that in the text titled *Televisión*[16]—and in "Posición de lo inconsciente"[17] ("Positions of the Unconscious")—Lacan asserts that the analyst is part of the concept of the unconscious. I believe that it is an admirable way to treat the analyst as presence. It is the presence of the analyst that is part of the concept of the unconscious, for it is that presence the latter addresses. Consequently, we should agree that the concept is not simply a theoretical idea, an abstraction, since the concept "takes shape," it corporealizes.

The unconscious thus possesses operative effectiveness and accomplishment (*efectuación*), if the analyst exists. This constitutes an example of the fact that the fundamental concepts not only can, but should be, articulated according to various angles. What we are doing now is relating the terms linked to the transference based on this definition of the concept that I see as subversive, so much so, that it renders the concept certainly aconceptual. The concept, therefore, is not something that exists merely on paper, or that is effective as a recitation. It necessarily involves the interlocutive dimension at play. We can talk about the unconscious as a concept, but also as a field on which we may operate. Our daily practice accounts for this; we are concerned with this every day. To end this exposition, the unconscious is not, therefore, a fundamental concept on which we may preach out of the presence of the analyst.

QUESTIONS AND ANSWERS

Q: You pointed out that psychoanalysis does not do introspection, but does the transference not relate in some way to the dimension of the introspective?

A: I don't see why it should. Let us take as an example Freud's views in *Beyond the Pleasure Principle* (with which we will deal more thoroughly

---

16. J. Lacan *Télévision*, Seuil, Paris, 1974, p. 26. [*Television*, trans. D. Hollier, R. Krauss, and A. Michelson, W.W. Norton, New York, 1990.]

17. J. Lacan, "*Posición del [de lo] inconsciente*," *Escritos II, op. cit.*, p. 370. ["Positions of the Unconscious," trans. B. Fink, in R. Feldstein, B. Fink, M. Jaanus, eds. *Reading Seminar I and II*, SUNY Press, Albany, 1995.]

next meeting). The analysant does not remember having been an un-ruly child who systematically opposed his father, but he presents such a behavior now—he repeats his failure in act, with his analyst. This observation requires an analytic interpretation. It is not characteristic of the subject of representation, the one who sees himself seeing him-self. When Lacan defines the unconscious as the discourse of the Other, he adds that the latter returns from the outside through the analyst's said (*el dicho del analista*). As you may appreciate, we are getting farther and farther away from the introspective.

Q: Could you distinguish between transference and the effect of transference?

A: All right. We should ask ourselves why we must distinguish between transference and effect. Maybe it is that, if we want to be rigor-ous, transference is, in short, what may be analyzed in psychoanalysis. The effects of transference may occur, and do so, in many situations in life, but such effects are not processed in the terms we have discussed earlier, and are not suitable to be referred in—and to—a metaphorical mode, but are lived imaginarily.

On the other hand, we must pay attention to Lacan's insistence on saying "effect of." If there is no effect, there is no possibility to work on any issue. This procedure involves insisting on the fact that in analy-sis we are not dealing with an inner, introspective dimension of the inner world and objects, since all these are theories within an intro-spectionist episteme, even though they claim otherwise. The resort to "effect of" brings about manifold consequences, for it refers precisely to such consequences.

Q: Would it not be more exact, concerning the matter of being and ap-pearance, to refer to the distinction between being and entity? The en-tity is what is shown, insofar as we must reveal through knowledge (*conocimiento*) the being that conceals behind it.

A: The point we want to highlight, especially regarding those issues linked to the decoy, does not allude to a cognitive dimension but pri-marily to the order of the drive—in other words, to the specific combi-nation of the life drive with the death drive. What is substantive here is not the yearning or the impossibility to know, but, for instance, how it is possible that the veil arouses, or how it is that the act of pretending to be more than a subject is, intimidates. Our intention is to try to account for the roots in the drive (*raíces pulsionales*) of what in the field of philosophy is customarily posited in strictly cognitive terms.

Q: Does the diagram of the gaze Lacan presents in this seminar have anything to do with the experience of the inverted vase, or with the formation of the virtual image?

A: The optical model in the *Ecrits* attends particularly to the dimension of ideals, which is not considered in the diagrams you mention. In that opportunity, Lacan focused on the formation and the elucidation of the pair ideal ego–ego ideal.[18] Here we are dealing with something different, very delimited, for Lacan is concerned with highlighting the significance of the way in which castration is eluded through that object *a* called the gaze. The diagram in Seminar 11 is a very elementary— geometral, even—and bidimensional support. Lacan uses it so as to be able to ponder certain issues and to posit a segment of structural analysis. The fact that both triangles—that of vision and that of the gaze— are oppositive is not coincidental. Then Lacan will present the chiasma as a simile for the interweaving of fibers. At this point, let us say that Lacan is the first to analyze the effect of synthesis. He thus tries to process the ways in which we are incessantly "caught" by the scopic— especially by the infatuated subject of representation. At the same time, he does not fail to note the occasions in which this object *a* gaze can be detected.

---

18. J. Lacan, "*Observación sobre el informe de Daniel Lagache: 'Psicoanálisis y estructura de la personalidad,'*" in *Escritos II, op. cit.*, pp. 289–305. [I could not find an English edition.]

6

Deception, Knowledge, Ideal: Transference II

Today I want to tell you something that happened when I started to read the newspaper advertisement for our meeting. I found that I had been transformed into a man whose last name was *Hareptos*. As you may realize, such a term starts with the first letters of my last name and continues with the last letters of the word *conceptos*[1]:

The word *conceptos* obviously slipped in from the title of this course. When I read the ad, I couldn't understand the name at first, until the condensation emerged clearly. This is an interesting example to look at in considering the role of the proper name function. I present here what happened without being able to give you any details, obviously, about the way in which this formation of the unconscious came to be configured. A process of metonymic gliding (*corrimiento*) took place here that

---

1. "Concepts" in Spanish. (Translator's note)

derived later in a condensation, in Freud's terms, or a metaphor, in Lacan's. The metaphor[2] essentially, crucially alludes to the founding condition of the subject, who is such due to paternity—it is from paternity that the proper name occurs. I am referring to the paternity strictly due to the slant of the last name. In the face of this ad, I must point out that I still bear my own, and not the one the paper attributed to me.

This *lapsus* is interesting because it evoked in me how, faced with the insistent mistake in the spelling of my name when I was at school, I took to designate myself as "Harari with an aitch and all together." When others would ask my name, I would answer thus, so that the bearing of this mark, of this inscription, would remain sharp and present. These are common reactions when one finds oneself suddenly "insulted" in one's proper name, for a mistake in this matter is not equivalent to any other *lapsus*. Despite what I have told you, this time I feel flattered at having been so closely tied to the concepts of psychoanalysis. I do not fail to acknowledge that the unconscious process whose conclusion is this new last name resulted in a compliment.

Let us go on then to the concepts. Last class we started with the third one, namely, that of the transference, on which we had offered a few basically indicative, phenomenological notes. To continue with this matter, in Seminar 11 Lacan organizes the following strategy for his exposition: he starts with the third fundamental concept so as to immediately give the cue to the fourth, that is, the drive. I, in turn, will develop a different course, founded on a didactic motive, if you will accept such a justification. I will do so because there are points further along in the seminar where the concept of transference is taken up again. I think it is more appropriate, given the nature of this brief course, to apprehend the theme of the transference as it gradually appears, through partial but defining strokes.[3] We will reserve the last meetings (we are starting the second half of our meetings today) for the fundamental issue of the drive, a topic that will allow us to include the decisive Lacanian

---

2. Cf. Chapter 10.

3. This is the sense in which the author has used "*espigadamente*," a neologism. (Translator's note)

problem concerning the constitution of the subject, or even better, the causative operations of the subject.

I will only announce these operations at this point, and we will return to them later. They are alienation and separation. Our immediate itinerary will attempt an introductory reading of Chapter 12 of the seminar, titled "Sexuality in the Defiles of the Signifier." Right after that, we will resort to certain parts of Chapters 18 ("Of the Subject Who Is Supposed to Know, of the First Dyad and of the Good") and 19, titled "From Interpretation to the Transference." Our following conceptualization on the transference will hinge on those chapters.

In the first class we specified a definition of transference that we now incorporate again. Lacan says that the transference is the enactment of the reality of the unconscious. Notice, of course, the reference to reality, and not to the Real. As we already know, this is a crucial distinction for Lacanian theorization, which calls for very precise criteria. Why the insistence on this issue of reality? To answer this question we must take a brief detour that will also serve as a recapitulation. You will recall what we worked on last class regarding the theme of the scopic, with the development of the gaze as our starting point. We pointed out that the special characteristic of the scopic was a certain idea of the decoy and the mask—a covering-up appearance, suggestive of a beyond. We did not deal with essences, for our purpose is not to substantialize the concepts. We agreed then that such an idea allowed us to clarify the relations between appearance and what is beyond it, in order to derive from that the transference, which refers to something different from what it seems to be. We can support that idea, with the awareness that it entails an almost banal, and even tautological, approach.

Within this register, we brought up the division between negative and positive transference, and we also included the recourse of not taking what the analysant has to say about the analyst too seriously, as if it were a reality. The matter just started there. A traditional line of post-Freudianism emerged from these elaborations whose curative goal lies in trying to situate the analysant within the frame of a reality, setting aside the deformation entailed in the transference. These trends assume that transference deceives. The role of the analyst, consequently, would be to succeed in transcending this deception by means of interventions such as the following: "What you believe is not so in the real world; it is this other way." Nucleus of truth: even in these conceptions, the idea of deception is tied decisively to the transference. It is possible then to establish a very elementary statement to begin with, namely, that the transference is firmly tied to the dimension of deception:

Transference ⟶ Deception

Lacan's reflections on deception are very sharp, particularly regarding something quite common. I am referring here to an erroneous maneuver in analysis that occurs when deception is interpreted reflexively (that is, to self-deceive). In what sense do we consider that the denunciation of the analysant's "self-deception" constitutes an out-of-place maneuver? In the sense that what is being addressed is the much talked-about "healthy part" we mentioned in our last meeting. This strategy involves appealing to the good judgment, the sensibility of this healthy part, summoning it to combat the ill part. The foundation for this action consists in an argument at least as old as Socrates, namely, the postulation of a sort of irresistible power the good exerts on the subject. If the subject knows (*conoce*) the good, knows (*sabe*) about the good, he will choose it, and this is taken for granted. If the subject does something evil, it is obviously only because he does not know.

According to this peculiar morality, in sum, knowing (*conocer*) the good would suffice for choosing it spontaneously. To self-deceive would mean, ultimately, not to know, which would determine that the subject be implicated (*incurso*) in a malevolent morality. Based on these arguments, this trend appeals to the analysant's good sense, information, and knowledge, all of which would lead him to travel the right path. The universe of the "psy," as we know, offers this type of product to the citizens at large. If they know the "psy" data, this trend assumes, they will act "right." Not long ago, I had the opportunity to address this issue critically in a brief journalistic essay. I recalled there what Freud expressed to a woman who demanded advice concerning the right upbringing of her young son according to the psychoanalytic rules, in order to prevent any psychic disorder. Freud answered that she shouldn't worry; whatever she did, it would be wrong. Was this answer due to skepticism on the part of the mastermind of psychoanalysis? Or did it intend to point out that we all are—and will be—irremediably neurotic? In that essay I argued as follows: the answer did not assert that whatever she did she would do *him* wrong. It only said that she would to *it* wrong. I believe this is a radical difference. The issue is not about the harm to, or the possible neurotization of, the child, but about the fact that if the mother forced herself to abide by certain norms, such an endeavor would not be possible, because in fact she would do what her desire dictated, insofar as the abstract and general norm has the (veiled) role of inducing the *"mass-media" jouissance*. It functions as a parasitical superego, inducing discomfort in the subject when he verifies the inexorable fulfillment of the "beneficial" injunction, in this case for not implementing—concerning her son or whomever—an upbringing such as psychoanalysis dictates.

We heard right: such behavior renders psychoanalysis equivalent to what is expectable from God. Indeed, in this type of proposal psychoanalysis is transformed into a religion. Thus, it is asked, it is demanded to bring about a moral reform of society, so that the latter may finally be comprised of "healthy individuals." We derive all this from the function of deception contained in the fallacy of Socratic morality—it is not exaggerated to qualify it thus—that is still prevalent today, with the help of decoys. How often, faced with a certain discovery in the session, analysants appeal to the request for "innocence," placing the analyst as superego dimension! The consequent "response" to the irruptions of the unconscious is then: "Ah! But I didn't know this was like that." Claiming ignorance manifests a way to skirt around the register of desire.[4] Lacan points out then that the dimension of deception is utterly constitutive of transference. The alluded-to deception, however, is quite different from the presumption that it constitutes a deformation of consensual reality. Let us include now the definition of transference and the oppositive relation reality-deception in the graph we designed earlier:

---

4. Without overlooking the fact that ignorance is a passion of being, and that nothing justifies the pretension to postulate an epistemophilic drive.

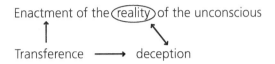

Does deception with respect to reality exist in the relation reality-deception? Doubtlessly so. Yet this does not happen due to a sort of moral ignorance, to the lack of knowledge of the parameters of good and evil, but due to a different cause, something quite more puerile, common, and customary that has determined the incessant production of so many joys and sorrows among the speaking beings. I am referring specifically to love. If there is deception in the transference, it is precisely because love is at play there:

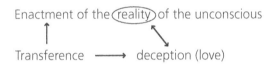

What does it mean that there is deception in love? Might we believe that this affirmation refers to the distinction between a deceiving love and one that is not so? Doesn't true love exist? The issue here is not to fake love where it doesn't exist, but to affirm deception as constitutive of love. It happens that when one says loving, what one means is being loved. Such is Freud's crucial discovery[5]: this is the deception constitutive of love. Returning to our fundamental concept, the fact is that transference is constituted in terms of love. Let us resort to Freud's classic text, *"Puntualizaciones sobre el amor de transferencia"* (*Observations on Transference-Love*).[6] We may ask ourselves why he was concerned with and why he wrote exclusively about transference love and not about any other manifestations of this phenomenon. It is because he went to the core, to the very node of what transference means. He

---

5. S. Freud, *Introducción del narcisismo [narcismo]* (*On Narcissism* [narcism]: *An Introduction*), O. C., *op. cit.*, vol. 14, pp. 84ff.; and *Psicología de las masas y análisis del yo* (*Group Psychology and Ego Analysis*), O.C., *op. cit.*, vol. 18, pp. 105–110 [pp. 89 and 111–116].

6. In *Papers on Technique*, S.E., *op. cit.*, vol. 12. (Translator's note)

did not consider, therefore, that positive transference is love transference, and negative transference is hate transference, because love transference both enables and blocks analytic work.

In the transference there is an opening of the unconscious, for it is there that the analysant articulates himself to analysis under the figure of the analyst (we will clarify this point later on). At the same time, paradoxically, transference is the closure of the unconscious—we should remember here the hoop net—for the analysant, as Freud describes so well, dodges the referral of one situation to the other, assigning total veracity and legitimacy to what is happening in the here and now. If we read carefully the quoted text, we will notice that in no way is transference love considered false. Very often the maneuver, the analytic steering of love transference, is reduced to voicing considerations such as the following: "In fact, you don't feel what you are feeling toward me but toward somebody else. You deceive yourself. I am only your analyst." This comment usually refers to a character from the past. It is then that the already-mentioned confusion between transference and repetition occurs. The analysant repeats with the analyst something that refers to somebody else. Here, now, and with me becomes way off in the distance, before, and with somebody else.

Even if it is not said precisely with this wordplay, what Lacan affirms is that transference cannot be thought aside from love, but love cannot be thought aside from the transference. Love indeed implies transference. In the previous session you asked me about the discrimination between transference and effects of transference. I repeat it: the analytic situation is not in any way required in order for the effects of transference to be triggered. The latter happen along with a factor that does not strictly require the perimeter of our praxis. What is needed is only the appearance of somebody who will embody—we should take this term literally, em-body, to give body, to throw oneself into (*poner el cuerpo*)— somebody who will embody, as I was saying, the set square decisive for the transference: *le sujet supposé savoir*.[7] I quote it like this in order to

---

7. In French in the original. It has been translated into English as "the subject supposed to know" or "the subject who is supposed to know." Sheridan sometimes uses the French expression without translating it. (Translator's note)

offer you my own translation of this Lacanian expression that I believe has been usually poorly translated. It is worth noting: the subject supposed to knowledge (*el sujeto supuesto al saber*), that may also be presented as a triple "S," with the intermediate one in lowercase: S.s.S. It has been sometimes translated as the supposed subject of knowledge (*sujeto supuesto de saber*), a definition that, frankly, suggests the imaginarization of somebody as the bearer of a certain knowledge. This somebody is, of course, a subject. According to this suggested translation, a dimension related to self-deception is once again postulated. In this way, it is believed that there is a person who is the repository of a certain knowledge, and hence, supposed subject of knowledge. If I said knowledge supposed to the subject (*saber supuesto al sujeto*), or subject of whom knowledge is supposed/subject who is supposed to know[8] (*sujeto al que se supone saber*),[9] we would be confronting the same problem. To say, on the contrary, subject supposed to knowledge (*sujeto supuesto al saber*), as I suggest, implies to have knowledge (*saber*) precede the subject. It means, congruently, to take into account that there is a preexisting structure to which a subject offers his being. Evidently, this development refers to a knowledge (*saber*) not in the sense of a knowledge (*conocimiento*)—and I am being purposely redundant—cognitively conceived. It is, conversely, a knowledge (*saber*) about the dimension of desire that constitutes the subject—the unconscious as an articulated knowledge (*saber*) that is not known.

Yet the locus of the Other knows about me, can answer the queries of my existence. It is consequently upon psychoanalysis that transference ultimately materializes; the subject with a name and a last name, claimed as analyst, will take that place. He will be the partial embodiment of the lacking knowledge—a knowledge (*saber*), therefore, precedes him, in the same way as the Symbolic precedes the subject, as we have said before. If the embodiment is partial, the maneuver will con-

---

8. Since *saber* can be both the infinitive of the verb "to know" and the noun knowledge, this phrase may be translated in two different ways. (Translator's note)

9. The latter is the option suggested by the new version of the seminar (Buenos Aires, Paidós, 1986, pp. 238ff.), which, by the way, claims to be "the first Spanish edition" (*sic*, p. 6).

sist at the most in supposing that the subject possesses a certain knowledge (*saber*) as a resulting effect. It will not consist in endorsing the identity, the overlaying equivalence.

To affirm a certain subject as a subject of effective knowledge (*saber*)—and not to suppose him such—runs the sure risk Lacan pointed out in "*De una cuestión preliminar a todo tratamiento posible de la psicosis*" ("On a Question Preliminary to Any Possible Treatment of Psychosis"): the uncannified psychoticizing encounter with what he designates as A-father (*Un-padre*).[10] This is a particular character who, at a certain point in a subject's life, operates as real A-father, triggering psychosis. He does not determine it, but appears as a detonator in the face of the subject's call, induced, from then on, to an eroticized field of aggression. I believe that this A-father might be Knowledge (*Saber*), not supposed anymore, but affirmed without inconsistency, without castration. In this respect, it is interesting to note how Lacan thought that in the field of psychoanalysis there was one who knew. The one who knew—not qua supposed to have knowledge—was Freud.[11] Yet his knowledge did not deal with theory or concepts; Freud knew about the defining desire of the psychoanalyst as such.

To be a psychoanalyst means to confront the constituting order of desire. That is why we situate as the central pivot of analysis what we dealt with, basically, in our second meeting, namely, the desire of the analyst. As we have already pointed out, there exists a (fallacious) Socratic morality of which the psychoanalyst would be the contemporary deputy. How? By supposing that, since his task is oriented to lead the other to the irresistible juncture with that which would do him good, the psychoanalyst is the one who wants that other's good. Yet the seminar warns that when, following such a Socratic morality, he appeals to the healthy part of the analysant and invites him to abide by that good, the analyst does not take into account—does not analyze—a nodular dimension of desire, that is, the one that may be characterized as an apparent non-desire, as

---

10. J. Lacan, *Escritos II, op. cit.*, pp. 262–268. [English translation in *Ecrits: A Selection, op. cit.*, pp. 215–221.]

11. J. Lacan, *Los cuatro conceptos . . . , op. cit.*, p. 237 [*The Four Fundamental Concepts . . . , op. cit.*, p. 232].

a not wanting to desire. Do we need to recall that such a mode is characteristic of the psychoneurotic? In the latter we can grasp the fact that not wanting to desire is wanting not to desire. It is, precisely, a defensive phase by means of which a decisive feature is ratified in the Freudian cogito, baptized as *desidero*. This is only a way to express, resorting to Latin, that the articulation of the subject with desire is of the nature of a fundament. Desire is the ultimate sediment of the action of the signifier upon the subject to which it gives rise. Let us recall that the subject can be constituted precisely because the unconscious is structured like a language. This constitution, however, determines that such a *desidero* be the last—or first—where the way in which the subject regulates his life may be found. It is advisable to emphasize this point we have already made, that is, that the analyst's desire is not the desire to be an analyst, nor each analyst's desire. The latter, particularly, is located in the rancid order of subjectivity characteristic of introspectionism—malicious as epistemological orientation—and is precariously founded on: "I feel that," or "I think that." The recourse to a "felt" cognition, instead of the *desidero*, the set square of truth and irrefutable testimony, culminates in an ineffable. Doubtlessly, the "I feel" alludes to an inner world, but, how to convey it? Of this, what can be processed? The fact that somebody feels something belongs to the order of the subject of representation, who finds in rationalized affect a maximum and nontransferable bastion. The desire of the analyst, on the other hand, aims at locating knowledge in the place of truth. It is a function to which the subject offers his being. The subject must seek to settle in the analyst's desire, which we might define, maybe, as the analysts' desire. I believe that it is, provisionally, a viable formulation, for it allows us to highlight, concerning the concept, the common denominator implied in the fact of appointing oneself as the one who summons the transference. The analyst's desire, Lacan tells us, is that upon which the field of our practice is founded. This is important, because it entails considering that it is not just the analysant's desire that is founding. The person who comes as the analysant arrives, and carries out his transference.

The novel aspect is this Lacanian emphasis, namely, not the fact that the analyst's desire has its own status, but that its circumscription is the very pivot of analysis. This move entails quite a sudden twist imprinted in the global elucidation of our praxis. Then, if the pivot weakens, the analysis itself may end up "falling," or may be abruptly interrupted (let us recall here the *acting-out* and the *passage à l'acte*).[12] This consideration leads Lacan to recommend that the analyst be cautious, that he ask himself the following: "What is my part in the maintenance of the disorder I am denunciating?"[13] He approaches this matter in a way that is apparently persecutory, and likely disagreeable to his colleagues—indeed, the analyst must be sat in the dock. He must give his reasons, or else every violent transferential effect will be constrained, in his "intellection," to the fact that it originates in a hypothetical untreatable pathology of the analysant's.

By stressing the analyst's desire, Lacan is also emphasizing that the *desidero* of the analyst must obviously confront sexuality. It must do so because the origins of psychoanalysis have been marked in this way. I am referring to the founding moment when the patient par excellence—everybody knows about this already—enables the beginning of our discipline. Anna O. launches analysis paradoxically by means of the articulation with the weakening of the condition of her therapist, Breuer. We can identify here in which way sexuality plays a role in the analyst's desire. If we read Anna O.'s case history, we find almost no reference to sexuality. There was nothing manifest until the unforeseen appears in the most unusual way—a pseudocyesis, a hysteric pregnancy. This effect emerged in a surprising way, unsettling Breuer. The reaction of the therapist is well known: he abandoned his patient and traveled to Venice with his wife on a second honeymoon. According to Ernest Jones—and Lacan followed this information—during that time the Breuers conceived a daughter who would later end her days by suicide in the United States, no doubt due to the conditions in which she was conceived. This information dates back to 1964, but later testimonies have changed this map.

---

12. Cf. Chapter 2.

13. J. Lacan, *"Intervención sobre la transferencia,"* in *Escritos I, op. cit.,* p. 41. ["Intervention of Transference," trans. J. Rose, in J. Mitchel and J. Rose, eds. *Feminine Sexuality,* W.W. Norton, New York, 1982.]

I have here a book by Lucy Freeman published in 1971. Its title is *La historia de Anna O. (The Story of Anna O.)*. It has not been published in Spanish so far, which might mean it is not seen as potentially profitable. It is a pity, for the reading of some passages in this work is very valuable to clarify the so-called origins of psychoanalysis. A letter by Freud to Stefan Zweig (numbered 265 in his *Correspondencia*) is also useful to elucidate what happened to Breuer. In this letter, Freud reveals the details of the emergence of Anna O.'s transference in such a peculiar manner (as unexpected sexuality) through the pseudo-cyesis. At that time—we add along with Lacan—there suddenly occurred a weakening of the analyst's desire, in favor of the desire of a particular analyst (Josef Breuer) for the apparent search for a new child, a child verbalized by Anna, in the midst of her abdominal cramps, in this way: "Dr. Breuer's child is coming!" In the cited letter Freud wrote: "At this moment, he [Breuer] held in his hand the key that would have opened the 'doors to the Mothers,' but he let it drop."[14] (There is here a literary reference taken from Part 2 of Goethe's *Faust*.) Evidently, Breuer could not bear the situation, and overwhelmed by "a great conventional horror," adds the letter, he fled. Nevertheless, today we have other historical data that I will read to you: "Dr. George H. Pollock, director of the Chicago Institute of Psychoanalysis, also investigated the case of Anna O. He discovered the mistake Jones made when he stated that a daughter had been conceived after Breuer terminated the treatment precipitously . . ." Here comes what I already told you, namely, the trip to Venice, and so on. The text continues: "Dr. Pollock obtained proof from members of Breuer's family—taken from the archives of the city of Vienna—which showed that this girl—Dora, Breuer's youngest child—had been born on March 11, 1882. The treatment of Berta Pappenheim (Anna O.'s real name) ended on June 7th of the same year. Consequently, this daughter had been conceived on the preceding year."

---

14. S. Freud, "Carta a S. Zweig del 2/6/32," in *Epistolario (1873–1939)*, Bibioteca Nueva, Madrid, 1963, p. 457. [*Letters of Sigmund Freud*, Selected and edited, E. L. Freud, McGraw-Hill, New York, 1964, p. 413.]

Here, then, is a first mistake. Pollock discovered also that Dora committed suicide not in the United States, as Jones wrote, but in Vienna, when the Nazis knocked on her door to take her to a concentration camp. This was confirmed through repeated interviews with her relatives.[15] These are mistakes that need to be corrected according to the facts, in honor of the truth, but they in no way modify the decisive reference to a sudden and unforeseen irruption of sexuality. It was the latter that brought about Breuer's frightened flight when confronted with the little ball. He evidently knew that it wasn't his child. What was then the matter? What would we have done in his place? Say that the supposed child was a demand addressed to another, or account for the dimension of deception that constitutes the transference?

With his customary acuteness, Lacan understood what happens with the vicissitudes of love already in the beginnings of the analysis. When transference love is established, the analysant wants to transform himself into someone lovable.[16] He succeeds in proposing himself for that place, situating the analyst in the place of the loving one (*amador*) (forcing our Spanish a little bit).[17] The loving one and the lovable form a pair that the other psychoanalysis has recognized and named as "honeymoon"—maybe detaching it from Breuer's story. This is a crucial moment, for it establishes deception as constitutive of the relationship. I believe that it is necessary to point out that if, as it actually happens, there exists something likely to trigger a situation not created by the analysis but from which the latter profits, that "something" is no less than the fundamental psychoanalytic rule—free association. As you will recall, the latter constitutes neither a guided introspection nor a recount

---

15. L. Freeman, *L'Histoire d'Anna O*, Presses Universitaires de France, Paris, 1977, pp. 248–249. [*The Story of Anna O*, Walker & Co, New York, 1977]

16. The rest of this sentence in the original refers to the fact that *amable* means both "lovable" and "amiable": ". . not in the sense of kind but in that of someone liable to be loved." (Translator's note)

17. The right Spanish word would be *amante*, "lover" in English. The author has replaced it with *amador* in order to avoid the connotation of a third person participating in the relationship given both by the Spanish and the English terms. That is why I have translated "loving one."(Translator's note)

of affective states. This command (*consigna*) to make the analysant speak, to make him say whatever it is, is valid because as an analyst—as the embodiment of the subject supposed to knowledge—I am implicitly empowered to interpret concerning the analysant's desire. As a structural effect, the systematic maintenance of free association positions the analyst in the locus of the ego ideal. Such position demands a complementary pole on the other end: the ideal ego, the lovable:

$$\text{Ego ideal} \longrightarrow \text{Ideal ego}$$

$$\text{(loving one)} \qquad \text{(lovable)}$$

Concerning this ideal ego, Freud pointed out that it consisted in the ego being once again, as during childhood, its own ideal. Paradigmatically, this circumstance is attained at the initial stage of the analytic cure, even though it is not reduced to this stage. The analysant resolves to be his own ideal once again, as he was during childhood, but only to the extent that the analyst exists. For doesn't the listening to a driveling and sillerile (*tonteril*) parlance indicate a loving one?[18]

Let us move now to the last part of Seminar 11. Lacan focuses here on the clarification of two chapters in Freud's work that are indispensable for any analyst. I am referring to Chapters 7 and 8 of *Group Psychology and the Analysis of the Ego*, titled respectively "Identificación" and "Enamoramiento e hipnosis" ("Identification" and "Being in Love and Hypnosis"). The beginning of analysis constitutes a logical moment in which the existence of hypnosis may be allegorically postulated. In other words, as Freud succeeds in detecting, both in analysis and in hypnosis, there is a loss of critical judgment on the part of the analysant, as well as a devotion to an agency (*instancia*) of ideal. This does not happen through subjection or naive dependency, but because our starting point is the deception of love. This is the way in which, in loving, this deception is constituted, isolated in its present, in transference, in other words, the deception that affirms that in loving, I make myself

---

18. Yet not a blindly unconditional listening, for the cutting of the session also constitutes a symbolic punishment in the face of empty speech.

loved. Let us think then how much this transferential situation has in common with the dimension of being in love.

Psychoanalysis's conception regarding love is generally quite disappointing. Something that is apparently as lofty, as sublime as love, is relegated, for instance, to the affirmation that one loves in the other what one does not possess, in order to reach one's own ideal. Love is nothing more than a somersault of the ego to re-enthrone itself as ideal. If one finally idealizes the object of love, it will only be to declare: "If an object this marvelous loves me, how splendid I must be." It is on this highly elementary reasoning that the establishment—often at astounding levels—of the lack of criticism, of the loss of the least degree of objectivity, is founded. We enter thus into the strict dimension of idealization. We are dealing then with two ideal formations, namely, the ego ideal and the ideal ego. They constitute two planes that hinge on love one way or another, even if they exceed this perception.

In Chapter 7 of *Group Psychology and the Analysis of the Ego* Freud distinguished among three types of identifications. Methodologically, we are not interested now in the way in which Freud threaded them, but in the way in which Lacan lucidly exploits this discrimination toward the comprehension of the cure. For such a discrimination offers indeed a privileged slant to subtly enter into the advent of the analytic cure. Regardless of its genesis or of the way in which Freud theorizes it, what takes place in the cure is an identification pertinently designated as narcissic that is related very clearly to love. In Lacanian terms, we may call it imaginary or specular:

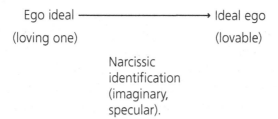

We can place a letter in this schema to indicate one of the functional localizations at play. It will be an I, through which we come close to the idea of the place of the analyst qua ego ideal:

In the seminar, the I means the idealization of identification. We must not confuse this notation with that which Lacan writes as I (A), which means ego ideal.[19] The I is not exactly the same as ego ideal, because it is the idealization of identification. What is interesting is the observation that this is precisely the locus "embodied" by the analyst according to the analysant's request. The analyst, then, is being called by the analysant to occupy the locus of the I insofar as symbolic support of the specularity.

We must take this I in analysis as a demand effect. We introduce this term here due to its considerable conceptual appropriateness in Lacan. Obviously, demand does not equal desire. We must discriminate between them. Let us start with the criticism of the way in which the demand has usually been considered. First, this notion does not strictly denote the sole, clear, neat sense of explicit request. No, because we must also attend to the litigious element the word *demand* transports. Moreover, when we scan the word *repetition*, we must not fail to listen to the emergence there of a re-petition, that is, a requesting again. The demand factor, therefore, also comes into play, taken in the repetitive—failed—angle of the requesting again.

The demand is not manifest content insofar as desire is latent content, even though we should add that through the paths of the demand crawls desire. Yet there is also unconscious demand, so that this discrimination is not valid. It is often said that the demand is the demand of love. Whatever is requested, it is finally love that is demanded. I think that this is a very fine grasp of what takes place, obviously, in so many of the

---

19. J. Lacan, "The subversion of the . . . ," *op. cit.*, pp. 306ff. [Harari maintains the Lacanian notation that corresponds to the French word *Autre*. Sheridan uses I (O), for Other.]

analysants' requests. On the other hand, nothing can be done about desire but fence it in so as to gradually circumscribe it, but in the order of desire there is no possibility of naming as there is in the case of demand.

To formalize the function of the demand in analysis, a demand that is a demand of love—always in terms of the first identification, the love identification—the seminar introduces a very simple topological resource, namely, the interior eight:

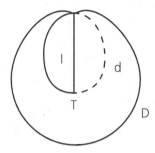

We must consider this diagram as representing a continuous surface with a return lobe that enters from behind, which accounts for the dotted line. The drawing makes us think of a dimension of depth at play. Something is located in the hidden lobe that attempts to break the whole "natural" sense of the figure. We signal it with the letter d, which represents desire. With this schema, Lacan shows how transference T is that which facilitates leading the demand D to the identification, represented in the graph as the line of intersection I we mentioned before. It is very simple—the analysant experiences that his analyst is somebody marvelous, and wants to be like him. That is his request. That is why the analyst is called to embody, via the demand, the ideal, in anticipation of an identification. If there is idealization, the way in which such idealization will bind later on determines that the analysant will seek identification with the one with whom he has a claim to be in love. That is why we are saying—along with Freud—that there exists a capturing oscillation between being in love and identification. Transference leads the demand toward identification, but the d remains behind—in the hidden lobe; in the cure—the analyst's desire. The latter is the one who tries, precisely, to prevent the accomplishment of such a passage. He attempts, then, to prevent the transference from leading to identification, advocating the reestablishment of the demand. We must point out that this very thing that takes place in every analysis—and prospers in those that are inappropriately theorized—has been worshipped in certain analytic schools—the paradox is worth noting—as the very goal of analysis. These schools seek, foster, the identification with the analyst, which, if on the one hand constitutes an out-of-synch narcissic compliment, on the other hand it hypnotically alienates the analysant behind the person (in the Greek etymological sense of mask) of the analyst.

This identification is actually a moment of arrest in the analysis. It may certainly give rise to similes, where it seems that there is psychoanalysis when what is going on once and again is that the analyst is offering—the word is too brutal yet illustrative—satisfaction to a demand. To tell the truth, such a satisfaction is utterly impossible, but what does take place is a highly effective narcissic bait, so that the demand may lead to identification. We must make clear at this point that identification is not merely a globalizing, totalizing process. Freud postulates a second type of identification designated as identification with the feature, with the trait.

It is not necessary that the identification happen in the sense of some sort of totality that is "imitated." A single feature or trait is enough, Freud warns us: an *einziger Zug*. Lacan punctuates and privileges this term. It is doubtlessly his merit to have highlighted it in Freud's work, as he did with so many other concepts. It suffices then with one single feature or trait for the identification of the second type to happen. Consequently, the *einziger Zug* is rendered as a unary feature. This identification may give rise, for instance, to the formation of many symptoms. One may have the same symptom of somebody one loves. Eventually, one may also suffer the symptom of somebody one hates. In the first case, it means to possess in oneself the loved object. In the second case, the symptom appears as a possible punishment in the face of hate.

The examples are manifold, and there is a crucial element we must take into account. We understand that this ideal formation, this ego ideal, bears in its nucleus a unary feature. Every ego ideal starts indeed through an identification with the feature, with the trait, which allows, starting from a nucleus, the gestation of the ideal. This second identification can be sometimes detected in the various analysants of the same analyst. Such an iterative feature causes the analysants to recognize each other and to appear, in a way, as belonging to "the same family," because they share "a likeness." This occurrence may very well obey to the limits of the analysis by this particular analyst, in which case it will bear testimony of a weakening of the analyst's desire. On the other hand, this shared element is not necessarily a product of an inference or of a vague assumption, but may be clearly identified in traits tied to speech and/or in unexpected behavioral manifestations. Usually, neither analyst nor analysant has the least idea of this identification, for it possesses a condition—to say it in scopic terms—of scotoma, of blind spot.

In sum, this is only one among many issues linked to the particular way in which we understand this stage of deadlock in the cure. In this respect, the proposition consists once more of inviting the analyst to relinquish the glitter obtained thanks to his ability to occupy the locus for which the analysant continually nominates him as an effect of the structure characteristic of psychoneurosis, allied with the analytic artifice. Instead of this infatuation, of this strutting, what Lacan proposes is to occupy a more modest place, namely, the one that enables the analyst to set himself up as support to object *a*, the cause of the analysant's desire. Now, if this happens, the problem will be to be able to detach oneself from I in order to isolate oneself as object *a*:

If one succeeds in taking this place of the object cause of desire— to "semblance" (*semblantearlo*) it—what one will attain, instead of fastening the analysant as lovable, will be the production of what Seminar 8 designates as the metaphor of love. The latter entails, denotes, the phenomenon of inversion of places. Consequently, from the prior lovable would emerge now a barred subject. This promotes a decisive change in the plane of identification:

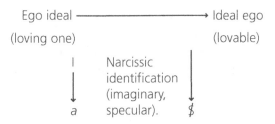

Such a displacement implies that we mustn't fathom anymore what is going on exclusively in terms of the deception of love, for the subject of desire has been established. In writing it as a barred subject, we must think of another dimension that is being summoned—we have gone from love to desire. The issue is to be able to aim at the analysant's desire and "free" it, precisely through the destitution of the analyst from this locus of the ideal. It is a process of dispossession that may be carried out through various maneuvers that claim the analyst's desire. It is worth noting one of these maneuvers whereby Lacan understands that the analyst may divest himself, destitute himself.

The analyst's sliding away (*corrimiento*) from the I does not take shape from one moment to another. Being determined not to be I anymore in a voluntaristic way is not enough. It is an arduous process, mainly because we run into the fundamental obstacle of the narcissic bait of "an" analyst, which invites him to consolidate himself as I. In the text *The Subversion of the Subject . . .* , for instance, we find a small reference that should be considered in all its technical quality and precision—it implies a *Techné*, thence the term. We read there: "A calculated vacillation of the analyst's 'neutrality' may be more valuable for a hysteric than any amount of interpretation—though there is always a danger of frightening the patient."[20]

The concept of a calculated vacillation of the analyst's neutrality could be dismantled as follows, taking into account each of the terms.

---

20. J. Lacan, "The subversion of the . . . ," in *Ecrits: A Selection, op. cit.*, pp. 321–322. [Harari's translation differs from Sheridan's. I offer here a translation of Harari's translation: " . . . a calculated vacillation of the analyst's 'neutrality' may be worth more for a hysteric than any interpretation, running the risk of the (transferential) driving to madness (*alocamiento*) that may result from it."]

Calculated vacillation means something that does not emerge as an untimely *acting*[21] of the analyst, but as a product of the calculation of the effects of such a vacillation. The analyst will not exactly vacillate in the locus of I, but in the way to divest himself of the locus of the ideal. A calculated vacillation of "neutrality" postulates the decision not to be neutral. Conversely, it points to a particular taking of a stance at a certain point. This "recommendation" certainly goes against every reproductive canon regarding the analyst's expected behavior, that is, those that rule that an analyst does not give advice, does not indicate, does not suggest, does not give an opinion, and so on. Moreover, if we gauge its effect, this maneuver is worth more than countless interpretations, and even if it refers to the case of the hysteric, I consider this "indication" as utterly fertile for the steering of the cure in general. The calculated vacillation may be worth then more than innumerable interpretations. It is a kind of intervention that brings about an impressive effect of interpretation, an analytic act, of course, a signifier.

Congruently, the text talks about this at length right afterward, suggesting to the analyst the occasional appropriateness of "preserv[ing] for the other the imaginary dimension of his non-mastery, of his necessary imperfection."[22] I understand that what is at play here is the question of identity, and of what the analysant expects will be the analyst's behavior at all times. Often, the way to provoke an analytic effect is precisely to do in a calculated way what the analysant does not expect the analyst to do. I will offer you a very simple example: An analysant arrives at the session half an hour later than the agreed time. When he comes in, he points out that he only came to "let the analyst know," and that he is leaving because "his" time is up. In this case, to have him come in would be an intervention of this sort. It does not matter whether there is another patient coming afterward. In this case, it would seem that the analyst gave a session when he wanted, or that he yielded to the demand, or that he did not frustrate it, and so on. If we think, on the contrary, of the proposition that calls for singularity and not for the generation of

---

21. In English in the original. (Translator's note)

22. Harari quotes "conveying the imaginary dimension . . . ," but I have quoted from Sheridan's translation. (Translator's note)

norms, as if they were recipes, the situation changes. The analysant was late to the session, taking for granted that he would find the analyst in a certain position. The analyst's causing the analysant not to find him in the expected place refers to the order of the calculated vacillation of neutrality. It aims, then, at a failed encounter. This movement is part of a series of maneuvers of the transference. It is an intervention in act, an analytic act, because from such an act there emerges—is brushed—an effect of (half-said) truth from which the dimension of interpretation is not absent. I recall this because there has existed for a while a certain book originated within a section of the local realm that claims itself Lacanian, titled *Acto e interpretación* (*Act and Interpretation*), yes, as if they were two disjointed terms. In my view, this has nothing to do with what Lacan teaches in his Seminar 15—*El acto analítico* ("The Analytic Act"). Lacan conveys there that such an act is tied to the signifying order, a position, on the other hand, that he never changed.

Returning to the "technical" recommendation, it serves also to take into account how we must respect the principle that in the cure the analyst must pay even with his own person, as Lacan points out in *La dirección de la cura* (*The Direction of the Treatment*).[23] This does not entail the playing of various roles during the psychoanalytic treatment in the manner of psychodrama, which would not demand that high a degree of involvement for the analyst. There is something much more difficult in the Lacanian proposition, which is that in order to be an analyst it is necessary not to be one, not to be one according to the canons whereby apparently everything is regulated, whereby one knows exactly what to expect from the analyst. Lacan says it very clearly: the only thing one should expect from the analyst is an analytic cure. Obviously, this statement is very far from being a coarse tautology.

To end for now, it is worth retrieving some additional notes on the word *knowledge* (*saber*), ambiguous in itself and easily understandable—that is what is deplorable. The knowledge (*saber*) we have referred to in this meeting is not, I repeat, about the cognitive or the epistemic. It aims, in any case, to what is thematized in the text "Variantes de la cura-

---

23. J. Lacan, *Escritos I, op. cit.*, p. 219 [*Ecrits: A Selection*, p. 227].

tipo"("Variants of the Standard Cure"):[24] what the analyst must know (*saber*) is to ignore what he knows (*sabe*), that is, to be able to undertake each analysis as a truly novel one. The analyst must not embark upon the search of the reencounter of the same, but must suspend his knowledge (*saber*) in accordance with an attitude of learned ignorance. This is not a negation of knowledge (*saber*), but its most elaborate form. It is the request of a virginal listening as *desideratum*, and not a ratification of the already known (*conocido*). This is one of the prerogatives, in my opinion, that I would define as a substantive feature of the function desire of the analyst.

QUESTIONS AND ANSWERS

Q: Concerning the calculated vacillation, I would like to know if the latter is always related to the demand, that is, if one should vacillate there where the patient makes demands to the analyst.

A: Precisely, if we do not see the demand as a claim formulated punctually in a certain request. That of the establishment of a certain comfort in the analysis, in the sense of letting everything happen in a predictable manner, where everything is more or less silenced and those moments of Real that lead to a third logical instance in the analysis do not appear, can also be a demand. This third movement in the course of the analysis will necessarily remain unsaid until the next encounter. It is the movement in which the detachment of object *a* occurs, a circumstance that produces a certain singular state in the analysant.

Already in his Seminar 1, *Los escritos técnicos de Freud,* Lacan elaborated on this momentary, instantaneous—but beneficially recurring—state of the analysant that borders with depersonalization.[25] Such

---

24. J. Lacan, *"Variantes de la cura-tipo,"* in *Escritos II*, pp. 117–129. [I have not been able to find an English edition.]

25. J. Lacan, *Les écrits techniques de Freud. Le Séminaire, livre I*, Seuil, Paris, 1975, p. 258 (there is a Spanish translation published by Editorial Paidós). [*The Seminar, Book I. Freud's Papers on Technique, 1953–1954*, trans. J. Forrester, W.W. Norton, New York, 1988.]

a moment indicates that the ultimate certainties concerning the being start to rock. We do not notice this state, for instance, in cases taken to supervision, because "nothing happens" in them. A third must be introduced here, also of an empirical sort—the supervisor—so that an analysis may start to circulate again. In these static cases, anyway, there is also demand, albeit established in terms of inertia. I find Freud's explanation for these situations very worthy of consideration. In analysis, as in life, it is unlikely that the subject will abandon a libidinal position he has attained. A state occurs then in which one finally makes do with very little, according to the celebrated proverb: "Better the devil we know . . ." And yet we are summoned to operate in such an appropriateness.

7

Erastés, Eromenós: *Four Terms, Five Vicissitudes of the Drive*

I want to devote the first part of today's meeting to a recapitulation and synthesis of the most important issues we dealt with last class in speaking of the transference, the third of the four fundamental concepts to which our course owes its title. In this opportunity we will also make some progress on this concept. I will constrain myself, then, at the beginning, to emphasizing a few points so that this introduction to the third fundamental concept will reach its conclusion, or in everyday language, I will wrap it up.[1]

The figure of roundness is not very pleasing to Lacanian thought because such a figure imaginarizes the sphere, and the latter implies a dimension that does not help us formalize the structure of the analytic problematic. Why? Because our respective surface is bullic (*tórica*), bullized (*torizada*).[2] This quality responds to a particular topological object, namely, the bull. Lacan insists repeatedly on resorting to this object to propose it, among other contexts, as a valid alternative to the

---

1. The Spanish expression I translated as "to wrap it up" is *redondear*, to "make round." Thence Harari's following comment on roundness. (Translator's note)

2. J. Lacan, *Seminar 24, L'insu que sait de l'une-bévue s'aile à mourre, Ornicar?*, pp. 12–113, Lyse, Paris, n.d., p. 12. [I haven't been able to find an English edition.]

sphere, in regard to which it presents the decisive advantage of consider-ing the function of the hole. I don't intend to dwell on these matters; I simply enunciate them to note that in everyday speech we unwittingly slip in certain types of prepsychoanalytic considerations, such as the plan to "wrap up" (*redondear*) certain stances. It is worth then noting the fol-lowing: the sphere constitutes a "good form" to graph the feasibility of the hypnotic encounter, situated in the antithesis of analysis.

The first noteworthy point is the reason why in Seminar 11 the concept of transference is barely touched, immediately passing on to the concept of the drive. As we define the transference as "the enactment of the reality of the unconscious" and we claim such a reality as sexual, the very appearance of the sexual—and hence pertaining to the drive—refers unavoidably to the detour through the slant of the drive in order to conceptually elaborate on the transference. You will remember that we had resorted to a small license and had skipped the references to the drive in order to take on two late chapters of the seminar and return afterward to the treatment of the transference as the fourth fundamen-tal concept. In this way, we may not follow strictly the order of reasons offered in the text. Our recourse was founded on a didactic intention, a certainly arguable goal, although we may also question the need to fol-low the text only in terms of the order of reasons claimed in it.

We have established, then, that the decisive weight of the transfer-ence lies on its sexual reality. We had dealt with the question of sexual reality not only because of its relation to the sexual desire that has to do with the analysant, but also, crucially, due to its articulation with a Lacanian innovation, a Lacanian "invention." Such punctuation refers to the analyst's desire. In this way, this supplement leads to the com-prehension that takes place not in terms of the analysant's or the analyst's desire, but precisely by relying on the link, the knotting, between both desires.

We have already offered some notes—empirical, if you will—on the analyst's desire. Let us mention here that, even if it was coined rela-tively recently as a psychoanalytic concept, the subjective position that serves as its foundation is not an unheard-of datum in the history of Western thought. We may find at least one illustrious precedent in Plato's *Symposium*. In a certain passage of the dialogue, Socrates appears interpreting—renouncing—according to a simile of the analytic mode: "What you think you are telling me, Alcibiades, you are actually telling Agaton," Socrates more or less states. The statement strikes as an accurate psychoanalytic intervention. It is as if Socrates put things into place, attempting at disarticulating the transferential dimension from where Alcibiades raises his inflamed panegyric to Socrates.

This desire of the analyst—that is neither countertransference nor feelings—does not consist in imposing on the analysant a certain behavioral model or pattern, a sort of defined scheme of values, of beneficial vitality, profiting for this purpose from the powers conferred by the loving deception. These aspects allude precisely to some of the risks to which the psychoanalyst exposes himself when he weakens from his position as support of his place (*desfallece de su lugar*). When he makes these mistakes, obviously, he quits being an analyst, no matter his title, nor his years of devotion to our practice. The analyst may "fall" from his place, for instance, if he starts a sort of implicit sermon whereby he tries to shape the analysant to his own image. In fact, in the Lacanian—in the sense of Freudian—sense, transference implies the possibility to give up the power with which the place of the analyst invests us. Otherwise, if we make use of—abuse—such power, we will slide toward the antipodes of psychoanalysis, namely, suggestion. By processing a scansion of this term, we must remember that, concerning the analyst's behavior, su-ggestion[3] must not become suggestion. The management of the treatment must pivot on the transference, and not develop into an influence whose result is that what the analyst utters becomes a ruling issued from a particular position. We always speak from the transference, whether or not we recognize it and interpret it. This is certainly not the same as the so-called analysis of the transference. It is not enough to just keep this matter in mind, for there is another very important vector to consider. The seminar enunciates it with great sagacity in the following way: it is not just what the analyst wants to make of his patient, but also what the analyst wants his patient to make of him.

---

3. Harari is playing here with the meaning of the two words that result from such a scansion in Spanish: "*su-gestión*" (suggestion) gives us "*su*"—his-her—"*gestión*"—management. (Translator's note)

This statement, then, claims that we may "recognize" the desire of certain analysts. In such cases we will not be facing the analyst's desire anymore, but Abraham's, or Ferenczi's, or Nunberg's desire, evinced in their particular theories, in their ways to direct the cure, and in what they expect as the end of analysis. All these elements, among many others, are tinged by these analysts' desires. We can then verify how Abraham intends to be a sort of complete mother. We can think with strict logic that this intention reaches its zenith with Kleinism's desire. Indeed, from this perspective, the analyst must come to be both a good and a bad object. Starting with the dissociation between a persecuting and an idealized object—as Melanie Klein states it[4]—the object integration and the ego synthesis are finally attained. Being a complete mother is what the analyst demands from the patient that he make of him.

In a different conceptualization, such as Nunberg's, an ideology of divine aspiration decants congruent with certain arbitrative postulations about life and death, such as can be appreciated in the theories of this nonetheless brilliant psychoanalyst, author of a valuable *Teoría general de la neurosis*.[5] [I have been informed that a publishing house is about to reissue in Spanish this book written while Freud was alive and prologued by him. In terms of its quality, this text is light-years away from Otto Fenichel's famous work on the same topic, *Teoría psicoanalítica de las neurosis*. (*Psychoanalytic Theory of Neurosis*).] Equipped with the capital instruments afforded by Lacan's teachings, we can rethink a series of conceptions around the question of the transference, whereby the analyst situates himself without renouncing to the locus that we signaled with an I, with no more additions, in our last meeting. The I denotes the idealizing aspect of identification, and as you will remember, we discriminated this I from another well-known matheme, the one written as I(A).

---

4. M. Klein, "*Algunas conclusiones teóricas sobre la vida emocional del bebé*," in *VARIOS Desarrollos en psicoanálisis*, Hormé, Buenos Aires, 1967, pp. 177–207. ["Some Theoretical Conclusions Regarding the Emotional Life of the Infant," in *The Writings of Melanie Klein*, vol. 3, Hogarth Press, London, 1975.]

5. H. Nunberg, *Teoría general de las neurosis basada en el psicoanálisis*, Pubul, Barcelona, 1950. [*Principles of Psychoanalysis: Their Application to the Neuroses*, International Universities Press, New York, 1969.]

The second matheme reads rigorously as ego ideal. The I is another agency (*instancia*) related to the former one. Yet the differential notation implies, as is obvious, the purpose of marking a conceptual difference. What the analyst wants his patient to make of him indicates, amidst its variants, how the analyst demands an idealization from his analysant as an ensnaringly identifying vehicle. That is, the analyst demands not to be dispossessed from the idealizing locus of identification. What did Lacan suggest as an alternative, as that which should remove the function of this I? Neither more nor less than object *a*:

Object cause of desire, object of the drive, surplus-*jouissance* (*plus-de-gozar*): different ways—and these are not all—of reading this object *a*. Removing oneself from the idealizing locus of identification in order to "semblance" (*semblantear*) the locus of object *a* is the displacement to be carried out, and it concerns the analyst. Based on this elaboration, we could reformulate what has been said about the analyst's desire—not Abraham's, Ferenczi's, Nunberg's, or anybody else's. If the analyst cannot vacate this narcissic locus where *his* desire places him, the assumption of the analyst's desire—which implies situating oneself in a locus of remnant, of debris qua object—is not possible. The analyst's is not that unitary, whole, spherical, full, and complete realm characteristic of the narcissic dimension but, on the contrary, a site like that of the remainder of an arithmetic operation of division. Such a remainder is precisely what enables the analysant to set himself up in the following way:

The barred subject is the desiring subject, so that a first twist or inflection of what is happening in the analysis takes place. To say more precisely how we understand this process in Lacanian terms, we may state, first, that due to the rule of free association, the analysant sees himself as lovable. Not, I repeat, in the sense of somebody who has a gentle attitude and good manners, but in the sense of somebody who may be loved from I.[6] This is the fundamental rule of psychoanalysis, the decisive element that situates the beginnings of the analysis from a narcissic positioning. To this settling of the analysant in the locus of the (lo) lovable corresponds the respective positioning of the analyst as the loving one:

Analyst   Analysant
   | Ideal ego
Loving one   Lovable

The loving one relates from the position of I as the necessary complement to the lovable. As we have already punctuated, this corresponds not, strictly speaking, to Seminar 11, but rather to Seminar 8. When closely analyzing *The Symposium* in this seminar, Lacan takes up again the characteristics the ancient Greek called *erastés* and *eromenós*,[7] which correspond respectively to the categories of loving and lovable:

Analyst   Analysant
   | Ideal ego
Loving one   Lovable
(*erastés*)   (*eromenós*)

Starting from here, the next movement in the analysis will attempt then to produce what we call the metaphor of love. Without going too deeply into this problem, the word *metaphor* alludes to a dimension of signifying substitution. It is not just a substitution, but an interverting (*interversivo*) replacement. We may say this differently so as to clarify this process. It consists in the operation of exchanging loci:

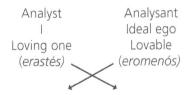

Analyst   Analysant
   | Ideal ego
Loving one   Lovable
(*erastés*)   (*eromenós*)

---

6. See note 16, Chapter 6. (Translator's note)

7. J. Lacan, *Seminar 8, op. cit.*, class of July 12, 1960.

As you can see, it is a reciprocal move. This metaphorized *eromenós* does indeed correspond now to the passage from I to *a*, as long as the analyst succeeds in sustaining the locus of the remainder. What empowers him to do so? As we mentioned in our second meeting, it is a particular desire, a desire of death. Due to its somber connotation, such an affirmation incites us to ask ourselves what leads an analyst to become such.

This query, this perplexity, are highly attenuated, however, when we run into the desire of someone like Melanie Klein, for example, the conception rendered in *Envidia y gratitud*, highly representative of her position.[8] It would seem that the author of this text wails mournfully for not being sufficiently loved, in the style of a *yiddishe mama*.[9] She systematically complains that she is not being sufficiently thanked. She constantly insists on positing that the analysant is in debt, for he owes something to her. We may think of precisely which phallic dimension and which unsatisfied desire is Melanie Klein speaking about when she repeats once and again that envy prevents the emergence of gratitude, postulating the latter as a crucial vector in the "reparatory" cure of the object. The Lacanian formulation, with its castrating tinge, uncomfortably and rigorously states that as analysts, we mustn't expect to be "repaired" by our analysants. The analytic artifice is not a repair shop where repairs are performed on the enveloping imagery of the analyst.[10] Furthermore, the point is neither that the analyst should be a bitter pessimist, nor that he should not know how to hear gratifications or gratitude. The point is that these statements can be produced for nonmanifested motives, in the same way as on so many occasions many analysants cannot account for their libidinal bind with the analyst and frequently cultivate a hostile confrontation during the sessions. To remain in this plane of constant "envious" rivalry—a special danger in the analyses of obsessives—insisting on the

---

8. M. Klein, *op. cit.*, in *VARIOS, Las emociones básicas del hombre*, Nova, Buenos Aires, 1960, pp. 105–194. [*Envy and Gratitude: A Study of Unconscious Sources*, Basic Books, New York, 1957.]

9. In Yiddish in the original. (Translator's note)

10. The Spanish word *reparación* corresponds to M. Klein's word "reparation," and also means "repair," in the sense of "repair shop" (*taller de reparaciones*); thence Harari's pun. (Translator's note)

issue of aggressiveness, and thus achieving only to reduplicate it instead of incorporating the unavoidable libidinal factor, would mean not to transcend the manifest. The analyst's desire, the desire of death, lies then in the act of semblancing (*semblantear*) the object that causes desire, without tirades, of course, about the hate resulting from the occupation of such a destiny. A way of writing it into our schema is placing the final terms, resultants of the interverting (*interversiva*) relation I just highlighted:

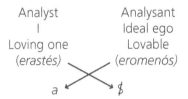

The reference to a cause of desire constitutes an intelligent recourse, for it can elude any idealism summoned by the subject of representation. In this way, desire does not emanate from the inside to later search for an object, placed before it, with which to be satisfied. On the contrary, it is an object situated "behind" that acts as a causal decoy. We must recall, furthermore, that desire does not pair with its corresponding object in a harmonic way. It is the sudden, unexpected presence—the one connected with *Tuché*, with repetition happening as if by chance—the one that counts, because it recycles, in the subject, his barring. Such a barring must also be considered qua schizia, such as the one detected between the eye and the gaze.

There is still another movement in the analysis, since we are not finished yet with what we can posit concerning this crucial deception involved in the transference. Such a deception consists, we reiterate, neither in not seeing someone properly nor in having one's perception of reality distorted, but in the local and current characteristic of love, a characteristic, as Lacan perspicaciously reads in Freud, that is in itself deceiving. That is why it is so important to expose how the analysant—not in bad faith but just led by the movement of the unfolding of his pathology in analysis—tries to deceive the analyst, that is, tries to love the analyst, or rather, wants to have the analyst love him by attempting to convince him of the fact that what is important is the cure through love.[11] This is a Freudian concept that is extremely valuable in apprehending the crux of the analytic unfolding. Yet a cure through love does not refer only to the obvious sense already pointed out (the one whereby the analysant will aim at being loved by the analyst). No, because as important or more so than this circumstance is the question of certain providential objects that emerge often in the course of the analysis and to which the subject practically entrusts his life, and, certainly, his happiness.

Freud assesses such cases very wisely. In principle, of course, there would be nothing wrong with them—the analysant says he is happy because he found the right person, the love of his life. There shouldn't be a problem, except for the nature of extremely forced, of oppressive dependence of the subject with respect to such a providential object. This datum indicates the establishment of a highly precarious tie that might jeopardize the subject's adduced, demanded balance anytime. On the other hand, what happened, adds Freud, to the "inability to love" characteristic of the analysant? It is very often "solved"—in fact worsened—by means of the positing of an alternative to choose between the providential object and the analyst. This "either . . . or" proposition is situated within a context where the interest in the analysis starts to fade, and appearance indicates an evident (pseudo) improvement of the symptom.

On the other hand, the choice of this person may be extremely precise, to the extent that it could be someone blindly hostile to psychoanalysis. There are more of such cases than one may believe. Consequently, at some points an option may be established where the position of the analysant as lovable can be neatly grasped, which indicates how crucial and complex the problematic encompassed within the cure through love is. This fact does not happen only in the obvious case of the patient who, cured through love, impulsively abandons his analysis in a perfect *passage à l'acte*. If you will, this is the most nakedly pathognomonic case, even though there are many more—conceptualizable—subtleties related to it that are at play in this deception called love of—within—the transference.

---

11. S. Freud, *Introducción del . . . op. cit.*, pp. 97–98. ["On Narcissism" [narcism] . . . , p. 101.]

For instance, another element positions itself in the transference that Lacan analyzes very perspicaciously from his first seminar on. It is the analysant's fear regarding deception, but in a different sense from the earlier one. It is not fear of being deceived by the analyst, but rather of the possibility to be able to deceive the analyst. In this seminar, Lacan reports the case of a patient who had visited a series of analysts. The episode is quoted by Michael Balint, an analyst whose conceptions Lacan criticized often, their close friendship notwithstanding. (Lacan's criticism, on the other hand, was addressed to Balint's theorization, not to his notorious clinical sagacity.) Lacan narrates that on a certain day, a man comes to Balint's office, and starts telling him a very strange, rich, and long story, to which Balint listens very carefully. In this way, several interviews follow one another, until finally this person, a veteran of interviews with analysts, demands that he be told if they would start the analysis. Balint answers that that would not be possible, because there are some things that aren't clear, despite their being very interesting, and that he cannot manage to understand this confusing story. Faced with this statement, the interviewee, satisfied, confesses that Balint is the first honest man he has found, because everything he has told the analyst were lies, and the analysts visited previously believed his tale blindly, which indicates that if they could be deceived, they must be charlatans and liars.[12]

The dimension of the "I can deceive him" hence marks the limits of the careful and open listening (*escucha*). We must note here, in any case, that truth and lie are not valid parameters for analysis; in the enunciation there is no possible lie. The example is nonetheless important in order to take into account that the analyst, from the locus of I, will often outline complaints about why the analysant did not provide him with an eventually essential piece of information at the right time. In the face of this claim Lacan will answer: because the analysant was afraid that the analyst would interpret everything in terms of that information. Let us suppose, for example, that the analysant belatedly informs him that he had had syphilis. He will say, "I didn't want you to believe that every-

---

12. J. Lacan, *Les écrits techniques* . . . , (*The Seminar*, Book 1) *op. cit.*, p. 253.

thing was due to an organic problem and to interpret always in that sense. I don't come here for that purpose." The dimension of dread appears very clearly here—not of being deceived by the analyst but of the latter as an easy victim of deceit. In other words, the fear is that the dimension of love will betray the analytic work.

A few minutes ago I mentioned tangentially something about the obsessive analysant. In the same way, I believe that we can punctuate a few clinical notes to support the fact that the matter of love in the analytic device does not circulate only due to the naive fact that the analysant declares his love for us. On the other hand, the clinical aspect—another merit of Lacanian teachings—also appears more convincing in the exposition, even though our goal concerns the construction of an order of reasons and relations. In this respect, it is possible to offer a tripod deducible not only from Seminar 11, but also by means of a journey through the most decisive stretches of the teaching that concerns us. We might define it in the following terms: love in the obsessive appears especially through the demand to be recognized in the locus of the slave, that is, of an obedience toward the one situated in I; here, the locus of the Master.

This fact brings about a logical and expected consequence, namely, that the slave does no more than wait, in a way, for the Master's death. In other words, the continuous aggressivizing tension characteristic of the obsessive neurotic emerges. The joyous expectation of this death, however, reveals a slight trap. It is not the expectation of what will happen in the future, since the psychic consequence of this situation is that, awaiting the Master's death, the slave is already dead, due to the very fact that he has resigned himself to the locus of slavery, yet identified with the anticipated death of the Master.[13] Faced with this situation, the slave adopts a (second) attitude in which a demand, a request of permission continuously appears.

Such recourse may show in a highly evident way at some points in the analysis. These are the cases where people will say, "He won't do anything without his analyst's permission." This is precisely what the analysant

---

13. J. Lacan, "Función y campo . . . ," *op. cit.*, pp. 131–132. ["Function and Field . . . ," pp. 99–100.]

hopes to achieve, among other things. Very frequently, as we know very well, we have the analysants say what we want to hear so as to point out later, "He told me so." Here we should ask the analysant what part he is playing in what refers to his analyst having him say what the analyst wanted to hear. It is an elementary questioning, the ABC of the analytic question. Yet the fact is that an analysant with an obsessive slant will claim his condition of slave, always expecting the sacred word of the analyst as well as, decisively, the acquisition of the harassed permissiveness, inquiring at every point whether or not it fits into a certain type of norm (in a broad sense). Given this situation, the acts of the analysant's life will be inevitably tinged with the nature of feats or exploits about which we are inclined to ask: So much fuss about that? How can this analysant think that he has done something titanic, a heroic deed out of the average human's reach? In these questions, of course, there is no interpretation whatsoever. They consist rather of an immediate, emotional, and consensual psychological reaction, if these terms apply. Such a dimension of feat—the third one under consideration—emerges because, when chained in such a way, the fact that as a slave who has asked for permission and is defenseless and helpless, he has done some things, and necessarily provokes a tinge of exploitness (hazañosidad). The issue is very closely related to the notes characteristic of the fantasme,[14] a topic we will only be able to mention in our course.

In the obsessive, then, this trait of the exploit, of the crossing of the Rubicon, of the condition we could even call epic with which he wants to crown his actions and develop his life, bears an insistence truly proverbial. It is not a coarse intention to impress. His goal is more elementary, because it concerns the order of the constitution of the subject. It is precisely the way to try to arrange his place in the field of the Other, of succeeding in answering that decisive query circumscribed by Lacan's teachings that says, Che vuoi?, What do you want?, or better yet, What does he want of me? [as the question about desire appears in Subversión del sujeto,[15] extracted from Cazotte's fantastic tale, El Diablo

---

14. J. Lacan, "La dirección de . . . ," op. cit., p. 269. ["The Direction of . . . ," p. 273.]

15. J. Lacan, "J. Lacan, "Subversión del sujeto . . .", op. cit., p. 326. ["The Subversion of the Subject . . . ," p. 312.]

enamorado (*The Devil in Love*)]. This question allows us, then, to take into account the following conundrum: What does the analyst want of me? We mustn't forget the following: in these developments, "I" is the locus we are led to—or that we are led to embody—by the analysant's demand. The subject requests, demands, an I, even though nobody suggests it to him, and without resorting, on the other hand, to any kind of special artifice. Conversely, the maneuver will be carried out by the analyst so as to remove himself from such a location, where he has been settled by a movement characteristic of the structuring of the analytic situation. The diagram of the interior eight—a surface with topologic properties we mentioned in our last meeting—accounts for this fact. The way in which demand circulates consists in taking the transference to that moment of stagnation in the analysis called identification.

Such a moment is inevitable, and many analysts have conceived it as the *non plus ultra*—nothing beyond this, enough is enough, that's it—of psychoanalysis. Nonetheless, once we are in the presence of the identification with the analyst—a "success" of the demand, for it is a demand to be like the analyst—this plane must be crossed. I once ironically titled one of my papers as follows: "Being (the) Analyst: End of Analysis?"[16] Of course this will not happen if we proceed to a first operation, a first inflection—from I to *a*. There must be still another moment in analysis. I am obviously speaking of logical moments, not of those pertaining to a chronological successiveness. What I am positing in a diachronic form must be apprehended in a synchronic sense, that is, in the syn-chronos, in the Other chronos. If we take a cross section, we will notice that this passage may occur even within one analytic session—that the analyst will establish himself in I so as to pass later to *a*, according to the following linear (but nonmetric) schema:

We will see later why the third segment remains, not coincidentally, blank. On his part, the analysant starts situating himself in the locus of

---

16. R. Harari, *Discurrir . . .* (Pondering . . .), *op. cit.*, pp. 106–160.

the ideal ego to emerge later as subject with schizia—insofar as he is "broken in half" by the *a*. Yet later another inflection takes place in the analysis, the one characterized by *The Seminar, Book I* as "an experience at the limit of depersonalization." Rendered in a schema homologous to the previous one (with the same observations), we obtain this design:

Ideal ego $\$$ depersonalization

The term *depersonalization* will undoubtedly resonate harshly, because it seems to bring analysis close to an exercise of iatrogenic butchery. It is a concept extracted straight from the field of schizophrenia. There is no reason, however, to be afraid of the conception the term denotes, as it is taken up by Lacan.

Going step by step, we find that the statement "at the limit" does not mean, does not point at, a strict depersonalization. Nonetheless, what occurs does approximate to it, because in this circumstance the subject loses the narcissic strongholds that support him as ego. The loss, of course, is not definitive, neither are we dealing with a possible psychoticization. If someone is neurotic, we will not transform him into a psychotic through this inflection. Such an assumption, in fact, is nothing more than another illusion about the alleged unlimited powers of analysis. It is undoubtedly possible that maybe due to haste, to a poor grasp of what happens during the preliminary interviews, or to both, an analysis might trigger (not determine) a psychosis in a prepsychotic subject. In this case it will be argued with certainty that psychoanalysis is to blame. In a sense this is true, insofar as psychoanalysis was the practice through which the psychosis was triggered. Yet the latter was not conceived, was not produced *ex nihilo*—out of nothing—in the analysis. The analysis constituted, I repeat, the triggering factor.

The depersonalization to which we are referring involves momentary, instantaneous dimensions where a fall of meaning in terms of its blocking plenitude suddenly occurs. Such a fall lasts only an instant, because it will be promptly overlaid with a different meaning. I think that this is the point on which Lacan insists—in the last chapter of the seminar, titled "In You More Than You"[17]—when he states that what the end of analysis is about is traversing the *fantasme*, looping the loop—alluding to the support of the interior eight.

This (logical and experiential) moment must occur several times, since the end of analysis does not exactly mean its termination. It does not allude to the fact of the cessation of the encounters between analyst and analysant but to an experience that must be traversed several times in the course of an analysis. Depersonalization is then possible because *a* ceases to operate as cause, detaching itself from its location in the analyst. By means of such a detachment of object *a*, the subject (punctually) "loses" the barring that singularizes him with respect to his analyst. In this regard, we mustn't forget that the split subject can only be so, can only be enacted to the extent that this split is supported by object *a*. That is the reason for the blank space in the segment of the previous schema—the segment of the analysant. That is why, also, the detachment of *a* entails more than the loss of the supports of the ego—it involves the brushing of the real of the drive. As Lacan puts it, "The experience of the subject is thus brought back to the plane at which, from the reality of the unconscious, the drive may be made present."[18]

This point serves us, therefore, in our entry to the fourth fundamental concept, that is, the drive. Consequently, we will transfer our attention to the slant with which sexuality is tackled. We will notice how, in Seminar 11, sexuality is grasped through its relation to love. We have defined the transference as the enactment of the reality of the (*lo*) unconscious, a reality that is above all sexual. Our exposition moved immediately from sex to love. We should ask here the most elementary question: Is this true? Is such a passage viable?

---

17. Harari gives the title of this chapter as "In You More Than to You" (*En ti más que a ti*). I have quoted the title of the chapter in the English edition of the seminar. (Translator's note)

18. J. Lacan, *Los cuatro conceptos . . .* , *op. cit.*, p. 277 (modified translation). [*The Four Fundamental Concepts . . .* , p. 274.]

The fact that sexuality is not alien to love can be detected not just in clinical practice. Let us resort to the texts, especially to the crucial psychoanalytic work on the fundamental concept we intend to tackle now. As you must have correctly inferred, the text in question is our well-known *Pulsiones y destinos de pulsión* (*Instincts and Their Vicissitudes*). In our first encounter we used precisely the epistemological opening of this essay in order to present the problematic of the fundamental concept (the *Grundbegriff*). We will now return to the specific developments explicitly stated there.

If we undertake a careful reading of Freud and we ask ourselves whether sexuality and love are homogeneous, we will be able to perceive their situation: they are clearly discriminated. The first part of the text deals with the drive and its vicissitudes to give rise later to a significant reference to love, posited almost as a border function with respect to sexuality. Freud approaches it, but at the same time he points out that it is not exactly comprised within the sexual. He highlights a dimension in love where unity, totality, predominates; in sum, synthesis, the narcissic structure. It doesn't happen thus, instead, with the drive. In the latter we may in fact recognize different elements, components, or terms that cannot be isolated in love. In the same way, according to other variables, we might ponder desire, a concept in which different terms and vicissitudes cannot be identified. When we are confronted with the drive, on the other hand, an identifiable diversification immediately appears.

When several meetings ago we elaborated on the question of the scopic,[19] we designed a schema with four types of drives as they present themselves in the Lacanian conception, namely, oral, anal, scopic, and invocatory. We will now take up this classification again in order to analyze first the composition of each drive, and then, what is its respective vicissitude. In what concerns us now, there exist three different paragraphs regarding the drive in which the number four insistently emerges. We can notice this in the (noncorresponding) three columns that we may arrange in the following table, in whose first column we place the just-mentioned drives:

---

19. Cf. Chapter 4.

Drives	Terms	Vicissitudes
– oral – anal – scopic –invocatory		

In the second column we must locate the four "terms"—it is the Freudian word *Termini*[20]—which may be isolated in the drives. Regarding this point, we can follow the definitions included in the quoted work. The source takes place in a dimension of lack, impelling its filling, its straining. The object is that in or by which the drive may attain its aim. Besides, it is possible to be equipped also with a plane that will take into consideration a force whose impact is constant, to put it in Freud's terms. I am referring now to the nature denoted by the term *pressure*.[21] Lastly, we must think about a point in which the drive attains, albeit temporarily, the aim propelled by its operation: satisfaction, which can be obtained if the state of excitation of the source is suppressed. Therefore:

Drives	Terms	Vicissitudes
– oral – anal – scopic – invocatory	– source – object – pressure – aim	

The vicissitudes of the drive are also four, so we will include them in this matrix. They are reversal into its opposite, turning round upon the subject's own self, repression, and sublimation.

---

20. In a coincidental way, Lacan designates as "terms" (*termes*) the four components or occupants of the four places in the four discourses mentioned in Chapter 1 (cf. J. Lacan, "Radiophonie," *Silicet*, 2/3, Seuil, Paris, 1970, p. 99; there is a Spanish version). ["Radiophonie," trans. Stuart Schneiderman, in M. Blonsky, ed. *On Signs*, Johns Hopkins University Press, Baltimore, 1985.]

21. Harari uses the Spanish *presión* (pressure) as the equivalent of the German term *Drang*. Sheridan, however, translates as "thrust." I have chosen to use "pressure," both to respect Harari's choice and because it is the classic English rendition, as it appears in the English version of Laplanche's and Pontalis's *The Language of Psychoanalysis*. (Translator's note)

Drives	Terms	Vicissitudes
– oral – anal – scopic –invocatory	– source – object – pressure – aim	– reversal into its opposite – turning round upon the subject's own self – repression – sublimation

The second and third columns summarize then the formulation suggested in *Pulsiones y destinos de pulsión* (*Instincts and Their Vicissitudes*). There is a small element, however, that breaks this beautiful "wholistic" (*todista*) harmony—as I like to call it.[22] It is the discovery of an unpublished text by Freud that was recently found, as they say, among Ferenczi's papers. Its title is "Síntesis de las neurosis de transferencia" ("A Phylogenetic Fantasy. Overview of the Transference Neuroses"). It consists in a sort of draft where there are some phrases ready for publication, and others in the manner of notes an author writes to himself so as to expand them later on, and hence they admit—or require—various interpretations due to their multivocal sense. Well, this text breaks any harmony within the order of the drive, for Freud postulates in it regression as the fifth unequivocal vicissitude. The latter is so important that it deserves its own place in the corresponding column:

Drives	Terms	Vicissitudes
– oral – anal – scopic –invocatory	– source – object – pressure – aim	– reversal into its opposite – turning round upon the subject's own self – repression – sublimation
		– regression

The addition of regression emerges then from this text belonging to the *Metapsychology* that Jones, once again erroneously, had deemed destroyed.[23] On the other hand, we should keep in mind that, based on the

---

22. Concerning such a harmony (and number four) the seminar states: "It is curious that there are *four* vicissitudes as there are *four* elements of the drive" (J. Lacan, *Los cuatro . . .*, *op. cit.*, pp. 171–172; author's emphasis). [*The Four . . .*, p. 165.]

23. E. Jones, *Vida y obra de Sigmund Freud*, Nova, Buenos Aires, 1960, vol. 2, pp. 200–201. [*Life and Work of Sigmund Freud*, New York, Basic Books, 1953–57.]

one-sided surface known as the Moebius strip, Lacan notes that the life drive and the death drive are actually but two aspects of the drive located on the same surface. If we traverse the course of a drive—in the Moebian strip—conceived as life drive, we will see it suddenly transform itself—on the "other" surface, which is the same one—into death drive, to revert later, once again, into the first. We are not dealing thus with larger or smaller quantities of one or the other drive, nor with metaphysical leaps from one type to the other, nor with the coarse idea that alludes to an interweaving. Freud undoubtedly delimited the concept of the drive, but its formalization occurs with Lacan. In the *Ecrits*, the latter reflects upon the translation of the term *Trieb*, suggesting, among other alternatives, to translate it as *dérive* (drift).[24] It may be strange at this point to refer to life *dérive* and death *dérive*. Yet the term is valid and accurate because it connotes the nature of itinerary, of sliding (*deslizamiento*), of the drive. Moreover, above all, *dérive* takes into account in an unsurpassable way the unstable, the variable character of the object of the drive.

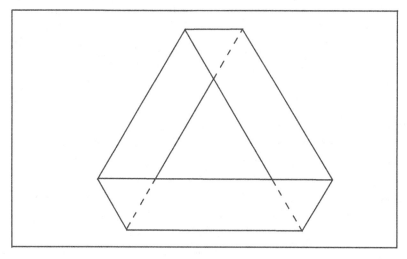

Moebius strip[25]

---

24. J. Lacan, *Subversión* . . . , *op. cit.*, p. 315. [*The Subversion* . . . , p. 301; Sheridan maintains the French term.]

25. J. Granon-Lafont, *La topología básica de Jacques Lacan*, Nueva Visión, Buenos Aires, 1987, pp. 31–46. [I have not been able to find an English edition.]

The classification I just posited requires that we at least situate the definition Freud offers in his text. This work points out: "It appears to us as a concept-limit between the psychic and the somatic." Since we are working on the fundamental concepts, we must already point out here some thoughts on the "concept-limit." Freud does not say that the concept is riding between the psychic and the somatic. The idea of "limit" implies that the concept ought to be analyzed as a knot in which the psychic and the somatic participate. On the other hand, the text does not allude to the fact that the drive has a necessary empirical referent either. In any case, we can grant it the status of fiction in the sense suggested by Jeremy Bentham, the British utilitarian. Fiction is not the opposite of truth; it is not a falsehood. Rather, "fiction," as we saw in our first class, is what will enable Lacan to define truth itself. "Truth has the structure of fiction," he will go as far as to say. In this way, we must not "overcome" fiction in order to go on to the truth. On the contrary, insofar as truth is said—and saying it all does not entirely exist— there is no alternative but to endure it as fictional. Fiction, as narrative shows, is not classifiable according to the formal, traditional canons that divide true from false.

In the Freudian conceptualization, there is no naive empiricism that tries to find a palpable, quantifiable drive. In positing it as a concept-limit between the psychic and the somatic, it is clear that Freud is referring to a *Begriff*.[26] The definition goes on as follows: ". . . like the psychic representative of the excitations, originating in the interior of the body and reaching the psyche." We must note in this respect that the origin of the drive establishes an interesting difference with everything that is involved in the problematic of the instinct, since the latter is entirely a-subjective, thus eliminating the signifying order. Concerning the drive— one of its readings—we are dealing with a psychic inscription represented for another one. In the instinct, conversely, psychic inscriptions are not contemplated, for the former bears the condition inherent to blindness, that is, to that which pertains to the order of the innately programmed.

---

26. Concept, in German. (Translator's note)

Every instinct is conceived as an adaptive mechanism, effective for the purpose that a certain specimen will attain the perpetuation of its being by attending to its vital functions. In the field of the drive, we find instead "a psychic representative of the excitations, originating in the interior of the body and reaching the psyche, as a measure of the demand of work imposed on the psychic as a result of its bind with the bodily." If Freud is speaking about work, he is also speaking about change. This brings as a consequence, among others, the inability to endorse conceptualizations such as the Kleinian. In her solvent presentation of Melanie Klein's ideas, Hanna Segal defines the unconscious fantasy as "the mental expression of the instincts."[27] There is no work there. This conception does not take an initial raw matter to articulate it with a certain instrument of application and thus obtain as a result something different from the original matter. If there is work, there must be mutation, change, transformation.

Let us think of the process that goes from cutting a tree to transforming it into a wooden bench. This process may indeed give rise to all kinds of philosophical or metaphysical disquisitions. Yet we will not dwell on this, but will pay close attention to the way in which Freud privileges the dimension of work. This demand of the body that ends up in a psychic order does not concern the realm of the instinct at all. It "ends up" insofar as there is no postulation of a crowned epiphenomenic copy, as I believe happens in Melanie Klein's work, where the psychic is conceived as a mere subordinate and mechanical correlate. Among the Kleinian current, through the term *instinct* the authors end up maintaining that the fantasizing (unconscious) universe is preconstituted in biological functionalism.

From these ideas—and I bring this up to show that the issues mentioned are not abstruse matters regarding which people debate about nonsense—it has been viable to think things such as the fact that envy is determined by the functioning of the liver, responsible for the "manufacturing" of the specific fantasies. It is possible to reach this conclusion by

---

27. H. Segal, *Introducción a la obra de Melanie Klein*, Paidós, Buenos Aires, 1965, p. 20. [*Introduction to the Work of Melanie Klein*, New York, Basic Books, 1980.]

considering the decisively catabolic, "destructive" function of the liver. Of course, this function pertains to digestion, and is therefore necessary and imperative. An author stated then that this process bears a mental expression, namely, envy. According to him, the envious person will be the one who tries to break and destroy the supposedly valuable thing possessed by the other. With Lacan, instead, we have learned in this seminar that *invidia* is linked to the gaze, to the evil eye, which has little or no connection, in terms of intrinsic value, with what the other has. It is simply that the other appears tied to what he has, offering "the image of a completeness closed upon itself."[28]

One envies the image of completeness offered by the other with such an object, whichever it is, and not with that which "makes one want" (*da ganas*). In the light of these affirmations, we may understand better some of the problems that emerged in this field, alluded by that figure (so valuable clinically) Freud designated as narcism (*narcismo*) of the small differences,[29] small differences that certainly often engender the most ferocious arguments. Rather than what is far away, we envy what is nearby. This dimension contemplates a wise, rational comprehension of the contending rivalry, which is called envy, concerning how the other has the *a*. If not, led by the Kleinian reasoning, we might conceive (as it has already been done) that just as there is a hepatic-envious fantasy, there is a cardiac one, a pulmonary one, and so on. In sum, based on the organic functioning, an allegedly psychic fantasy is copied that fulfills the same role in its field as the organ does regarding the global functioning of the biological organism.

We must take into account punctually what Lacan has shown, namely, that *Trieb* is a novel concept whose arrival revolutionizes theory. Translating instinct for *Trieb* spoils the Freudian edifice. It is not a matter of mere words. No, because in saying instinct we already begin to tinge a direction of the cure and to orient toward the operation in terms of the desire of an analyst, not the desire of the analyst. On the other hand, Freud has rigorously circumscribed the scope of the term *instinct*. We

---

28. J. Lacan, *Los cuatro . . .* , *op. cit.*, p. 125. [*The Four . . .* , p. 116.]
29. S. Freud, "*El tabú de la virginidad*," *O. C.*, *op. cit.*, vol. 11, p. 195. ["The Taboo of Virginity," p. 199.]

can locate five passages where he writes *Instinkt* to allude strictly to the biological instinct, to the zoological endowment. When he names the fourth fundamental concept, the drive or drift (*dérive*), he writes *Trieb*, which indicates that he knew very well what he was talking about. Is there more evidence of this? What he writes in *The Question of Lay Analysis*, as follows: "'*Triebe*' [instincts], a word for which we *are envied* by many modern languages."[30]

QUESTIONS AND ANSWERS

They asked me if I can expound on envy; if the image or the idea of the complete other is more important than the alleged value that other possesses. Lacan believes that a quote by Augustine where he describes (the quote is not literal but this is the idea) how he had the opportunity to see a child who, pale and writhing with envy, watched his mother breast-feeding his younger brother is a *princeps* site to approach this matter.[31] Was this reaction due to the fact that this child needed milk, that milk was of use to him? Was this what was valuable to him? Or, in the Kleinian manner now, was it the good breast that he wanted, and what his younger brother was taking away from him? Isn't the latter, in fact, hanging from the separate *a*, taking pleasure from it? On the other hand, wasn't this image of the mother with the child hanging from her what envy was trying to cleave?

What is unbearable is this mother-hanging baby (we mustn't forget the phallic value of the son as an attempt to occlude the hoop net, as we have already described), and what matters is not the organic satisfaction but the very special juncture, the amboceptor completeness produced in that breast-feeding act. It is there that envy appears, remarks Lacan, doubtlessly recalling Freud, who had meditated about the "evil eye" and its link to envy in "The Uncanny."[32] This is an order where the

---

30. S. Freud, *O. C.*, *op. cit.*, p. 187, emphasis added [p. 200].
31. J. Lacan, "*La agresividad en psicoanálisis,*" *Escritos II*, *op. cit.*, p. 78. ["Aggressivity in Psychoanalysis," in *Ecrits: A Selection*, *op. cit.*, p. 20.]
32. S. Freud, "*Lo ominoso [siniestro]*" (The Uncanny), *op. cit.*, pp. 239–240. [p. 240]

scopic is at play. Where is the evil eye aimed? We will work later on the answer to this query, accounting for the (more encompassing) context in which it is inscribed. Let us say for now that the *separating* dimension of the eye makes its appearance here, in the sense that it tries to separate, for instance, the mother from the child hanging from her, and the latter from his hanging from *a*. For it is not, I repeat, the breast-fed younger brother the child envies; it is the fascination of this image itself that captures him. If it crystallizes in a significant way, this situation may give rise to a particular condition—requirement—for eroticization. Such a fascination may establish itself—articulated, of course, with other factors we will leave out—as a condition of unavoidable excitation with respect to *jouissance*.

Q: How should we define prepsychotic?

A: It is one of those classifications that I actually don't like. The problem is that it is difficult to say it in any other way. There appears here a conflicting tendency for psychoanalysis, namely, that of making a sort of forecast. In our first meeting we posited one of the elements that differentiated us from scientific discourse as determined by *Tuché*. The practice of psychoanalysis is a practice of the random, detached from the one that corresponds to science, which tries to maintain the foreseen variables and zealously advances forecasts. Fore-see, that is, to see before what is going to happen. Science vindicates the consideration of this causal plane in the realm of forecasting. The establishment of analysis tries to seek a different status for itself. The prefix "fore" alludes then to the anticipation of something that will inexorably occur later. This is related to the issue of diagnosis, a slippery problem Freud considered in one of his *New Introductory Lectures to Psychoanalysis*, the one titled "*Esclarecimientos, aplicaciones, orientaciones*" ("Explanations, Applications and Orientation"). Freud resorts there to a tale he attributes to Victor Hugo (even though the information seems to be the product of a paramnesia) in order to design a simile of the problem brought about by the possible production of diagnoses in psychoanalysis. The fable tells about a king who claimed to know whether or not a woman was a witch. According to this character, it sufficed with taking the woman in question and putting her in a cauldron with boiling water. Once the cooking was done, the resulting flavor when tasting the broth produced would allow one to verify whether or not the woman was a witch. Freud commented in his lecture that something similar takes place in analysis. We can make a diagnosis in the manner narrated in this half-funny, half-tragic literary reference, namely, always a posteriori.[33] This might seem like a truism, but it is not the same thing to be in the analytic situation than not to be in it. There are phenomena that only set in within the analytic situation, and not before. The delicate part lies in the "fore," that is, in the preliminary interviews. I would venture to say that other than indicating in the medical-psychiatric manner whether certain symptoms or signs appear, the symptom implicates us as analysts insofar as it constitutes a signifying articulation, and a possibility on the part of the analysant to displace the a to the locus where it constitutes us in our practice.[34]

In that first moment we need to verify the emergence of the metaphor and the subject's tolerance to it. We must notice if there is the chance of substitution or if any eventuality of metaphor is blocked by a narrow-mindedness where, for instance, either a slant of obsessive argument or one of paranoid persecution is tenaciously adopted. A possible border, to give a somewhat "technical" indication, is to practice the possibility to interact in the register of the metaphor (*posibilidad de metáfora*) in the preliminary interviews, since the use of the metaphor entails the operance (*operancia*) of the signifier Name-of-the-Father.

Ultimately, if there is metaphor, it is because there is paternal metaphor. If one can talk in an allusive way, or if the analysant can tolerate the fact that if he says one thing the analyst hears a different one, the practice of analysis can start there. Conversely, if there is no metaphor, our comprehension aims to the psychotic structure, for certainty rejects metaphor.[35] Yet evidently, the problem is "glassy" (*vidrioso*). We must admit that often the matter has to do with the plane linked to experience.

---

33. S. Freud, *O. C.*, *op. cit.*, vol. 22, pp. 143–144 [pp. 155–156.]

34. The "broth" in question, isn't it what "poured" from the sacrificed women? Is it a diagnosis proposed in terms of the (a posteriori) location of a?

35. As we can deduce, this punctuation of the metaphor does not (deliberately) emphasize the consideration of the psychotic stabilization known as "delirious metaphor" (cf. J. Lacan, "*De una cuestión . . .* ," *op. cit.*, p. 262). ["On a question . . . ," p. 217.]

Lacan himself will go as far as to allude to the "knowledge (*saber*) that experience deposits in each of us." This perception relates ultimately to the analyst's *training*,[36] and is hard to conceptualize. We can only point out a few fragmentary data. In sum, what is the psychoanalytic technique as a whole? Any grade-school child can understand it fully and reproduce it, but from there to being able to perform according to it there is a long haul. Or is it that it does not exist as such?

Aside from its conceptualization, a prepsychotic state may be noticed due to the absence of metaphorization and the appearance of certain effects triggered by an interpretation. In this case, we run the risk that what would have detonated elsewhere anyway will detonate here. In any case, it is the ethical responsibility of the analyst not to trigger it at his own particular risk. It is possible to think this problem through in terms of constituting structures or operations, or, as I prefer, in terms of the dimension of the specificity of desires. The critical point is the particular way to understand the structure generally and particularly. Ultimately, the crucial factor an analyst must consider to make the decision about conducting or not an analysis is not so much the label as the decision whether or not analysis will help the prospective analysant. We must retrieve these concepts once and again, and not in a shameful way, because if we don't, we run the serious risk of losing ourselves in abstractions without paying attention to concrete elements whose assessment must be done case by case.

What does it mean to decide whether or not analysis will help? From a perspective tied to the personal, we would say that analysis must aim to the fulfillment of the analysant's satisfaction. Now, satisfaction is what relates to the aim. If the drive's aim is to obtain satisfaction, analysis shows that satisfaction can be achieved in a number of ways. The analysant reports that he is unsatisfied with himself—that is why he seeks analysis. When he betrays this dissatisfaction, the analyst will reveal to him how satisfied he proves to be. Then, what justifies our intervention? Very pertinently, Lacan remarks that in order to achieve this very peculiar satisfaction comprised within neurosis, analysants grieve too

---

36. In English in the original. The author refers to the degree of experience of the analyst. (Translator's note)

much, they make too great an effort. We analysts start from the premise that things could surely be achieved through shorter paths, rectifying the mode of satisfaction.

There is analysis because that surplus of work captures the psycho-neurotic's life. That is why he is extremely surprised when the cure determines a more lively life for him, when he appears more awake, more creative and sublimating. The latter is possible because something of the libidinal involved in the maintenance of the order of the symptom may now be applied to other realms and interests in life. We could repeat here the classic Freudian motto regarding the goal of the cure, namely "to love and work." Analysis may actually help in these orders, usually affected in the subject who consults us. In short, the process consists in changing the conditions of *jouissance*, in being able to respond differently to the demand of the Other; in being able, in sum, to conquer a place before the Other that will not be that of the slave (that is, the place of the deadly, ceaseless restlessness where there is an attempt to staunch a Name-of-the-Father that is continuously weakening).

8

Partiality, Border, Layout[1]:
The Drift (Deriva) in Circuit

Today I want to start by commenting upon an encounter. Pleasant though unexpected—for a change—it confronted me with the imbalance of an asynchrony. Why? Because I would have wanted for that encounter to have happened before our first meeting, and in fact it happened only for the eighth one—today. Indeed, a few days ago I had the chance to be affected by something that belongs in that order we have tried to clear up some meetings ago, namely, that of *Tuché*, the encounter with repetition given as chance. In this case, the repetition occurred based on the publication of a text by Martin Heidegger that appeared recently in France, and that includes some of his courses that had remained unpublished during his lifetime. They belong to a series dictated in 1941. The original publication is from 1981. The translation into French came out last year. What interests us is the fact that this text is titled, as is the course, *Fundamental Concepts*. Of course this title was not chosen randomly, even though chance is not absent here in the sense of repetition, of the *dustuchic* encounter.

Heidegger's reflections deserve some comment, for they are interesting in relation to our attempt to better delineate the *Grundbegriff*. It

---

1. According to the author, his use of the Spanish term *trazado* (layout) refers both to the already laid path, and to the new marks produced by traversing it. (Translator's note)

is the same term Freud used in *Instincts and Their Vicissitudes* and on which Lacan insists when he starts his revision of the fourth fundamental concept of psychoanalysis. As you will recall, the fundament is related to the *pudendum*, so that it is something that is connected to the genital dimension, or rather, to the sexuality of the drive. Insofar as he was not a psychoanalyst, Heidegger grants a different sense to the term *Grundbegriff*. Yet there is a shared intention, that of pondering precisely this particular term. We think, therefore, that it is possible to draw a certain line that goes from Freud, through Heidegger, to Lacan. We are not interested specifically in whether or not the Lacan of Seminar 11 knew about Heidegger's classes. This information is irrelevant in terms of a criterion such as the one we are maintaining, where the specific knowledge (*conocimiento*) is not as important in terms of influences as is the sharing of a certain cultural climate. If some thoughts "permeate" the atmosphere, then eventual direct influences needn't be postulated—this is not the only way a precursor may exert his influence.[2]

I don't intend to assert by this comment that the title with which Seminar 11 was published, *The Four Fundamental Concepts of Psychoanalysis*, has been taken from Heidegger. It is just that Lacan always mentioned his respect for the ideas of the German philosopher, of whom, moreover, he was a friend. That is why it is worth mentioning some of such ideas in our course. The fact is that we do not invoke just anybody randomly. The seminar has taught us how chance always involves a limited structuration of the situation. It is not about relating one thing to another through mere whimsy. Certain binds are possible and others enter the category of the impossible, that is, of the Real. The purpose of both authors is similar in what concerns us here—it articulates with the way in which the fundamental concepts are being thought.

In his 1941 classes, Martin Heidegger asserted: "We call 'concepts' representations in which we place before us an object or entire domains of objects in their generality. The ground concepts are then entirely general representations of as large as possible domains."[3] In my view,

---

2. Cf. Chapter 3.
3. M. Heidegger, *Concepts fondamentaux*, Gallimard, Paris, 1985, p. 14. [*The Fundamental Concepts of Metaphysics: World, Finitude, Solitude*, tr. W. McNeill and M. Walker, Indiana University Press, Bloomington, IN, 2001.]

this is a meaning utterly sharable by the Lacanian trajectory. Heidegger formulates another, even more successful explanation. In a summary written in a certain passage of the introduction, we read: "By 'fundamental concepts' we usually understand representations that delimit for us a domain of objects, fully or according to particular but directing perspectives."[4] These last words indicate an element linked to a term dear to the teaching that summons us here, namely, that of *direction*, which will certainly evoke in you the direction of the cure. Besides the usual sense of this term, we can relate it to one of the possible translations of another Heideggerian notion, that is, *Sorge*, translatable as "care" or "cure."

This is really a significant background to keep in mind. When we allude to the direction of the cure we are dealing with a field ruled by *ground-concepts* and concerning the *Dasein*, to use the philosopher's own designation. To conclude, let us read one last paragraph as a testimony of my encounter: " *'Ground-concepts'* means to conceive the ground of everything, that is, to go as far as to relate to the 'fundament' of everything. What 'fundament' means here must be classified gradually. What must also be clarified, then, is in what consists the relation with the fundament, to what extent this relation implies, refers, to a knowledge (*saber*), and to what extent this relation is in itself a knowledge (*saber*)."[5]

If we substituted somewhat boldly the dimension of the unconscious for such "fundament," we might notice, thanks to that slant, how Lacan argues and demonstrates the unconscious's condition of articulate knowledge (*saber*). This going to the depths[6] is but another way to take into account the consequences inferable from the etymology of the term *Grundbegriff*. This is all I wanted to mention to you regarding my unexpected encounter with these Heideggerian developments, within the strict scope of our course. In our last meeting I mentioned in passing that there were five places in Freud's work where the term *Instinkt* appeared explicitly. After the meeting, I was very pertinently asked about

---

4. M. Heidegger, *op. cit.*, p. 25.

5. M. Heidegger, *op. cit.*, p. 34.

6. Harari plays here with the two meanings of *fondo*, namely, "ground" and "bottom" or "depth." (Translator's note)

these texts, which mark a clear discrimination between the order of the instinct and that absolutely novel one implicated in the term *Trieb*. The places where Freud produces this evident distinction are *Totem and Taboo*, *The Unconscious*, the case history of *The Wolf Man*, *Group Psychology and the Analysis of the Ego*, and *Inhibitions, Symptoms, and Anxiety*.[7] You will find there a categorical, doubtlessly emphatic discrimination, since *Instinkt* is inscribed in relation to the condition of a "reproductive" behavioral cycle that is linked, or alludes, to the animal kingdom. Taking advantage of the ambiguity of the word, with the term *reproduction* I wish to imply that in the instinct a hereditary package is present that serves as a vehicle, as Heidegger would put it, for a wisdom, a knowledge (*saber*). What does the instinct know (*sabe*) about? About something quite unique—it knows about preservation. It possesses a sort of programming with which each species is equipped in order to survive as such, and by virtue of which each individual belonging to that species may last, besides making the species last through its offspring. Lacan often refers ironically—because he formulates it in the Freudian sense of the joke, not by mistake—to a death instinct. He does it precisely for the paradoxical value of the concept, because he wants to account for an unheard-of idea. Indeed, if the animal instinct aims at the prolongation, at the preservation of life, what would a death instinct be?

In rhetoric this is called an oxymoron. Saying death instinct produces an effect similar to the one achieved when referring, for instance, to a bright darkness. If we think carefully what instinct means, we may verify how the Freudian proposition—not Lacan's, but Freud's himself—is unarguably revulsive with respect to any conventional characterization of the instinct; hence the insistence in pointing out that the concept of *Trieb* is a new one. This whole opening is lost, however, if—as they do in the English edition of Freud's work, the classic *Standard Edition*

---

7. S. Freud, *O. C.*, vol. 13, pp. 124–126; vol. 14, pp. 191–192; vol. 17, p. 109; vol. 18, pp. 112–113, and vol. 20, p. 157, respectively. We should point out the following circumstance: most of these references do not appear in the indexes of the *O. C.* (Complete Works). [Vol. 13, pp. 124–126, vol. 14, pp. 194–195, vol. 17, p. 120, vol. 18, pp. 118–119, vol. 20, pp. 154–155.]

directed by James Strachey—both *Trieb* and *Instinkt* are indiscriminately translated as "instinct."

Fortunately we have had at our disposal for some time now Etcheverry's Spanish version, where *Trieb* appears as drive (*pulsión*). Yet we are forced to emphasize another translation problem regarding this topic. When we refer to the terms of the drive, we find a suggestion that, in my view, is inappropriate in what refers to one of them. We will see which one it is, and I hope you will share the reasons I will bring forth here. Lacan affirms very wisely that in the direction of the cure, the drive is a decisive concept. What does he mean by this, if we leave speculations aside and we refer to clinical practice? What does the concept of the drive connote and denote? We could say, first, the following: it denotes the type of circumstances where what emerges from the interior of the body presents itself with such force that it is unstoppable. There is no valid, effective coercion when the irruption of what we call the drive exists. Then, if with this concept we account for an incoercible, ungovernable agency, we state about it that, logically, it has to go onto a course of action, that is, in a way, it implies motility. It is here where we have to start to be careful, because the problem becomes more complex. If we were only dealing with what we just said, then the drive would simply constitute a sort of motor discharge. Let us recall in this respect the very basic schema of the reflex arc:

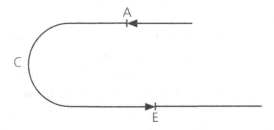

The diagram represents the ingress of an excitation, the journey through a certain path, and the later motor exit. There is here a nerve cell called afferent (A), another considered central (C), and a final one labeled efferent (E). Let us take, for example, the kneecap reflex. If an external stimulation is applied, a spontaneous kneecap reaction is produced by means of a prescribed path. The reflex arc is precisely the starting point to distinguish what the Freudian *Trieb* is about. In other words, we can start from this schema in order to realize what the *Trieb* is not.

Freud starts by saying that there are undoubtedly excitations, that is, stimuli applied from the exterior to the organism. He then points out that what we are interested in, however, is another matter—that of endogenous stimulation. That is why he alludes to something that emanates, that surges from the interior, having to translate quickly into action, into its motor materialization. We need to discriminate, then, between an exogenous afference and another one that, in order to somehow make it present, we consider as emerging from the interior (or endogenous):

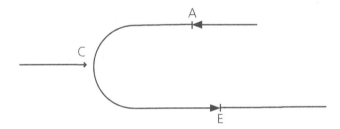

The schema of the reflex arc certainly appears early on in the Freudian theorization. We find it already in *La interpretación de los sueños* (*The Interpretation of Dreams*).[8] As in *Instincts and Their Vicissitudes*, we are surprised by the detectable explanatory strategy. In both cases, the procedure entails starting from certain developments accepted by the current scientific convention. When we succeed in getting an approximate idea of what Freud is suggesting, he states that it is not that, but something else. In *The Interpretation* he starts indeed from the model of the reflex arc in order to build a design of the psychic apparatus. Right after finishing it, he warns us that such a model is not viable because it is incapable of accounting for an anomalous situation in terms of the possibilities it considers. Which situation? The fact is that the excitation might also follow this course:

---

8. S. Freud, *op. cit.*, *O. C.*, vol. 5, pp. 530ff. [pp. 537ff]

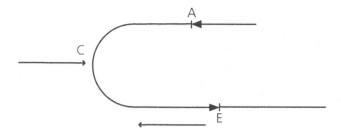

The resulting circuit has no reason to exist in terms of a biological basis. Freud tries to ponder a problem alien to the realm of biology by means of a theoretical-biological *fiction*.[9] Confronted with these punctuations, some hasty or malicious people have branded him as biologistic. We should respond to this accusation saying that Freud works with the models provided by the disciplines of his time. That is his frame of reference, yet he actually subverts it in order to be able to process his own experience, and not trace it from the discipline from which he adopts his theoretical fictions. There is nothing biologistic here. With such a criterion, one may accuse Lacan (as it has been done) of linguicist, topologistic, anthropologistic, etc., when his behavior consisted of the importation of other (contemporary, current) systems of reference in order to relaunch, to renovate psychoanalysis. His crystal-clear intention was to avoid the weakening effect of the *ad infinitum* reproduction of the Freudian quote, which condemned our discipline to a death by starvation.

Going back to Freud, the recourse of starting from this reflex arc in *Instincts and Their Vicissitudes* does not have as a goal to focus on the matter that he had called retrogressive direction (←) in *The Interpretation of Dreams*, but on the problematic that may be characterized as that of the endogenous stimulus:

---

9. *Fiktion*, a term (it is worth noting) present also in *La interpretación* . . . (*The Interpretation* . . .) (*op. cit.*, p. 592). The frequent Lacanian reference to Bentham, therefore, implicitly acknowledges Freud's.

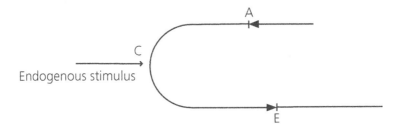

A problem emerges here: we are using the same word for the endogenous and the exogenous stimulation, but these stimulations are sufficiently dissimilar. We don't solve the matter by naming one as inner, and the other as outer. It is to this, precisely, that the problematic of the drive refers.

To attempt to elucidate more rigorously the singularity of the endogenous stimulus, the seminar takes up again what we had defined last meeting as the four terms of the drive, following Freud carefully and adding the display of certain necessary precisions and contributions as well. As you will recall, the four terms are as follows:

$$\text{Terms of the drive} \begin{bmatrix} \text{– Source} \\ \text{– Object} \\ \text{– Pressure} \\ \text{– Aim} \end{bmatrix}$$

Source, object, pressure—it is here that the translation problem we will tackle right away is located—and aim. These are the terms of the drive.

The terms present themselves in a relation of disjunction. Each one can be separated from the rest, which means that they are implicated as elements of a combinatory that admits many combinations among them. To clarify this idea, we can bring up an example of combinatory and combination: telephone numbers. The combinatory is constituted by all the numbers present on the keypad, that is, ten elements. Yet the millions of possible combinations in series of seven or ten numbers indicate an unrepeatable singularity for each of them. If not, one telephone number could belong to two or more customers, and we know that each customer has a singular series of digits that is *his* telephone number.

The disjunction in the terms of the drive entails the lack of solidarity among them, since they are located on the plane of a combinatory.

Doubtlessly, when we think of any drive we must take the four terms into account, but that does not determine that when we postulate one of them it will involve, as if by a "dragging" effect, the others. This warning allows Lacan to establish in the corresponding chapter that if anything, the drive resembles a montage whose elements in no way bear in them a predictable form of assemblage, a formative legality.

Yet we must clarify another point that I had the chance to discuss outside the class in a previous meeting. I was asked about the possible relation between Lacan's postulations and surrealism. This is precisely what we are talking about now. If the drive is a montage, we must understand it as that which is characteristic of the surrealist collage. I think it is an important simile, for one of the very first points about this collage is that it constitutes something different from the reproductive copy of a representational world, obvious for everybody. Nothing is further from reproduction. Another point to highlight: the elements combined in the collage are, furthermore, heteroclite among them. They don't possess, for instance, the typical homogeneity implicit in the various colors, forms, lines, and textures of classic canvas painting. It could be present, but a newspaper clipping, a rag, a spoon, a lightbulb, or the wire coil of a television set, for example, also participate in the collage. Due to their customary condition of disjunction, such elements truly surprise us when they are assembled.

Through this effect of surprise, of unsettlement, the subject is "taken" by this valuable experience of nonsense, which the seminar calls *nonsensical*.[10] In this nonsense, experiences of a very diverse nature are lodged. Prior to its "retrieval" by psychoanalysis, this issue had been treated prevalently within the fields of literature and logic. Lewis Carroll holds a distinguished place in this practice. Of course, not just for *Alice in Wonderland* and *Alice Through the Looking Glass*, but also as the writer of recreational logic, where he presents those paradoxes that bring about the sudden paralysis of the subject confronted with nonsense.[11] I would also add Edward Lear, Carroll's predecessor and author of a book that has been

---

10. In English in the original. (Translator's note)

11. L. Carroll, *Matemática demente*, Tusquets, Barcelona, 1983, and *El juego de la lógica*, Alianza, Madrid, 1976. [*Curiosa Mathematica: Pillow-Problems*, part 2, Classic Books, 2000; *The Game of Logic*, Classic Books, 2000.]

published in Spanish under the title of *Disparatario*.[12] You will be able to find there many of these logical games (and mockery, why not), in which we cannot perceive language to be the copy of anything, or to represent something that may be particularly recognizable as external to it.

We must underscore another matter related to the topic of the combinatory and the combination, namely, the leap from the general to the particular. Instinct bears the nature of the general. It is universal, it encompasses every individual in the species. The drive, conversely, accounts for a sort of singular formula—if we can put it like that. Instead of postulating, as the instinct would have it, that the individual is just a member of the species, the drive respects the value of singularity.

As you can see, this strange element, the drive, becomes less and less recognizable in relation to the details characteristic of the instinct. We just pointed out that the *Trieb* is inherently ungovernable, incoercible, something that becomes action. All these characteristics incite us to situate the term pressure in the first place. This term is often confused with the concept of *Trieb* as a whole. The Freudian original term is *Drang*. Lacan will translate it into French as *poussée*, preserving that nuance that relates *Drang* to the order of an almost explosive urgency. In the new translation of Freud's work, *Drang* is rendered as effort (*esfuerzo*). The term provokes serious misunderstandings, since it gives rise, among other things, to the (in my view) erroneous translation of concepts such as secondary repression (or repression, strictly speaking), which is transformed into "effort to give chase." Such translation is the result of the need to remain within the same type of semantic family. On the other hand, in the translation of Seminar 11 published by Seix Barral, *Drang* appears also as pressure (*presión*).[13] This *Drang* has other connections, of course, if we try to incorporate the teaching effects of the reflections on language to articulate them in our treatment of the ground-concepts or fundamental concepts. If we situate ourselves within the realm

---

12. E. Lear, *op. cit.*, Tusquets, Barcelona, 1984. [*The Complete Nonsense Book*, Book Sales, 2001.]

13. On the other hand, in the most recent one by Paidós (*op. cit.*) it is translated as "thrust" (*empuje*) (pp. 169ff). The observations we will bring forth next are also valid for this alternative. [The term *thrust* coincides with Sheridan's translation.]

that concerns us, the *Drang* is then related to the *Verdrängung*, a word that is translated as repression. On this issue I disagree with the new Spanish version of Freud's work, which proposes in this case "effort of ejection and supplantation." Why? Because *Drang*, as a particle, is present in the term *Verdrängung*. Homologically, we can—we must—articulate pressure (*presión*) and repression (*represión*), for they account for the following: if we do a simple scansion like the ones we so often do during sessions, when we "cut" the prefix of the second word, we will obtain re-pression (*re-presión*).[14]

I believe this is a pertinent way to understand the concept, for it locates the latter at the maximum distance from the allusion to any pseudo-volitive attitude such as, for instance, the expression "effort to give chase," with its unavoidable connotation of the intentional homunculus. Let us recall that when there is repression, a signifier didn't disappear or fall into oblivion, lacking in potency or effectiveness. Repression is that which exerts pressure again. What is repressed is what returns exerting pressure, not what disappears. As we have already said, the Freudian unconscious is effective—it is not a diluted, pale subconscious, lacking in strength. This fact is solidly based on our understanding that we are dealing here with the impelling, coercive condition of the drive. These data are enough, in my view, to establish the need to translate *Drang* as pressure. It is important to clarify these issues, because if we resort to the new translation of Freud's work we will constantly run into "effort." If we choose other terms, we must at least justify our choice. Ours is an option founded within psychoanalysis itself, and not only from the linguistic (etymologic or semantic) perspectives. In this way, we may rigorously deduce that repression does not indicate the action of anything that provokes disappearance, but the exact opposite. We will also be able to grasp the link between a term and a vicissitude of the drive.

What is the action of repression, in sum? To bring about the return of the elided signifier, a return that is verified in a displaced or substituting way. As we have pointed out, the notion of pressure may

---

14. The Spanish word *presión* means "pressure." (Translator's note)

give rise to the supposition that it in itself defines the drive. If we say that the drive is the incoercible, and immediately afterward we mark this element as a key trait of the *Drang*, a coarse syllogism is produced almost spontaneously. What is definitive about the drive would seem to be precisely the pressure as irresistible urgency. Such a confusion has brought about numerous deflections among the post-Freudians who, although they maintained, without acknowledging it as such, a field we have learned to call the field of the signifier, they also endorsed, on the other hand, a "beyond" that escapes the condition ruled by the signifier. This beyond would be something elementary, primitive, where the symbol has no chance to enter. If this conception resonates in our ears in a theological way, I think it is viable to credit it as such. Indeed, there is a reason why we are speaking of a "beyond."

On the other hand, the drive is not an internal, indescribable, ineffable emanation that, once it has appeared, we can only, in the best-case scenario, partially curb. The drive generates specifically in the field of the Other. It is not characteristic of the species, like the instinct. It gestates precisely in a crucial structure, that of the binds recognizable in psychoanalysis as belonging to the field of Oedipus, which comprises relations much more complex than those contemplated by the classic tale we all know. To orient ourselves here, let us think, with Freud,[15] of all the relations detectable in *fantasmes*, whose analysis is not our purpose in this course. We will only notice their design as a network quite richer and more intricate than the typical reduction to the dialectic of incest and parricide.

If we consider the drive also as an effect of the operations constitutive of the subject, there emerges an alternative entirely different from the proposition of the instinct, which is already-given with the individual of the species. Hence, the confusion that considers the *Drang* as an equivalent of the drive also starts from a misunderstanding. Lacan asks: Could it be perhaps the pressure characteristic of an individual urged by a certain need? For example, is what happens with someone desperately hungry the same or different from what Freud writes about

---

15. S. Freud, *"Sobre la sexualidad femenina"* ("Female Sexuality"), *O. C., op. cit.*, vol. 21, p. 228 [pp. 229–230].

pressure? Of course, the answer is that it is something different, and such an answer is based on the following: the tension provoked by the need, that discomfort that also leads to action, entails the involvement of the organism as a whole. Pressure, the *Drang*, in turn, concerns only the nervous system, the real I. It is constrained only to a partial dimension.

This last word—*partial*—is decisive in our entire development. I wish to linger here because the elucidation of this term also allows us to understand the problem of the object. In the theorization of Kleinian analysts, the object has been divided into partial and total. Then, if we speak about a "partial" trait, we should comment briefly on this issue. The said current supposes the existence of a preformed development, which is presented as closely tied to the ideology of the instinct as a whole. Kleinians postulate a sort of prototype of the species that follows, in the best-case scenario (and, possibly, helped by the environment), a certain path in each individual. The process starts amid a diffuse, chaotic, and disintegrated experience. Then a precise location occurs whereby things are grasped (perceptively and emotionally) as a totality.

This argumentation is easily understood. It seems to possess an overwhelming logic. This is indeed the case, for it bears the logic of the Imaginary, which, always convincing, is immediately grasped in an intuitive way. This pseudo-theory is highly persuasive. Nonetheless, if we state that the matter is not so aptly integrative, we come much closer to the formulation by means of the orientation of truth, since the object with which we are dealing from the perspective of the drive is immovably partial. When the object is defined as total, we are in the presence of a different dimension, namely, that of the object of love. And, as we know, the drives and their vicissitudes are one thing, and love is a very different one. This is categorically written in Freud in an almost literal way. Those who cannot see it that way simply don't want to notice it. We must discriminate between these two objects in a precise way. As you will recall, when we worked on the concept of transference we emphasized the fact that the object of love is related precisely to the terrain of the narcissic. In this way, the subject feels he is the loving one, *erastés*, when in fact what he seeks is to be lovable, *eromenós*.

It is here that the totalization of the object takes place, because we are in the narcissic axis, which, according to Lacan's teachings, is apprehended under the section of the mirror stage,[16] located in the Imaginary register. In this realm, the total object makes sense, according to the notation "I (a)."[17] There is neither a developing appropriateness nor a coupled re-encounter of totality, as Kleinians claim. Briefly, they believe that at the beginning there is a unity that will then dissociate, and that it will be reintegrated later. As far as I'm concerned, I have understood years ago that such a hypothetical trajectory constitutes a secular metaphor for the fall and redemption. Salvation occurs precisely through the reparation capable of twisting the guilt that derives from the original sadistic sin.

The notes in the Kleinian texts that serve to illustrate the search for "reparation" become effective through manifest behaviors pleasing to the empirical parents. We can easily find a protestant core in such theorization that is present as a true ground-concept. In short, in Kleinianism the drive doesn't appear; only the plane of the instinct is clearly evident. What is sought, then, is the totalization of the object. This information indicates at what level an analysis based on such premises may travel: it remains in the register of the Imaginary. And who says that the Imaginary does not have its own effectiveness? The results can be spectacular. We should keep in mind, once again, hypnosis. When the analyst remains in the locus we have designated as I, he will very likely reach "effective" results.

It would be necessary to define, of course, what are the ethics of this analyst—that of the desire of the analyst—and what he consequently intends as to the direction of the cure. Under the guise of an analysis, he certainly intends to maintain a hypnotic dimension, even if he doesn't ostensibly practice such a device. He may try to maintain a psychotherapeutic relation, instead of "in an upside-down hypnosis, to embody the

---

16. J. Lacan, "*El estadio del espejo como formador de la función del yo, tal como nos lo enseña la experiencia psicoanalítica,*" *Escritos I, op. cit.*, pp. 11–18. ["The Mirror Stage as Formative of the Function of the I," in *Ecrits: A Selection, op. cit.*, pp. 1–7.]

17. J. Lacan, "*Observación sobre el informe . . . ,*" (Observations on the Report . . .) *op. cit.*, p. 302.

hypnotized patient."[18] That is why, I insist, it is necessary to posit an imaginary effectiveness, paraphrasing the symbolic effectiveness described by Lévi-Strauss.[19] In such cases we notice to what extent this discrimination between a partial and a total object is not just a pun, or a simple theoretical option without major consequences. The distinction bears a truly enormous clinical impact. If the proposition consists of happily falling off a cliff within love, rejecting the split that constitutes us—since love totalizes—we are faced with an imaginary alienation that orders the subject to fall into a figure that can be designated as cure through love—for the analyst.

The object conceived as partial has, in addition, another defining characteristic concerning the discrimination instinct/drive. To our surprise, Freud points out that the object of the drive is indifferent. In the case of the instinct, in no way can the object be indifferent, for what happens is the exact opposite. The instinct must connect with a defined, outlined, and nontransferable object. This indicates a flexibility in the case of the drive antithetic to the rigidity characteristic of the instinct. The instinctive is even unintelligent, because it cannot adapt to changing circumstances. It blindly repeats a mechanism of successiveness, which, if interrupted at a certain point, when it re-settles, the animal guided by this instinct does not complete the circuit in the remaining stretch but starts again from the first step. The object and the mode of behavior to reach it are fixed, rigid, static.

According to the Freudian warning, the object of the drive is indifferent. It is not a simple coincidence that in one of Freud's crucial texts, *Tres ensayos de teoría sexual (Three Essays on the Theory of Sexuality)*, sexual aberrations are located at the beginning of the exposition.[20] The author has no intention here of dwelling on the category of pornographer, or of showing some morbid psychopathological curiosity. This

---

18. J. Lacan, *Los cuatro conceptos* . . . , *op. cit.*, p. 276. [*The Four Fundamental Concepts* . . . , p. 273.]

19. C. Lévi-Strauss, *Antropología estructural*, Eudeba, Buenos Aires, 1968, pp. 168–185. [*Structural Anthropology*, Trans. C. Jakobson and B. Schoepf, Basic Books, New York, 2000.]

20. S. Freud, *op. cit.*, O. C., pp. 123–156 [pp. 135–172].

opening is due to a discursive strategy—the best way to introduce what is at stake in the field of the drive. Freud's argumentative strategy continues, then, with infantile sexuality. There he presents in a very clear way developments that will trigger an epistemological rupture (using Bachelard's concept) with the prevalent prejudices concerning sex.

Let us review briefly what such prejudices entailed. Sexuality was a total biological function whose mission was the reproduction of the species, which was verified in a specific act, namely, heterosexual coitus; a fact possible, of course, after pubescent development. Freud must formulate his criticism and construe his postulation precisely against all of this. In such a conception—it is hardly necessary to point this out—the object appears as fixed and predetermined. By starting with an exposition of the aberrations, it is possible to show how they offer the model to determine that the object is not fixed in any way. The demonstration is configured precisely by these pathologies, which, for that purpose, must cease to be apprehended as hereditary deviations.

A certain psychoanalysis mistakenly conceives of sexuality in a prepsychoanalytic way when it advocates the ideology of genitalism. It assumes "the genital" as the stage normally reached in analysis; genitalism is then homologous to the Kleinian depressive position—the access to an alleged mental health. In this case, a conception derivative not only from the totalization of the object but also from the totalization of the drive is being practiced. As we may notice, starting from the partial aspect of the *Drang* we begin to pivot around two notions somewhat close to each other, that is, partial drive-partial object. What is curious is that they are two partialities that do not lead to any totality. They are not partial in the sense that at some point they will end in something superior or larger. Concerning this point, let us note that the drive is partial because it represents partially the biological—totalistic—aim involved in sexuality. Sexuality thus conceived possesses components that *will not* gather—"if everything works"—in a meeting point, or a guiding centering, for they will remain disjunct, as happens with the composing terms of each drive.

This is a first point to consider. The second one is something we already mentioned when we referred to the concept of repetition. As you will recall, we approached interesting formulations on the issue of developmental psychology and the stages of development. As we commented then, Lacan warned that this developmental conception (which even shows a nonnegligible degree of Platonism) is unthinkable from the psychoanalytic perspective. Confronted with such a conception, psychoanalysis insists on accidents or traumas, to use the Freudian vocabulary. We are interested in the unexpected as a vector of a twist in the position of the subject. The seminar postulates the same thing regarding the way in which the drives successively link, and their objects follow one another. There is no place where the fact that, in a sort of natural maturational transit, there must be a developmental passage from the oral to the anal, from there to the phallic, then to a latency period, and finally to a stage of genitality (following certain preestablished laws on libidinal migration) is pontificated. If one can predict a certain passage, such prediction is possible by considering the demand of the Other, yet, of what does this Other consist? Let us illustrate it.

There is a moment in which, due to her insertion in the symbolic order, the mother recognizes that, as Freud taught us, the time has come to request that her child's excrements be deposited in a certain place and time. Here we can see it clearly—there is a demand from the Other that requires the attention to a precise location for defecations, the knowledge of how to ask, and the taking into account that if one offers this present, one will receive something in exchange. This event founds the dimension of the gift, as the seminar points out. A dialectic of symbolic bartering is thus inaugurated. That is why the seminar emphasizes how related to anality the domain of exchange—and even that of oblativity—is.

If we imaginarized a statement of the demand of the Other, we would say: "I demand that you give me that." Even though this is not a very accurate formulation, it may give us a provisional idea of what we just discussed, that is, that psychoanalytically, we cannot speak about a prescribed evolution, about anything morphogenic or developmental, for whatever will happen will depend on symbolic requirements. There is not necessarily an explicit "I ask you for a part of your body," or a "Do it for my sake." It is a demand with an exchange value. It is not a value in itself, since the value is granted by the Other. "If you give me that, I will give you this other thing in exchange." Here we enter an obviously interlocutive plane.[21]

Let us return now to the schema we brought up at the beginning of this meeting, that of the endogenous and the exogenous. It is worth insisting on this matter, for we will tackle another delicate issue, namely, the allusion to motility, to everything ungovernable that occurs apparently in this plane, of allegedly nonviable deviation and control. This point is decisively tied to the fact that the condition of the endogenous is discontinuous. The drive, instead, is a constant force, Freud tells us. It does not admit a moment of decline. In a way, this other substantive difference with the instinct is related to the following point: the aim of an instinct is also satisfaction. Once satisfied, its need-provoked tension dies down. The biological function admits a rhythm—after one has eaten well, one is sated, is not hungry anymore. I don't like this very particular and elementary example very much. I am almost already criticizing myself for it, even though it serves as a scaffolding (to be taken out later) to punctuate what interests us here. Of course, we can't consider the noticing of hunger as an exclusively biological phenomenon, for it is also taken by the signifying order. In this way, food intake is not excluded from the drive, it does not concern solely a nourishing need, and we have both bulimia and anorexia to prove it. They both account for the fact that we are not dealing with a nourishing satisfaction inscribed only in the order of the chemical. Let us reiterate: object *a* is not the food, as Melanie Klein believes, her calling it bosom or breast notwithstanding. It is indeed the breast, yet not at the time of breast-feeding, but when the breast is lost. To somehow illustrate this we could talk about the breast constituted at the time of the weaning. It is there and then that this object is constituted. Only when it is lost it starts to be an object, for its condition consists in a sort of self-mutilation, a lost bodily organ that falls and summons the lack. Because the breast does not "be-

---

21. We have intentionally excluded the classic demand Lacan introduces in Seminar 19, . . . *ou pire*, which reads: "I demand that you refuse what I offer you, because it is not that" (class of February 9, 1972, unpublished). This demand, of course, relocates our "imaginarization." It particularly enables us to definitely state the nonexplicit nature of the demand, a point we have made in Chapter 6.

long" to the mother, it does not even represent her partially. Consequently, the Kleinian oscillation between instinctive satisfaction-good breast because it gives milk, and instinctive frustration-bad breast because it gives no milk, is not viable either. The presence–absence rhythm, that rigid rhythmicity of the instinct, is located in an order of satisfaction very different from the one suggested by the drive.

Let us go back to what I was discussing at the end of our previous meeting. I was referring to when and how our analysants adduce not to be satisfied with what they are. They claim that they are not happy, that they don't live well, that they are anxious, that they don't obtain what they yearn for, etc. Our problem, Lacan tells us, consists precisely of trying to show them that they actually attain satisfaction through their symptoms, thanks to which they are dissatisfied. The question would be to elucidate what is denoted here by the pronoun *they*. We will thus produce a very important turn that will help us understand certain matters, because they undoubtedly give joy to something. The seminar states that the drive is what basically attacks the rule of the pleasure principle. The drive is then responsible for establishing, determining, and enforcing something other than the mere pleasure principle.

Let us continue by quoting a question Freud poses: "How could the satisfaction of an instinct produce unpleasure?"[22] This problem is obviously tied to the issue we are considering, but instead of unpleasure, Lacan introduces the concept of beyond the pleasure principle (I am expressing it in an orienting manner, only to introduce the concept), that is, *jouissance*. The latter is not exactly pleasurable; it has very little of the decreasing pleasure of the excitatory accumulation. We say *jouissance*, and we produce an effect of meaning. Yet as a concept it is the exact opposite of what the word suggests.

What does Lacan want to indicate with this, besides the lexical trap he has set? In my opinion, he intends to show once again the arbitrary nature of the signifier. In a way, what Humpty Dumpty points out in *Alice in Wonderland* is what always takes place, namely, a word ultimately means what the Master decrees that it mean. Among other things, this

---

22. S. Freud, *Inhibición, síntoma y angustia* (*Inhibitions, Symptoms, and Anxiety*) *op. cit.*, p. 87 [p. 91].

fact marks the relation between a signifier and power, but at the same time, it registers the flotation that embraces any signifier insofar as it does not by any means have its "own" signified stuck to it. On the other hand, we have already verified how Lacan proceeds in a similar manner regarding the concept of the Real, a manner that might be characterized—as a teaching effect—as joking and ironic.

When he proposes his very special approach to *jouissance*, Lacan specifies that it must not be confused with pleasure. On the contrary, he points to it as that through which the drive subverts the all-embracing kingdom of the pleasure principle. In this way, the satisfaction of the symptom brings quite a few complications. First, it is not a satisfaction that hits you naively in the eye, for it hides behind a genuine mask of suffering. Here there is a paradox, namely, the fact that in this suffering there is also satisfaction, a satisfaction to which the adjective-wildcard "masochist" cannot be hastily added.

Yet not only the symptom raises problems regarding the satisfaction of the drive—there is a vicissitude that renders the matter even more complicated. I am referring, of course, to sublimation. The vicissitude of the drive known as sublimation is solidly related to that category so hard to grasp that Freud analyzed it in detail in *Group Psychology and the Analysis of the Ego*, namely, the aim-inhibited drive. By definition, the latter would be the drive for which reaching the goal of satisfaction is forbidden. Yet we must also point out that, concerning sublimation, there is a very elementary disjunctive relation that may be postulated between this vicissitude and the symptom:

$$\text{symptom} \quad \vee \quad \text{sublimation}$$

If we wanted to locate these two terms in a big conceptual map, we might say that repression founds the symptom, whereas sublimation occurs without repression, and nevertheless entails a vicissitude of the drive that reaches satisfaction through a substitute path. Insofar as it represents a detour from the goal, the aim-inhibited drive indicates, says Freud, "an incipient sublimation."

In *Group Psychology and the Analysis of the Ego*, Freud expands his idea about friendship, making some wholly unexpected remarks. Let us bring up the main one by means of the *Porteño* proverb: "Women pass by, but friends remain."[23] In different words, psychoanalysis teaches us something similar. When aim inhibition exists, a stable bind can be maintained. Among friends of the same sex, the homosexual libido says "present," even though there is no explicit, bodily sexual manifestation. As long as this drive component does not reach its aim, it preserves the object, fostering hopes that the subject himself—in unison—will make sure to contradict, to adulterate. Bodily satisfaction tends to the weakening of the libidinal agency. We can thus explain the maintenance of a friendly tie throughout the years, as well as the exhaustion of a heterosexual relationship.[24]

Certainly, we must qualify these extremes by means of the countless possible combinations in order to take away from such a conception its false Manichaeism. Briefly, let us point out that these data account for that special aim involved in sublimation as well as in the aim-inhibited drive. We confirm, therefore, how the drive cannot be reduced to a hypothetical ungovernable motor act. If we define the drive only by this circumstance, we will be wrong, because we would believe that it corresponds almost exactly to the reflex arc, albeit with an endogenous stimulation. It does not involve, then, the most bestial, the most intractable aspect of man, what instinct usually connotes. This is not the case, for a start, because sublimation exists as a vicissitude, and so does the inhibition concerning the drive's aim. This peculiar form of satisfaction constitutes another factor to indicate the serious distinction that must be formulated between instinct and drive.

In a way, to understand what kind of satisfaction pertains to sublimation and how it is reached, we must take into account the fourth—and last—term of the drive, that is, the source. This source is what Freud designates as the erogenous zone. It would be very easy to understand this if we instinctified the drive. Everything starts with a source from which the pressure that impels the search for the object emerges. When

---

23. The term *porteño* designates people from Buenos Aires. In the Spanish original, the ending of the word *amigos* indicates male friends. (Translator's note)

24. S. Freud, *O. C.*, *op. cit.*, pp. 131–132 [pp. 138–139].

the object is reached, the aim is obtained, and the latter usually consists in the assimilation, the incorporation of the object:

On the other hand, this last point is quite definitive regarding the issue of the instinct "modelized" according to hunger. It is evident that sometimes we are dealing with the opposite function, as is the case with excretion, whereby the body dispossesses itself of a certain biologically disposable element. As you may deduce, the problem is that the drive's aim is not located in the appropriation of the object. See also how difficult it is to expound on the term *source* without constantly bringing up the term *aim*. Then, when we think of an erogenous zone such as the mouth, we see that it does not have food as its object. Lacan will recall with extreme sagacity that perhaps where that which concerns the oral drive may be glimpsed most categorically is in the example of autoeroticism that Freud offers, which consists in the purpose of kissing one's own lips.[25]

What is summoned in this act of closing is precisely a void. It is not only the elementary sensory stimulation of the lips that is at stake in the act of kissing one's own lips, but—decisively—the object void generated so as to support the drive. We find here another, more categorical distinction between drive and instinct. The latter's object is grasped because it constitutes a palpable, tangible consistency. The object of the drive, instead, is not sought in order to incorporate it. Rather, there is an attempt to sustain a hollow, a void through it. This is a characteristic that is scarcely understood in our milieu—according to the reliable data I possess. In general, people start from the premise that the subject wants to settle in the realm of imaginary plenitude; consistently, the goal lies in incorporating more and more things—briefly, to totalize oneself.

---

25. S. Freud, *Tres ensayos . . .* (*Three Essays . . .*), *op. cit.*, p. 165 [p. 180].

This premise usually leads to clichéd and spurious interpretations, for example, that the subject "can't bear the lack" or "the absence," that he "wants phallic completion," and so on. Thinking exclusively in this way is a good indicator that reveals a philosophical worldview that explains everything in terms of a monothematic disavowal or foreclosure of a supposed intolerable lack. The lack is thus a curse we all try to escape—once again, the idea of the original sin. What Lacan points out is something entirely opposed to these notions, which are nothing more than another way to flatten out the three registers upon the Imaginary.[26]

It is true that the subject—or rather, the ego—tries to maintain a condition of complete virtuality. In the case of the drive, however, we insist that it is not about incorporating an object in order to block the lack, for a border-zone comes into play in the structure, which punctuates a decisive datum when considering the erogenous zone:

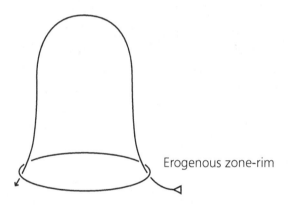

Erogenous zone-rim

If in the diagram the ellipsis is the erogenous zone, we have drawn in it the arc of what we will designate as the return into the circuit of the drive, marking the difference with the cycle, the rhythm, of the instinct. The title of Chapter 14 of the seminar is "The Partial Drive and Its Circuit." Now, the circuit to which it refers is produced around the object, which is located on this spot:

---

26. We should certainly include in this paragraph the blocking function of *a*. In any case, considering the goal of this exposition, the reading suggested is still conducive.

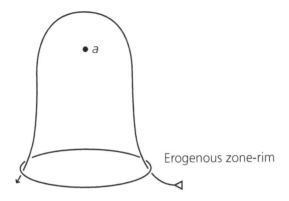

Erogenous zone-rim

The itinerary of the circuit consists in prowling around the object, taking its *tour*, Lacan will say, so as to emphasize the connotation of the double meaning of the French word, which the author clarifies by using the English language. It means both *turn* and *trick*,[27] that is, a limit around which one takes a turn, but at the same time a swiping twist, trap, sleight of hand even (*tour d'escamotage*),[28] to take it out of sight, which evokes the phrases "You never look at me from the place from which I see you," and "What I look at is never what I wish to see." This order of surreptitious concealment—clearly pertaining, as an example, to what we tried to develop concerning the gaze—refers to any object of the drive. It isn't, therefore, an action addressed to the object, as could be represented in our diagram by vertically inserting in it the one we designed in order to illustrate the operance of the instinct:

---

27. In English in the original. (Translator's note)

28. The second Spanish version opts here, entirely unexpectedly, for "conjuring trick" (*juego de manos*). Could it be because of the saying "*juego de manos, juego de . . . ?*" (*op. cit.*, p. 176) [p. 168 of the English version. Harari refers to the saying "*juego de manos, juego de villanos,*" which could be translated as "let's have no horse-play," according to Esteban Giménez, who explains it as a "warning about the perils of abusing of hand games among two or more people, since it could end in fisticuffs, in the manner of the *villanos*, a term that alludes to the primitive inhabitants of villages" (in *Del dicho al hecho*, San Pablo ed.)]

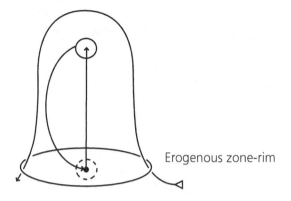

Erogenous zone-rim

It is in this way, then, that the instinctual would proceed—from the source, the pressure would impel toward the attainment of its object. It finds it, it incorporates it in some way, and it thus finally attains satisfaction. Things don't work like that in the drive circuit, for a return upon the erogenous zone itself takes place, without the mentioned incorporation. The object is not the drive's aim. It is that through which the drive attains satisfaction in the erogenous zone. Satisfaction takes place at the source. Its attainment consists precisely of the cessation of the local stimulation of the erogenous zone. What is produced here, therefore, is a back-and-forth itinerary, a "making oneself" (*hacer-se*): suck, poop, look, hear. It is a movement that synchronically condenses the conjugation of the drive, that is, active voice, passive voice, reflexive, middle voice.[29]

It is worth remembering at this point that the object of the drive bears the condition of being indifferent (as materialization if not as structure). On the other hand, in terms of this magnitude of the demand of work imposed on the psychic as a result of its binding with the bodily (a body that is, overall, a disjunct record of erogenous zones), the pressure shows very little of the order that relates to the biological body or the preestablished itinerary of the reflex arc. We can situate the Freud-

---

29. S. Freud, *"Pulsions et destins de pulsions," Métapsychologie*, Gallimard, Paris, 1972, p. 28; *O. C., op. cit.*, vol. 14, p. 123. [*Instincts and Their Vicissitudes*, p. 128.]

ian *Drang* in this conception, which accounts for the perforation to which it subjects the erogenous zone so that the cultivation of the "arounding" (*alrededoreo*) of the object will bear fruit:

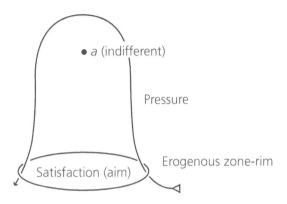

• *a* (indifferent)

Pressure

Erogenous zone-rim

Satisfaction (aim)

QUESTIONS AND ANSWERS

Q: Could you specify the differences between drive and desire?

A: I am grateful for this question, for it is one of the classic ones. Safouan also poses it to Lacan in this seminar, with particular reference to the respective objects. It is possible to start with a fairly obvious difference. Desire does not admit terms, and it therefore appears to have a different aptitude regarding the eventuality of being divided into elements of a combinatory. On the other hand, what characterizes and defines desire is tied to metonymy, regarding the slippage involved with respect to its object. In the case of the drive, the indifference of its object does not undermine its structural trait of stability. This is the plane that differentiates it decisively from desire. The latter is the target of interpretation, for desire and interpretation possess a structural homology. Desire and interpretation are both tied to metonymy, to a certain temporeity that entails the ability to move. This homology leads to the reference of the order of interpretation to that of desire. Hence, Lacan asserts that desire is its interpretation. The analyst interprets and seems to found desire through this act. There is much more to say—all these clarifications serve only as a first positioning.

There is another issue we shouldn't leave aside, namely, sexuality, through which we have gone from the transference to the drive. When we think of desire we are not in the presence of a pair set in opposition in a Moebian manner, as was the pair sexuality/death in Freud's work. On the other hand, the specific circumstance in which Lacan alludes to the desire of death is when he refers to the analyst's desire. Yet in the signifying articulation where desire crawls—that is, the metonymic chain—there is no inscription of death except as referring to castration. I think that this is an important discrimination. There is no unconscious inscription of death in the realm of the desiderative unconscious, as there isn't of the vagina. To believe the opposite would be to irremissibly move away from the Freudian premises. It is worth pointing this out because these are two fallacies into which the Kleinian current, for instance, falls.

Q: You pointed out that the passage from a certain stage to another during sexual development depended on the demand of the Other. Is this the case in all stages?

A: I am aware that sometimes in the exposition there arise examples that, being didactic, may even seem empiricist. This is the case when tackling the anal drive—in this case, its particular object cheats in its obviousness. It is evidently much easier to quote this type of example than one referring to the gaze, because in the latter case the detached, the fallen object is not as intuitive, as convincing. It is plain: defecation constitutes a clear act of detachment of something from the body that illuminates even the whole circuit of the gift and the symbolic swap. In any case, in the time that follows anality, there emerges the issue that Lacan designates, writes, in this way: $(-\varphi)$. This is the opposite of the phallic image, (φ), which could be partially homologated as the agency known since Freud as ideal ego.[30] As you can see, this issue relates to the register of the Imaginary.

The negativization of the phallic image occurs due to castration. It alludes to a pair that cannot be conceived in the absence of any of its

---

30. Another Lacanian support for this agency Freud postulated is the pair (fed in reciprocity) that is written thus: $m \rightleftarrows i\,(a)$.

terms, as Freud stated in "La organización genital infantil,"[31] a 1923 essay written as a complement to the *Three Essays on the Theory of Sexuality*, where he states for the first time the determining effectiveness—*après-coup*—of the phallic stage. We verify here a clear rupture with any form of naturalism of the biological functions. First, we find what we just mentioned, namely, that there is no inscription in the vagina, which indicates that there is no form of vital function at play. Second, Freud says phallic, and not genital. This means that in this order a clear symbolic dimension intervenes where the fall is produced in relation to a function, and not anymore to the detachment of a fragment of the body. It is a fall in the face of the absence of the monumental, perennial Phallus, which occasionally appears clinically as functional inhibition.

To clarify this we will resort to Chapter 3 of *The Ego and the It*.[32] "Like me—the father—you will not be," is the superego's sentence. We can express it in an imaginary way: "You will not be able to have this woman as woman, since she is not a woman to you: she is mother." It is the father agency that says that the subject cannot be like him. In a parallel way, the reverse of the injunction comes: "You must be like me."[33] There is an incitation to identification in the sense of ordering certain attributes, of granting the gifts to search for a woman when the time comes. In the phallic stage, nothing is cut nor anything bodily is lost, although its transit does involve a functional dimension. In empirical terms, this functional condition is equipped with certain alternatives in which numerous malfunctions may have a place that indicate in a way a lack of attention, a revolt against the injunction that commands: "Like me you will not be."

If it happens that the chosen woman relates to the maternal series in a scarcely metaphorical way, it means that with her "you can't." In this way, there is a functional obeisance to the "like me you won't be"; the "I am like you" is also obeyed, to finally—or firstly—disobey through

---

31. S. Freud, *O. C.*, *op. cit.*, vol. 19, pp. 141–149. ["The Infantile Genital Organization: An Interpolation Into the Theory of Sexuality," pp. 141–145.]

32. Following Lacan, Harari substitutes "it" (*esto*) for "id" (*ello*). (Translator's note)

33. S. Freud, *op. cit.*, pp. 36ff. [pp. 24ff]

the "I have the 'same' woman." A knot hard to untie is produced here, which, as factor in a constellation, may give rise to impotence, premature ejaculation, and so on. As I believe you can see, the whole matter originates in the demand of the Other, be it evident, implicit, inverted (as a demand *to* the Other), or even, at the level of desire, following the same alternatives.

Yet the situation gets even more complicated due to certain effects of structure that we may specify thanks to clinical referents. Lacan alluded to the fact that the man who is too much in love with his wife, for instance, may hinder the operance (*operancia*) of the Name-of-the-Father in his son, because it is the woman who lays down the Law. It is not an imaginary location of a phallic woman and a weak man. In this case it occurs that the man devoted to the founding idealization of love is located in a place from which everything that comes from the loved object deserves a *yes*. Promote the *no*, then? Indeed: if the *no* to the mother–child dyad is not a coarse, systematic oppositionism, it will serve as a vehicle for the paternal function by ordering the mother: "You will not restore your product. You will not reincorporate your son."[34] By emphasizing this structural moment of castration, the examples of the stages are de-imaginarized.

I have chosen, then, the example of anality because it is clearer in the first instance; even orality, in the punctual terms of weaning, may have its empirical referent. As we were saying, castration succeeds in having the intuitive phallic reference start to "escape" us, but we gain in understanding when we specify that castration denotes the place the mother grants the father so that the agency Name-of-the-Father will proceed with the efficacy of a double injunction. Castration also summons the gift of sexuality understood in these terms. Close to the end of his life, Freud (in the unfinished *Outline of Psychoanalysis*) goes as far as reiterating along with Goethe: "What thou hast inherited from thy fathers, acquire it to make it thine."[35]

---

34. J. Lacan, *Las formaciones . . .* (*The Formations*), *op. cit.*, pp. 84–90.

35. S. Freud, *Esquema del psicoanálisis, O. C., op. cit.*, pp. 208–209. [*An Outline of Psychoanalysis*, p. 207, quoted from *Faust*, part I, scene I, in German in the English translation, quoted in footnote.]

This maxim seems to me to be a smart avoidance, by means of an unheard-of solution, of any kind of labeling as to the fields of the innate and the acquired. Not even what is inherited can be owned if an operation capable of granting the possibility of acquiring it, of receiving it, does not mediate. If we understand this proposition in terms of the gift—for example, in the case of the male, the penile gift—it will read thus: Don't believe that because you possess the organ, the latter will function, for this will happen or not according to the vicissitudes of the desiderative dimension, that is, according to how you acquire what you have inherited. The "possession" of the body doesn't say anything. We can perceive here a huge difference with the species instinct. The body says nothing precisely because the saying (*el decir*),[36] the fall into the interlocutive field by virtue of which the body is immersed in the Symbolic, is missing. Certainly, Goethe's aphorism is very valuable because of the number of antinomies it solves or, at least, makes us rethink, for there is a whole "program" implied in this formulation.

Q: What would be the relation among drive, compulsion, and impulsion?

A: Compulsion is of the order of the obsessive. The term *obsessive-compulsive* concerns particularly rituals. Compulsion, furthermore, integrates into the plane of the repetition compulsion, characteristic of the death drive. Clinically, we can point out the compulsion as an injunction to be materialized, something that appears as pleasurable at the beginning, but that would increase unpleasure if it didn't materialize. A banal example: the typical "compulsive" washing of the hands many times a day. At a certain point it turns into an equivalent of masturbation, but at the beginning it was something the subject would have liked to avoid, and could not.

In the impulsion the way the subject is positioned before the drive comprises a localization where a schizia is not detected (as opposed to the compulsion). By means of a complete syntony, in the impulsion one ends in an *acting-out* or a *passage à l'acte* experienced as pleasurable. In

---

36. Harari is using here the Spanish translation of Lacan's term *le dire*, that Bruce Fink translates as "the saying" in Seminar 20. (Translator's note)

this way, because of its structure (not its phenomenology), the impulsion posits the perverse dimensionality. I think this is a very interesting question, because the relation between drive, compulsion, and impulsion is included in the same type of reasoning we have used with the terms *pressure* and *repression*.[37] They aren't just words. We must remember that it is with them, through them, that we can comprehend or not a whole series of phenomena.

Q: Wouldn't the compulsion be an exogenous phenomenon, produced by someone from the outside?

A: Not completely from the outside. In any case, if we think about this topologically, it would be an internal exteriority. The dimension of the discourse of the Other involves an agency "effected" from the field of the Other, but in the subject it is felt as another agency within himself to which his ego, however, is alien.

Q: Regarding the question of sublimation, I was recalling how Lacan characterizes this particular vicissitude of the drive when he talks about elevating the object to the dignity of the Thing. I would like to know, then, what this process typical of sublimation would entail.

A: In Freud, when the Thing appears as *das Ding*, it is connected to a slant of the primordial Other. Lacan transfers it—decisively, from Seminar 7 on[38]—to account for the fact that sublimation does not merely consist of a naive, happy, and successful adaptation to society and/or of an adaptive and successful defense mechanism. Sublimation is usually transformed into a phenomenon that cannot be confused at all with a sort of domestication of the drive. The more engorging, the closer it comes to the category of *das Ding*. Curiously, it may acquire a compulsive nature.

---

37. This is true in Spanish because the term for "drive" is *pulsión*. (Translator's note)

38. J. Lacan, *L'éthique de la psychanalyse. Le Séminaire, livre VII*, Seuil, Paris, 1986, pp. 55–194. [*The Seminar, Book VII. The Ethics of Psychoanalysis, 1959–60*, ed. Jacques-Alain Miller, trans. Dennis Porter, W.W. Norton, New York, 1992]

What Lacan shows is very interesting, because it does not point out that this is the pathology of sublimation but rather refers to its unfolding. In this way, Lacan succeeds in saving the concept from the sociological plane in which it is frequently diluted. Regardless of good adjustment or social success, Lacan's development is considering a process whereby the subject is incorporated more and more. As a pole of attraction, *das Ding* entails a trait of a certain uncanniness. One could interpret what it generates in terms of fascination, yet in a deadly sense. It is not the imaginary fascination, the one linked to the order of beauty and harmony.

Q: But wouldn't it then be assimilable to a symptom?

A: The symptom bears the condition of being experienced as actually bothersome, but must we conceive the sublimating entrapment in this way? If somebody, for instance, states that he will write, and goes as far as considering that he must sit down to do it because he cannot think of anything else, nor do anything else, until he finishes his writing, it is very hard to attribute this (in the psychiatric manner) to the nature of the symptom. On the other hand, in the sublimation (and this is quite crucial) an ability for symbolic exchange different from the privacy of the symptom is circumscribed. As long as the dimension of the Other is present—in terms of a demand addressed to him—a circulation is established, and what is produced is not a mere cathartic manifestation. The subject, furthermore, wants (in principle) to be cured of the symptom. Of this other type of circumstance, he doesn't. After all, psychoanalytically, the symptom is characteristic of those who claim to suffer it. He who does not say so, does not have it. The allocation is not produced from the outside but depends on the person interested in denouncing it.

9

Sexuality or Mantic? The "Vel" of Alienation

This is our next to last meeting, which posits a special obligation. I warned you in our first class that we would develop some issues expounded in Lacan's Seminar 11 according to my choices, which might be as arbitrary as anybody else's. In any case, we tried to set the foundations for the choices made in this course with regular insistence. Our classes don't intend to offer an impossible global reading—rather, they are an invitation to read Lacan. Such a proposition implies that what we have worked on here cannot be a substitute for your reading—it does not replace it under any circumstances. In any case, the motto is to think in somewhat simpler terms about certain developments that are evidently very complex.

We intend to expound on a series of concepts without bastardizing or degrading them, preserving their complexity, saying them in such a way as to stimulate further reading. This is the modest goal of our encounters, and it is obvious that many issues will be left pending. As I pointed out in our first meeting, I have no alternative but to insist on a sectorization, so that some points will at least be raised and supported according to Lacanian doctrine. I think it is interesting to be able to grasp of such doctrine the meanderings of its journey, its courses and recourses, in short, where this particular mode of working the dialectic experience in analytic practice will lead.

Today we continue with the display of the drive, in order to take into consideration—after some more punctuations on the topic—the causative operations of the subject. This is doubtlessly a transcendent problem, as indicated by its slightly pompous designation. We are dealing indeed with the way in which a subject is produced, starting from the rejection of the classic idea according to which the subject is—if you will allow me the use of the Latin expression—*causa sui*, that is, the cause of himself. In our view, the subject does not self-engender, for he recognizes an origin, a genesis, in what we have designated as the field of the Other. It is where we will identify the operance (*operancia*) of two decisive functions. The first one is designated with an already traditional term, very well known and popularized, of which the seminar will produce a highly different, original reading—we are talking about *alienation*. The other term at play, the other causative operation of the subject, is *separation* (we will just mention it now). We will reach the clarification of both notions gradually. Indeed, first I would like to raise some issues on the notion of sexuality, as it is elaborated in connection with the drive.

Let us recall how it was sexuality that led us from the transference to the drive. Here we are before the transference, that is, the enactment of the reality of the unconscious, which is sexual. Now, we know that in Freud there is, from the start, a drive dichotomy, finally rendered as life drive and death drive. In Seminar 11 a very appropriate formula is offered on this bipartition, by stating that the drive is leaning toward two aspects, that of life and that of death. This conceptualization certainly indicates a very different conception from that of the respective amounts of two dissimilar essences. What Lacanian teaching asserts is that there is a "moebianly" one-sided drive, with two faces. If we traverse it on one side, it will have certain characteristics; if we traverse it on the other side, the traits will be different, always keeping in mind that we are dealing with "the same" side. Thus the life and death drives imbricate, and we will see how.

There is another important point to make that indicates how it is precisely through sexuality that psychoanalysis succeeds in excluding itself from the practices usually known as mantic. The relation is given in terms of conceiving psychoanalysis versus the mantic. What is a mantic? The word is found, for example, as a suffix in chiromancy, oneiromancy, and so on. All these terms refer to divination by means of a particular recourse. In a strict sense, we call mantic a particular system of divinations that tends especially to foresee the future. Despite the fact that it goes back to the religious convictions of ancient Greece, there are others today of a very different sort.

Even many analysts from the other psychoanalysis have fallen into one of them by constituting systems of fixed, universal, and imagistic symbols. There are numerous dictionaries of symbols circulating, besides the more popular versions sold at newspaper stands.[1] For instance, there is a book titled *Psicoanálisis de los sueños (Psychoanalysis of Dreams)*, by Angel Garma,[2] in whose last sections a dictionary—"index"—is organized in the manner of a mantic. In the face of such confusions, we must then describe a precise way of delimiting analytic practice. For that purpose, a crucial element in that distinction is the primally repressed:

vs. mantic

Primal (or original)
repression.

Let us reiterate this: primal repression denotes that which has fallen through the action of repression and which will by no means become conscious—thence the designation of primal or original repression. Articulated to the secondary mode of repression, this element—deliberately not characterized—will give rise synchronically to what we know as symptom:

vs. mantic

Primal (or original)
repression.
Symptom.

It is possible to understand primal repression and the symptom as belonging to a homogeneous order, for they are both organized according to the chain of signifiers:

---

1. Newspaper stands in Argentina sell all sorts of books besides newspapers and magazines. (Translator's note)

2. Paidós, Buenos Aires, 1963, pp. 195–200.

vs. mantic

$$\text{Signifiers} \begin{bmatrix} \text{Primal (or original)} \\ \text{repression.} \\ \text{Symptom.} \end{bmatrix}$$

In the last analysis, and according to a certain reading, a symptom does not imply but a specific articulation of signifiers. In Lacanian theorization this constitutes a pole of analytic experience in which we find, as you will recall, an order of hiatusness (*hiancia*) where a temporal interval appears. We must keep this information in mind and include it in our diagram. Moreover, on the other end of the mentioned series, we encounter interpretation:

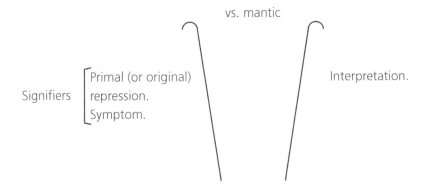

vs. mantic

$$\text{Signifiers} \begin{bmatrix} \text{Primal (or original)} \\ \text{repression.} \\ \text{Symptom.} \end{bmatrix} \qquad\qquad \text{Interpretation.}$$

Our next step will consist of crossing the interval between the poles, in the following direction:

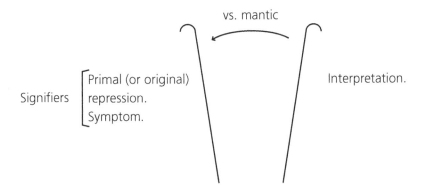

vs. mantic

$$\text{Signifiers} \begin{bmatrix} \text{Primal (or original)} \\ \text{repression.} \\ \text{Symptom.} \end{bmatrix} \qquad\qquad \text{Interpretation.}$$

In this way, with no more specifications, we would find ourselves in the heart of mantic land, contradicting the purpose considered by the "versus" in the schema. Indeed, "interpretation," taking a violent leap toward an experience built strictly of signifiers, would give rise to a mantic, in the first place. In the second place—and we must not fail to notice this—it would originate, depending on the case, a spiritualist, intellectualist, and speculative conception of "the analytic." You must know that the latter is one of the frequent refutations that are formulated to Lacan's work, out of naïveté or bad faith—when it isn't out of mere ignorance. His theory is branded as an intellectualist system. It would be so, naturally, if it did not locate itself (as it does) in that hiatusness (*hiancia*) where a leap is taken toward sexuality:

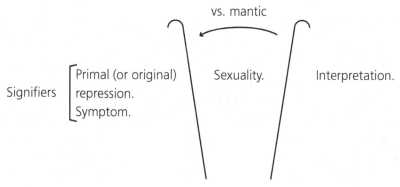

By virtue of having coincided with the same type of structure with which we approached the *Grundbegriff* of the unconscious, sexuality is related to a temporal pulsation:

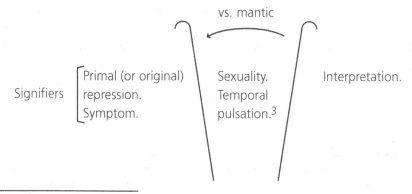

---

3. The "slight difference" with the diagram in Chapter 3 with respect to the realm where we signposted the temporal pulsation lies in the manner in which the emphasis

Resorting to our already-known chronological references, in front of the interpretation a relation of synchrony is located:

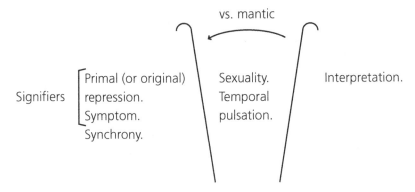

The synchronic denotes an action in unison. Let us recall what we said in our last meeting, namely, that if there is repression it is because there is re-pression—something that presses again. Strictly speaking, this pressing again is tied to the formation of a symptom. The symptom is not produced at a later moment but is the testimony of the action of repression. The work of repression consists precisely in generating symptoms, in the broad sense of the term. Here this synchronic nature becomes evident as a denotation of phenomena produced in a coinciding way.

The temporal pulsation, on the contrary, is related to the structure of opening and closing of the unconscious. We explained it thus in our second meeting. In that movement whereby a "trap" opens and closes is where there is a showing of the unconscious. This characteristic will be important when we consider that the erogenous zones of the drive—the orifices qua erogenous zones—are not simply excavated holes. Usually such erogenous zones are viewed as the site of contact with the world, in the sense of an exchange. They would seem to be border spaces that are being crossed, be it toward the inner or the outer zone. We must distrust an immediate move toward descriptive examples.

---

is placed, now, on the interval rather than on the operation as a whole, the way it did in Chapter 3, deception brought about, in short, by any imaginary scaffolding. Nonetheless, we take for granted that such a scaffolding does not veil the comprehension of the mentioned structure.

It seems to be extremely easy to understand the erogenous zones generically by giving the mouth as an example—the mouth opens and food goes in. Another simple example: the anal sphincter opens and feces are eliminated. This is very clear—something goes in or out of the body. The orifice can hence be thought of as a zone of exchange and connection. In fact, this argumentation is only a slight pseudo-psychological sophistication of the everyday imaginary experience; in other words, sheer imaginary effectiveness. Lacan, on the contrary, tries to offer a more serious formalization on this topic. That is why he points out that the mentioned orifices can become erogenous zones because they bear a topological commonality with the unconscious. There is something shared as to their structure (not, of course, from the empirical perspective), that is, the condition of being liable to opening and closing.

These are then the sexual, sexualized, drivicized (*pulsionalizados*) orifices, in which, precisely, the partial drive operates, which conforms to the condition of opening and closing of the unconscious. Lacan remarks enigmatically that only one of these orifices lacks this quality of opening and closing, and he adds that this will have consequences. In Seminar 11 such a circumstance is not elaborated, the consequences of the inevitable opening of the ear are not elucidated. Yet for now we must only note that the rest of the erogenous zones possess the mentioned condition. Certainly, if we think of our considerations on the gaze developed in earlier meetings, we must agree that the eye possesses the quality of opening and closing. On the other hand, it may be very stimulating (in the imaginary sense) to consider this organ as a zone of exchange with the world, or something like that. This would be the psychological degradation of the erogenous zone. What is truly significant is the movement of opening and closing indicated by the temporal pulsation. Based on it, a certain zone becomes erogenous thanks to a topological homology with the unconscious. Here we have the explanation, among other things, of why the partial drive emerges as the becoming present of sexuality in the unconscious.

If a total drive existed—let us speculate about this idea for a moment—there wouldn't be erogenous zones that opened and closed. It is the topological commonality with the unconscious that attracts the drive and makes it relate to the former through its specific erogenous zone.

This is how two fundamental concepts—the unconscious and the drive—articulate, as we postulated in our first meeting. Sexuality functions as hinge, as link, as locus of intersection, in order to allow the drive to have its insertion in the unconscious. Every drive is partial—this reiteration is by no means superfluous. When we refer to that which is total we are already entering a dimension different from the one that will account for the title of a chapter of Seminar 11, albeit with the terms inverted, namely, "From Love to the Libido." We punctuate here the passage from the libido to love. In the latter we may grasp the question of the total, that which immediately induces reciprocity—the latter being a defining trait of love. From this point on Lacan will offer a global conception when remarking, in various stretches of his production, that feelings are reciprocal. Under the appearance of a simple formula, this statement bears a transcendent clinical significance.

If we take it at face value, we will then grasp how countertransference speaks—conceding that it intends to account for the analysant's feeling—speaks, I was saying, about the analyst's feelings. It therefore indicates, as an operation of the analyst (if we can call it thus), a confession about what the latter feels regarding his analysant. This is true even when the analyst only intends to reveal the "failed" purpose of the analysant to provoke these or those feelings in the analyst. Yes, for the mere fact of verbalizing that the analysant wishes to induce these emotions in him shows how the analyst is already feeling them. If the analyst states: "You do that to irritate me, trying to make me feel irritated," he is already confessing everything. We are in the presence then of an imaginary, dual, specular way of "directing" the cure.

Let us dwell once more on the drive, continuing with our reading of *Instincts and Their Vicissitudes*. You will recall that we established in that text the clear division Freud draws between drives and their vicissitudes, on the one hand, and love, on the other. As a theoretical reflection or expansion, this is linked to the problem of the pulsation, of why its own pulsation enables sexuality to establish an imbrication with the unconscious. To better understand this circumstance we must point out that the interpretation is displayed within an order of metonymy:

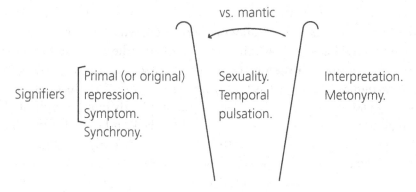

First, and in the most empirical plane, we must recall the apparent tautology that affirms that the interpretation is said. It might not be excessive to repeat this, for there is a certain (self-designated as "Lacanian") [*sic*] tendency to believe that interpretation may have nothing to do with speech (*habla*). It is no news to point out that every interpretation is comprised of words, but the fact of saying it has its consequences. Among other things, phenomenologically it implies that interpretation extends in time and is hence likely to undergo slippage, and it is in such a slippage, precisely, that we find metonymy. When we tie interpretation to metonymy we discover the presence of another common structure. If there is metonymy, what is the order immediately summoned in Lacanian teaching? What appears, of course, is desire:

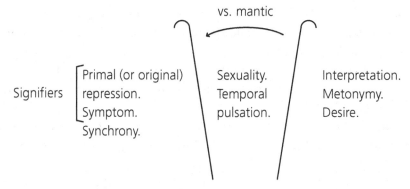

This relation is possible because the object of desire is metonymical, that is, it is that ungraspable object that slides away incessantly. The structure of desire is then metonymical. In this way, it ties to the lack that founds the subject. Lacan will ask himself, what is the being of the speaker? And he will answer: it is a lack, or better, he will refer to a lack-in-being. Desire will then be conceived as a search based on the lack that recognizes the object as that which is responsible for its causation, and the *fantasme* as its support. The formula, slightly more complicated, will allude to desire as the metonymy of the lack-in-being. I think that the earlier clarifications render this formula sufficiently intelligible.

When the analyst interprets, desire says "present." Let us recall what leads to the cure. Thus, when we worked on the fundamental concept of the transference, we specified that the pivot of analysis is the analyst's desire. Nevertheless, we find ourselves in front of another "turn of the screw" that will give rise to the title of one of Lacan's seminars that we have quoted earlier: *Desire and Its Interpretation*. We have both concepts in the same order, interpretation and desire. We may presuppose that the analyst interprets the desire that "is" in the analysant, according to our most common way to understand things. Now, the sole fact of taking into consideration that desire is the desire of the Other already complicates that imaginary way of elucidation quite a bit. If desire is the desire of the Other, I repeat, the matter lies in the fact that desire is its interpretation. This does not mean that interpretation is the interpretation of a desire located inside the head of the analysant. Somebody may object that according to the way in which we are positing this problem, the analyst would be leading the analysant in an almost suggestive, almost hypnotic way. The issue is doubtlessly different. In the interpretation, precisely, a dimension by which the subject is constituted is enacted. Isn't the latter constituted from the Other? And hence, isn't it precisely the interpretation of an enacting once again an operation of constitution of the subject?

It isn't true that the subject is constituted in a certain historical moment, once and for all. The fact that the analyst speaks to the analysant within the analytic situation indicates how a certain causative operation of the subject (that we will expound later) is enacted once again. Considering these issues, we may specify why desire is interpretation. There isn't thus a desire that "preexists" the analyst's discourse, for desire is that which is established by the analytic operation called interpretation.

Now, as this interval opened by sexuality in the form of a temporal pulsation appears, we should insert into our diagram, and name, a concept that we worked on at the beginning of this course. I am referring to a structure of hiatusness (*hiancia*):

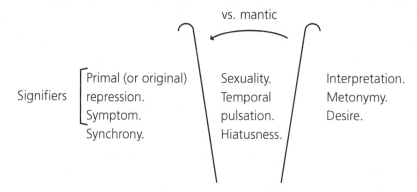

vs. mantic

Signifiers

Primal (or original) repression.
Symptom.
Synchrony.

Sexuality.
Temporal pulsation.
Hiatusness.

Interpretation.
Metonymy.
Desire.

In my view, hiatusness (*hiancia*) is an acceptable translation of the French *béance*, for it enables us to understand the determination at play in terms of signifiers. We should recall here how the hiatusness (*hiancia*) related to that known in poetry as a verse where there are hiatuses (*verso hiante*), with that cut, that caesura that conditions the cutting of, and in, the phrase.

Let us return now to a former matter. We have often pointed out that libido and love are opposing domains. To elucidate this point, Lacan painstakingly follows Freud's complex elaboration in the second part of *Instincts and Their Vicissitudes*. It is made quite clear there that Freud points out that it is the total ego that participates in love. The latter constitutes the possible condition for the understanding of a relation of reciprocity. This same notion of reciprocity enables us, for instance, to notice how those who are victims of the mistake Lacan calls Piagetic err.

The term *Piagetic* obviously alludes to Jean Piaget's conceptions, because the fact is that, at the most decisive stage of his inquiry, of his demonstrations, the Swiss researcher starts from the initial identification of a stage in the development of the subject that he calls egocentric. According to Piaget, this stage is overcome later when the child somehow accepts the presence of the other. Piaget points out that there is proof of this egocentric stage when, among other phenomena, the existence of a shared soliloquy is verified. Even though they are together, children soliloquize. No one pays attention to the other children, each one speaks to himself, each in his own world. One may infer from this the alleged—convincing—foundation of the egocentric. Development, therefore, would lead from egocentrism (being enclosed in one's own world) to the opening to the other in a reciprocal way. Certainly, this theoretical point of departure is not at all innocent. It can in a way be characterized as utterly opposed to the Lacanian conception, whereby the process starts in the field of the Other and is rendered operative by means of the signifier. The action of the signifier is the one responsible for the appearance of a subject where a simple living being existed. Where there was only the promise that there could be a subject, the signifier determines indeed the emergence of one. The priority is located without a doubt in the field of the Other. The Piagetic error consists in taking reciprocity as the only valid parameter. In its slippage toward reciprocity, we can extract from this theory love's totalizing dimension.

What is reciprocity? It is the I-you relation. I talk to you, you listen to me. The roles change immediately—you talk to me, I listen to you. It is an equivocal point of departure. About the soliloquy in particular, the seminar will note that rather than the alleged egocentrism, what can be punctuated is the taking into account of the presence of the others. The others constitute the condition of possibility, of existence, that will allow for the initial egocentric discourse to appear. Egocentrism, therefore, is not so, strictly speaking. Rather, the children who are present there, devoted to their games, are the ones who provoke his speaking; a speaking (pay attention to the joke that has been omitted in the translations) "à la cantonade,"[4] that is, the "speaking in an aside to the audience," typical of theatrical resources.[5] This approach derives from taking into

---

4. Alan Sheridan leaves the expression in French and writes in a footnote that "to speak 'à la cantonade' is to speak to nobody in particular, to the company at large. By stressing the first letters of the phrase, Lacan is punning on his own name" (*The Four Fundamental Concepts . . .*), *op. cit.*, p. 208. (Translator's note)

5. The first edition, more accurately, opted for "speak . . . off-stage" (*op. cit.*, p. 214); the most recent one chose "aloud but to nobody in particular" (*op. cit.*, p. 216). The loss of the reference to the stage is not without consequences, if we are agreeing witnesses (*contestes*) of the impact of "the Other scene," and of the discourse of the Other not as an autonomous soliloquy. "To speak to the curtain": "In theatrical lan-

account the gestation of the subject as not *causa sui*. Maintaining the opposite implies coming up against conceptions characteristic of the subject of representation.

Far from being present from the beginning, egocentrism is conceived according to the infatuated determinations of the subject of representation. Due to the fact that I have representations, I go as far as to believe I am the creator of the world. If I want to, I open myself to that world. If I don't, I shut myself off. This is an arrogant attitude, characteristic of every speaking being; as such, it constitutes a structurating condition tied to the narcissic positioning. As we have pointed out before, everything seems to be reduced to an exercise of the will—the other will exist depending on whether I want him to exist or not. It is this tendency that is called idealism in philosophy. Many exponents of the other psychoanalysis traverse this conviction: the neurotic is a sort of egoist enclosed in himself who will cure when he succeeds in opening up to the world. If in our everyday experience we see him constrained and almost surrendered to the demand of the Other, the (paradoxical) image these currents bear is almost that of somebody who is self-sufficient, who can withdraw from the world and do without it at will.

As you can see, the clinical danger of this conception is maximum, for it is not precisely decidable, arguable, whether we start from the egocentric subject or from the Other. Conceiving the neurotic as a dispensing arrogant (*arrogante prescindente*) implies a complete ethical and deontological offense, for it determines, regarding the direction of the cure, a formulation in the implicit sense of the reinforcement of the ego. Every analysis will thus be reduced to a reinforcement therapy. Even if we believe we are practicing psychoanalysis, the effect will not go beyond that of a support therapy, exerted indirectly. What is induced in these cases is ultimately the breathing into the analysant the conviction that he can enter and leave that imaginary world *a piacere*.[6] What a better

---

guage, behind a curtain or in the wings, or leaning out of any of the interstices or openings of the setting. It is said of the actor who thus placed observes or talks in the stage representation" (Real Academia Española, *Diccionario de la lengua española*, Espasa-Calpe, Madrid, 1970, p. 971).

6. In Italian in the original. (Translator's note)

ego therapy than the one consisting of prettifying (*maquillar*) the *fantasme* of the analysant's reality in order to give him a license to do as he pleases[7] that will read: "Puppeteer"?

Little by little, our topic is leading us toward the field of the Other. Prior to penetrating it, we will take into account some statements that emerged here that we must connect very closely to Lacan's text titled "*Posición de lo inconsciente*" ("Positions of the Unconscious") that we have already mentioned. There are many common elements between various stretches of Seminar 11 and of this essay, as well as differing aspects, of course. In both texts there appear references to a key concept, classic in psychoanalysis since its introduction by Freud—that of the libido. If we are speaking about the drive, the libido is an inevitable touchstone.

We have already recognized the four terms of the drive as they are detected in a disjunction situation. As to the libido, Lacan will explain that it is not a kind of force produced (transformed) by a dynamo that accumulates here and disperses over there, something that may tolerate ups and downs in tension. No, for he construes a definition truly striking, eluding the recourse to the energetic model—he asserts that the libido is an organ.

The term *organ* evokes at least two meanings: on the one hand, that of being part of an organism, and on the other hand, an instrument. How should we understand this? Is it a concept or maybe an ancillary representation? What status does it have in Lacanian teaching? Or, we could posit another query: Is the libido real, symbolic, or imaginary? The answer is to be highlighted, since Lacan does not solve the matter by choosing one of the three registers but enunciates that the libido is unreal, which in no way means imaginary. How to account then for this strange element called libido and considered as an unreal organ?

Our surprise increases even more when Lacan assigns it a special status through the recourse to the creation of a myth. The myth in question has the effectiveness of being articulated to the famous one of the androgynous Plato narrates (through Aristophanes) in *The Sympo-*

---

7. The expression used in Spanish, *patente de corso*, refers to the "warrant or dispatch with which the Government of a state authorized a subject to become a privateer against the Nation's enemies" (*Diccionario de la Real Academia Española*). (Translator's note)

sium.[8] As you will recall, that narrative refers to primal times where there existed a kind of complete being—man and woman at the same time—who after a series of vicissitudes was cleaved by the gods in punishment. That is how the differentiated sexes were created. Every subsequent attempt of these beings would seek to reconstitute that original androgynous, to be a unity again.

Lacan suggests another mythical option, audaciously renewing the valid status of myth for psychoanalysis. The fact that one would consider a myth analyzable and would assign theoretical validity to it is already hard to assimilate by positivist ideology, but the postulation of a new myth is considered utterly unacceptable. In the antipodes: if we take Freud's texts, we may find there all kinds of unheard-of, creative ways to "compose" psychoanalysis scripturarily (*escritureriamente*). As Ricardo Piglia states, *The Interpretation of Dreams* is, among other things, "a strange form of autobiographic fiction" that may be located in the genre of Rousseau's *Confessions*.[9] I believe that the invitation to see this work as an autobiographical work where the foundational moment of psychoanalysis is fictionalized (and I think we may coincide on this) is a very acute proposition.

From the very beginnings of our discipline, myths have in no way been excluded from it—on the contrary, for two basal pillars that articulate it are called Narcissus and Oedipus. Freud could become a founder thanks to the support of the oedipal myth through Sophocles's tragedy *Oedipus King*. Lacan may very well, therefore, propose a new myth. His contribution will consist of that particular one that he will designate as the *hommelette*. The term alludes to the well-known dish in a homophonic way. We may observe here, however, a play on words:

In French, this is a neologism. First, it summons man (*homme*). In condensation, erasing, as you can see, an H and an M, there appears the

8. Plato, "*Simposio (Banquete) o de la erótica,*" in *Diálogos*, Porrúa, Mexico, 1969, pp. 362–365. [*The Symposium*, trans. Robin Waterfield, Oxford University Press, 1994.]

9. R. Piglia, "*Crítica y ficción,*" *Cuadernos de extensión universitaria*, no. 9, Serie ensayos, Universidad Nacional del Litoral, Santa Fe, 1986, pp. 14ff.

popular omelet, which is not totally foreign because here we are also talking about doing something starting by breaking eggs. This could be translated into Spanish—at least this is the word that has been chosen, I believe
accurately—as lamella (*laminilla*). A thin sheet, conceived as an ultraflat
element (with almost no thickness) that can travel, go through any place.
Preferably, the lamella is usually placed in the rims of the erogenous zones,
thanks to its ameboid nature. Yet it is licit to ask what this myth would
explain if we considered its incorporation to the psychoanalytic corpus
as valid. Such a recourse, precisely, accounts for the fact that something
decisive occurs in the passage from the scissiparous reproduction of uni-
cellular organisms to sexual reproduction.

It is one thing that a microorganism will divide into two equal cells
(as Lacan points out, but also earlier Freud)[10] and will therefore be
immortal. Somehow, in this case the individual has not disappeared, for
it has become two. Here there is no death of the individual or of the
species. It is a different matter, however, when sexual reproduction
appears—here a loss inevitably takes place. Specifically, it is the loss of
the individual, who requires the necessariness of coupling in order to
attain by that means the production of a new being. If the latter emerges,
it is at the cost of the disappearance, sooner or later, of the being of the
former generation. In this way, we may see the implications of the appearance of sexuality in this step of zoology that we might call primitive. The establishment of sexuality, therefore, entails that of death.

In this bind between sex and death we find two crucial (initial,
permanent) coordinates of Freudian theorization, namely, sex and death,
one involving the other. This connection does not exhaust in the observation that a specimen lives, grows, reproduces, and then dies—that
would be a banal phenomenological description. The fact is that once
scissiparous reproduction (whereby the same is maintained) loses its
exclusivity, sexed reproduction introduces the nonidentical, the radical diversity existing among individuals. Referring to his *hommelette*,
Lacan points out that the libido represents that which has been lost to

---

10. S. Freud, *Más allá del. . .* , *op. cit.*, pp. 43ff. [*Beyond the. . .* pp. 47ff.]

the sexed living being in his condition as such, mythically, from his birth. With sexuality something is lost, something is left behind.

The condition of loss marks the living being. In my view, this is precisely the way to understand the situation religion illusorily maintains as characteristic of the original sin. The subject emerges permeated by the consequences of this action that impels him to leave something at his own starting point. This initial loss irremissibly condemns him to disappearance. Such an operation will be considered deadly, and this lethal factor will be renewed precisely by the very action of the signifier, by the relation with the Other. Certainly, the libido is also represented, as a figure, by that object to which we referred when we analyzed the terms of the drive—object *a*. The fact that it is something self-mutilated that the subject loses is a defining characteristic of this object. As we have pointed out, these circumstances were very clear in the case of certain examples, such as the feces. In other cases, such as the gaze, the defining elements were harder to notice. In any case, object *a* always refers to a certain self-mutilated element that is left behind, lost, in the path toward the constitution of the subject, and precisely through this self-mutilation it inevitably summons the order of the lack, of the central hole expressed in castration $(- \varphi)$.

It is very easy and customary to think that through the libidinal the subject seeks his harmonic complement, for this would respond to an alleged structural order. In this regard, the seminar contributes psychoanalysis's demonstration: what we are actually looking for is that part of the self that has been lost, attempting to reencounter it. Yet since what has been lost has been lost once and for all, such a reencounter is impossible. Of course, this statement is much less lyrical than that romantic approach that advocates a perfect and complete encounter. The Lacanian developments progress here toward what authorizes an "expanded" reading of the almost classic aphorism: "There is no sexual relation."

The fact that there is no sexual relation means that there is no dictate in the psyche capable of determining that somebody, whatever body he or she possesses, will be programmed beforehand to situate himself as man or woman in order to attain (consequently, like the androgynous) his "suitable" complement. Rather, the process will relate to the vicissitudes articulated in the field of the Other, and from there, the law of the non-mesh will be decisive, unavoidable.

As we have already noted, we are slowly reaching this dominance of the field of the Other. This is how Lacan is finally drawn to include in the seminar a notoriously decisive thematic, namely, that which accounts for the causative operations of the subject. Starting from the drive and from how the latter recognizes its genesis in the field of the Other, two essential operations will be posited whose articulation we will seek next. Moreover, from such an articulation will emerge, among other issues, a defined way of understanding the theory of interpretation.

The two said operations are alienation and separation. The first one is designated through a term that cannot but bother me somewhat, if you will allow this public confession. The manipulation this word has suffered and continues to suffer gives one grief. It has reached the every-day vocabulary in a repertory shared with expressions such as "having a trauma" or "having a complex." It is thus possible to hear often that someone is "very alienated." In this sense, Lacan's resort to the label of "alienation" is almost a challenging invitation. The word is a good one if one tries to clear out all the weeds and the scum stuck to it by its abuse. Yes, because even in its etymology the term alienation refers to the Other. In the Spanish version of "Positions of the Unconscious," the word was translated as derangement (*enajenación*),[11] although the reason for this choice—reiterated in the revised and augmented 1984 edition of the *Ecrits*—remains unclear.

First we must perform a distinction. It seems that this condition of alienation is related not only to the foreign but also to a mode of the foreign that is rather persecutory, uncanny. You will probably remember Ridley Scott's film *Alien* had truly uncanny effects produced by its hair-raising "protagonist." We could think that in the imagery created by its director, the "eighth passenger" occupies a place homologous to that of *das Ding* in the Lacanian conception. Since we are talking about movies, another similar film where this conception of *das Ding* is quite perfectly shown is the one by John Carpenter, known in Argentina as *The Enigma of Another World*. This work lost a lot when it was thus titled

---

11. J. Lacan, "*Posición* . . ." ("Positions . . ."), *op. cit.*, pp. 375ff.

for local distribution. Its original title in English was highly suggestive—
The Thing. If you watch it, you will be able to verify strikingly what the
term *das Ding*—the Thing—connotes, in the sense of a devouring and
hair-raising experience. Then, if we try to preserve in its designation the
threatening nature embodied in the alien, we may very well refer to alienation. We must utterly dismiss the popular conception of alienation. In
this sense, the term denotes the unnecessary but irreversible loss of a
certain valuable essence of humanness. In such cases, to be alienated
means to have sacrificed some inner thing in favor of a certain activity
or person. In the face of this situation, the consequent goal would be, as
they say, to disalienate, which is very similar to thinking that someone
falls ill due to a massive projective identification and is cured by the
reintrojection of what was projected. Melanie Klein (whose theory we
have glossed) actually considers that somebody fell ill due to having taken
too much out of himself. In a sort of ideology fenced by an elementary
intuitive space, the contents that have been taken out of the self may—
must—be reincorporated into the "inner world." Kleinism modelizes this
theory based on the (implicit) system of ideas of a pecuniary investment.
Lacan's point of departure—I repeat it once again—is the claim that the
subject is the effect of the signifier, and is constituted in, and from, the
field of the Other. In this way, there is no more or less externalized essence in alienation, whereby the latter would consist of a noxious, progressive extracting from oneself an alleged essence of humanness. Hence
the Lacanian stance is in no way essentialist, which does not mean that,
according to the classic dichotomy, it would be existentialist either. It
is not a question of positing existence as preceding essence, as a Sartre
would point out.[12] It is a subject conceived from the field of the Other,
but this does not mean that the latter is some sort of void, as I believe
the Sartrean (libertarian) reflection on existence posits.

You will doubtlessly have in mind that at the beginning of this
course we posited a punch. It is the following: ◊ Lacan profits from this

---

12. J.-P. Sartre, "*El existencialismo es un humanismo,*" in J.-P. Sartre, M. Heidegger,
Sobre el humanismo, Sur, Buenos Aires, 1960, pp. 14ff. ["Existentialism is a Human-
ism," in *Existentialism from Dostoevsky to Sartre,* ed. W. Kaufman, tr. P. Mairet, Merid-
ian Publishing, New York, 1989.]

notation to account for several psychoanalytic notions, among them, that of the *fantasme*, written as ($ ◊ *a*). In addition, the punch will also be used to write the drive in this manner: ($ ◊ D). ("D" means demand, as opposed to "d," which means desire).

Let us continue to work with this punch, now granting it a possible vectorialization after dividing it through its horizontal axis. The procedure provides us with the support to reflect precisely on two operations included in the little algorithm to which we have referred:

To discern these operations, we must place the subject to the right and, correlatively with him, the Other qua locus of the signifiers (to the left):

We may think then of a back-and-forth, counterclockwise operation. The action of the Other is what brings about the appearance of the subject, yet still unbarred, for he is only promised to become—in this logical moment prior to the barring—effect of the signifier. This action of the Other upon the living being we designate as alienation:

Alienation

It is a circular yet nonreciprocal operation (to include it in an order of reciprocity would be equivalent to conceiving it in a totalizing, nontwisting way), for in the return journey the separation characteristic of the barred subject occurs:

Separation

A $\quad$ $

Alienation

For now, we will just place this second vector in its relation, a relation whose nature we will see later on. Before doing so, let us continue with our attempt to characterize alienation. Lacan tells us that it is through the relationship with the Other that a subject may emerge. This seems very simple, but the history of the production of a subject is certainly complicated—what we just said is no more than a programmatic indication. As we have already stated, every subject is constituted leaving something of himself behind. He cannot appear, therefore, but as a subject taken in a conflict. If he appears as a subject, which actually happens in one of the movements of the operation, it is thanks to the fact that he is recognized as meaning in the field of the Other. The first thing that happens to the "virtual" subject is his being dashed by a wave of signifiers that, although allowing for his emergence, petrify him at the same time. This is a truly complex matter. The subject is born into culture through the action of the signifier, which grants him the only possible life for the speaking being and, at the same time, renders death present to him as a lethal factor. Because in the last analysis, the subject appears at the cost of a disappearance.

It is hard for the prestige of the ego to hear this kind of statement. It is not at all pleasant, because it forces one to think that the subject is not alienated due to having extracted something from himself, but that this is the cost of becoming part of the herd. It is in this sense that we may consider him petrified or even stupefied; placed, in sum, in a quasi-hypnotic condition, that is, the condition that can be categorized as the dimension of the impersonal pronoun (se)—the impersonality, the collectivizing. In short, this action of the signifier can be best verified, in my view, in the phenomenon Freud analyzed so accurately in 1920: the mass formation (or, more up-to-date, group formation). It is already possible to sound converging indications in "The Function and Field of Speech . . ." Indeed, we are crammed with words everywhere—stored, gathered, heard, written, and so on. All of this, which apparently indicates a vast richness of elements, raises a fence at the same time: it is the "wall of language."[13] In this construction the subject is petrified, he is dumbfounded (anonadado)—a precise word, since it denotes to become like a nothing, to disappear.[14] This condition will be designated as aphanisis:

1) Alienation – aphanisis

2) Separation

The term is drawn from Ernest Jones's work, who called aphanisis a supposed fear the subject experiences of not having desires, of the disappearance of the desiderative. Lacan retrieves this word but moves away from the sense Jones had assigned to it. It is not the fainting of desire but the disappearance of the condition of the subject, by virtue and in terms of what constitutes him as such. Here we must try to understand once again how Lacan continually processes the experience of analysis in terms of aporias, of contradictory propositions that, however, do not cancel each other. This aphanisis, disappearance, lethal movement can also be called *fading*,[15] thus introducing another novel word:

1) Alienation – aphanisis – *fading*

2) Separation

---

13. J. Lacan, "*Función y campo* . . . ," *op. cit.*, p. 21. ["The Function and Field . . . ," p. 101.]

14. Harari uses the word *anonadado*, which derives from the word *nonada*, no plus nothing. (Translator's note)

15. In English in the original. (Translator's note)

The subject's *fading* is precisely the mentioned condition of eclipse, of fall, of fainting. It does not allude to a phenomenological description—nobody disappears. What has fainted is the possibility (always in terms of alienation) to set oneself up as subject, as being something other than the product, the effect, of the signifying division.

In the face of this operation of eclipse of the subject captured by the signifier, we are left—fortunately—with the remaining operation, that is, separation. The latter is the reaction in the face of being aphanized, and appearing as meaning. To clarify this point, I will opt for drawing the area of partial overlapping of two circles, leaving the punch aside for the moment (although not completely). Actually, the alluded area in the following diagram derives, in my view, from a deformation of the punch, when we extend it in a curve until we form a lunule:

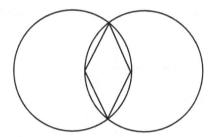

Here we posit the same terms again, the subject and the Other, inverting their locations. What will the subject "obtain" from the Other after alienation? Precisely, the possibility to be a subject. If he obtains being, he will be so qua barred subject:

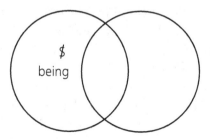

At the same time, what we will find in the field of the Other is meaning:

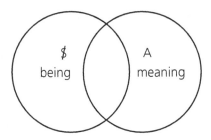

At this point, we must attend to the following: the Other operates as a producer of meanings that, as such, are incomplete, unfinished. Now, in the intersection of both circumferences there is a shared lunule, a place of interval between both fields where, we just said, it is possible to evoke the algorithmic figure of the punch. Then, in this area of relation between the subject and the Other, which appears as an area of pulsation, what will be designated not as meaning but as nonmeaning is inscribed:

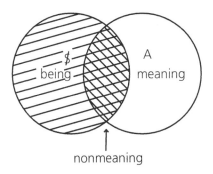

When meaning somehow materializes in a subject by virtue of the action of the Other, it leaves behind in its path a region of nonmeaning. This region is, precisely, that of the unconscious. In this way, the unconscious is a remainder of the operation of the constitution of the subject in the field of the Other.

This theorization of the causative operations of the subject will have a considerable impact in the way of understanding psychoanalytic interpretation, as we will see later on. Once he has shown this diagram, Lacan carries out a highly acute theoretical maneuver based on the precepts of a simple logic of classes. As we all know, the two circles allow the processing in their area of intersection of the operation that is known as joining in the most elementary set theory. [In the first Spanish translation it says union (*unión*), which is immaterial.] So, the seminar points out that alienation must be characterized as joining, and it discriminates: one thing is to add two sets, and a different thing is to join them. The formulation seems contrived, but it refers to something very simple.

If in set $ I have, for instance, five elements and in set A I have another five, if I add them I will obtain a total of ten elements. Now, if sets $ and A have two common elements, we must subtract two elements to the total when we carry out the joining operation, so that we don't count the shared elements twice. The total will thus be eight elements:

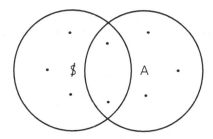

This diagram is a joining. The formulation leads to the discovery of the accomplishment of a particular *vel* in alienation. *Vel* means "or" in Latin, that is, it is a disjunction. Classically, disjunctions are divided into two kinds:

1) Exclusive
2) Inclusive

An example of an exclusive disjunction that is quite worthy of attention is: "I will go *either* here *or* there."[16] One must choose strictly between two options that exclude each other. An inclusive disjunction is instead:

---

16. Lacan adopts the direction indicated by a current tendency in logic according to which the *vel* encompasses also exclusive disjunctions. Traditionally, on the other hand, the *vel* ("*or*") only denoted inclusive disjunctions, identifying the other as "*aut . . . aut . . .*" ("*either . . . or*" . . .). Congruently, notations will differ: "V" for the inclusive, "⩲" for the exclusive.

"I will go to the movies *or* to the theater." This means that it is not necessary to choose between options that are mutually exclusive—a categorical discrimination between the terms under consideration is not at stake. Rather, it is an "I don't care either way." Now, Lacan suggests to us a third *vel*, that of alienation. Consequently, the *vel* are:

1) Exclusive
2) Inclusive
3) Of alienation

As we have already seen, this new *vel* is revealed in the operation of joining. It does not place two strictly opposing terms in disjunction. Neither does it refer to a disjunction where it doesn't matter whether we choose one term or the other. This *vel* indicates a highly paradoxical elective relation that has as its consequence a "neither one, nor the other," whichever the embraced option:

Vel

1) Exclusive *(either... or...)*
2) Inclusive *(or)*
3) Of alienation *(neither one nor the other)*

The *vel* of alienation is of inestimable value, in my experience, in clinical work with obsessive neurotics. In the obsessive, doubt options are usually posited in terms of this *vel*. If one listens analytically, one will notice that one is not dealing with doubts about doing one thing or the other. For instance, "If I do this, I can't do that. What would be better for me?" These are typical conflicts of the obsessive problematic. Even though Lacan posits these concepts in a high level of abstraction, they are of immediate clinical usefulness.

Ultimately, obsessive doubts concern the question of neither one nor the other. In these permanent ruminations and musings we may clearly verify the action of the *vel* of alienation. The seminar offers a general example, namely, that of "Your money or your life." Neither one, nor the other. If I choose money, I am left with neither. If I choose life, the latter will not be the same after losing my money. Even though this looks like an option, it is actually a relation where there is no possible choice.

Another alleged choice that may be postulated in accordance with the *vel* of alienation is "Your freedom or your life." Through these examples, we may easily see how the accomplishment of the suggested *vel* is posited. This recourse to joining as defined by set theory allows us hence to grasp many of the pseudo-conflicts characteristic of our clinical work with obsessive neurotics. It also bears witness—I believe we agree that we aren't talking about self-deception or bad faith—to how the obsessive neurotic is trapped by the signifying chain, petrified in the middle of that "neither one nor the other," trying precisely to enact the operation of separation. To keep the suspense, we will leave the matter of separation for our next "meeting."[17]

QUESTIONS AND ANSWERS

Q: Why is it that in the example given of the joining of elements in set theory there are two elements that cancel each other?

A: Lacan points out very well in the seminar that it is part of logic's silliness. He is joking, of course. Simply, these are operations that can be performed with certain elements. As for the Lacanian use, we should make clear once again that these resources are supports, buttresses of thought. The use of logic is just a scaffolding to think a clinical—and previously theoretical—matter such as that implied by the *vel* of alienation. What is certainly important, in my view, is that we are not always dealing with the two classic disjunctions.

Concerning one of the clinical repercussions of this development (the one mentioned here), what can be apprehended as pathology of thought in the obsessive is indicating that such pathology is but a hypertrophy and a stagnation pertaining to a function characteristic of every subject as a constitutive operation. It is just that as analysts we know that pathology doesn't invent anything—in any case, it goes deeper into certain preestablished lines.

---

17. The Spanish word for meeting, *reunión*, is the same as for "joining," hence the quotation marks. (Translator's note)

Q: When referring to the causative operations, I understand the issue of aporias as a figure, as movement. What I don't think I quite understand is the allusion to contradictions that don't cancel each other, for example, in the case of the signifier that grants both life and death to the subject. What would be the horizon of this? I think I understood that there would be a sort of "one" to whom life and death are granted. Despite the dialectical movement, this wouldn't escape the Piagetian error. What is granted life, and what is granted death?

A: The *vel* of alienation promotes the split of the subject, not of the "one," but of the subject as split by the action exerted by the signifier, that is, meaning/aphanisis. In this context, Lacan will wager a hard term—*freedom*. He does not do it in the naive sense of such a notion, for he is thinking of it psychoanalytically, in terms of the lack that founds the subject as split. This refers to the freedom to operate with one's own lack, and thus trying to perceive the lack in the Other. The subject operates by himself becoming lack, which might be condensed in the phrase "You could lose me," or "I could lack you."[18] The separation maneuver par excellence—as you see, this is a preview of our next meeting—is suicide.[19]

If suicide is the climax of separation, such freedom appears here as freedom to die, and to die purposefully.[20] This formulation, of course, refers to a being chained to the Other that is not, obviously, that of the subject of Sartrean freedom, that of the project determined from the for-oneself. There isn't then an all-encompassing freedom, far from it. Briefly, we are dealing with the freedom the subject has to work with his own lack. In this way, from the field of the Other, the signifier grants life and death to a sexed living being, promised to be split subject, in any case, but not there yet. Before the signifier and its impact (in logical time), we only count with a brood of the *sapiens*, the one Lacan calls *infans*, the mute, the one who doesn't speak.

---

18. I am translating literally from the Spanish translation of the French expression for "I miss you," which is *tu me manque*, you lack me. (Translator's note)

19. R. Harari "*Caída de un querer*," (The Fall of a Love") in *Discurrir . . .* (Pondering . . .), *op. cit.*, pp. 191–205.

20. I have slightly modified the original here according to the author's explanation of this phrase: To rid oneself of the weight *of* living, and to die *in order to* leave a message to the immediate survivors, without waiting to die of "natural causes." (Translator's note)

10

Separation, Metaphor, Interpretation

As you all know, this is our last meeting, and it is therefore accompanied by a certain inevitable eagerness to try to offer you all that is left. Nevertheless, if we consider Lacan's teaching regarding this issue of the lack in all its implications, we must agree that something will always be missing. Well, it isn't that bad if, when we finish, the lack persists.

The topic of the lack is precisely the decisive one about which I would like to articulate a few issues today that require that we take up again some problems we had raised in our last class. You will recall that we tried to elucidate two functions designated as causative operations of the subject, both related to the influence and effectiveness of the field of the Other in its connection with the subject. As we had the chance to point out, these two operations are called alienation and separation:

Alienation	
Separation	

We will arrange the two operations in this way in order to later distribute four columns that we will progressively fill. I will clarify something from the start: many of the items in these columns can be superimposed; we are not thinking in terms of exclusive disjunctions. There will be a certain degree of inevitable implications in this table, but I think that it will be useful to attempt this series of distinctions in any case. Before doing so, however, it would be interesting to go briefly over the problem of alienation and unfold that of separation, which was succinctly expounded in the answer to the last question I was posed last time.

As we tried to show, alienation is tied to the constitution of the subject in the field of the Other, insofar as it is an operation that determines the capture of the subject by the signifier. The latter gives the subject the chance to live qua speaking being. At the same time, and conversely, the signifier induces a lethal, deadly effect (in a metaphoric sense). This signifier does not kill, absolutely not, it rather inaugurates a function, that is, the one designated as aphanisis (a term taken from Ernest Jones's work), which constitutes a fainting, a disappearance, a petrifying. The effect of the signifier is to introduce a sort of *knockout* [1] whereby, as it usually happens under such circumstances in boxing, the subject faints. In this operation, undoubtedly, the primacy belongs to the field of the Other. From there, this dividing condition of revitalization and lethalization is produced. That is how the access to the level of subject of that which was no more than a promise to become one is determined. Subject, and therefore, speaking? It is redundant to refer to a subject who speaks. In Lacanian doctrine, alluding to a "speaking subject" implies a tautology. That is why we must refer to a speaking being. [2] Indeed, subject implies the fact of having been split through the action of the signifier. This is then the conceptual course to be privileged in dealing with alienation, that is, to be divided.

The splittings of the subject can be tackled according to a variety of dimensions. In Seminar 11 there is one that is developed in particular—the one we graphed in our last meeting. It establishes that whatever the option one chooses, between the subject and the Other such

---

1. In English in the original. (Translator's note)
2. Or, as Lacan himself suggests, based on a condensation, "*parlêtre*" (from "*parler*," to speak, and "*être*," to be). Thence "speakbe," in the sense of to be by virtue of speech (*habla*).

option is always taken away from—by—that intermediate locus designated as nonmeaning. If the option seeks to constitute itself searching for meaning, it runs into the nonmeaning. There is no total meaning in any speaking being, for a lack inevitably occurs that constitutes him, which, in the materialization of the subject, is the unconscious. There is no option between both conditions. Even when one believes that one chooses and wins, one always loses something of the chosen, which will not be what it was before the choice was made (let us just recall the example of "Your money or your life"). In fact, it is a false option, an assumption of a choice that is not so. Lacan will name this the *vel* of alienation. Yet this *vel* ("or" in Latin) does not point to any disjunction whatsoever but to the belief that one is choosing when such a choice does not exist. What it alludes to then is a lack—neither one nor the other. This is the action of the field of the Other in the constitution of the subject in its first movement, but we are still left with the other operation, namely, separation.

In *The Four Fundamental Concepts of Psychoanalysis*, the problem of separation is expounded and developed with extreme sagacity. Once the lack is installed in the subject, says Lacan, the latter proceeds to posit it in regard to the Other, that is, to search for it, even to induce it. There are those who consider (I don't know if out of bad faith or sheer ignorance) that the Lacanian Other is God, smuggled in. Coarse: they haven't succeeded in grasping (or haven't wanted to) how the Other is not an entity, an entelechy; the customary recourse to its lack, or to the attachment of some adjective to it, indicate that this is so.

For instance, it is the case of the primordial Other—to which we could refer as the mother. Why not call it thus then? What happens is that the mother has been, and is still being, so thrashed in theory (and in the "psy" counseling), that it is better to mention a primordial Other, for it accounts for a locus of the mother where she (usually) performs a mediating action in terms of the Symbolic order. This will not depend on her maternal instinct or on her feelings but on her place as presentification of the Other. This is the reason for the concept of primordial Other. It does not simply obey an attempt to complicate matters or to suggest unnecessary alternative words. In this term, therefore, there is a conception at play, that of the registering of experience, and its consequences. In sum, it is not the same to invoke the mother (which gives rise to all those child-care theories or the "cares needed so as not to neuroticize one's children," and so on) than to account for a primordial Other.

When the latter is interpellated, for instance, through the famous infantile "whys," we find an interesting datum. These "whys" are often hard to endure, for they confront us with the impossibility of an answer, with the fact that we can't answer every question. In short, they place the person asked before an ineffable real. It is not, the seminar says, an eagerness to know. There is an issue here where Lacan differs from Freud, who alluded to a *Wissentrieb*, a drive to know. The child does not ask in order to know, but in order to question: "Why are you saying this to me?" It is not just a why interested in content, but a why that asks about the desire of the Other. More accurately, we might formulate it thus: "You are telling me this, but what do you actually want to say? What do you want?" With these questions, the child is searching for, locating, something of the order of the lack. There isn't a univocal answer to this, and we are hence diving into the desire of the Other—desire means to think of the lack—and consequently into a conundrum.

Yet what is being answered about this desire of the Other? What is the first answer that emerges? It is not something vague, where there is nothing to say. The first object proposed to this dialectic of the "whys" is precisely one's own lack, but located in the Other. The slant with which the seminar presents this is very subtle. It is possible to formulate one of the usual ways to contribute one's own lack as belonging in the field of the Other as follows: "Can you lose me?" This formulation includes the fantasmatic a child customarily possesses regarding his being sent to his reward by his parents, which is simply a *fantasme* related to separation.[3] Thus, the "whys" are not an intellectual query. Understanding this allows us to clarify a disorder that we have learned to deal with effectively thanks to a specification formulated by Lacan. I am referring to anorexia nervosa, which consists in the subject's proceeding to "consume himself" in an attempt to become nothing.

---

3. Some who validate the *fantasme* punctually as a theory coin a filicide here that cannot account for the structure.

This "You could lose me" (now in the affirmative) addressed to the Other can be translated as "You need me," heard in a polysemic way.[4] Nothing better to achieve this than shutting oneself off, shielding oneself, intending thus not to give the Other his place. In this separation, the "function of freedom" strikingly appears, a fantasmatic freedom that denotes the attempt to get rid of the aphanisic effect. On the one hand, there is alienation, which bears the quality of capturing the subject, of subordinating him, of making him be, but at the cost of the lack-in-being. The function of the liberation of such capture, of freedom, is played out in separation. We will try to formalize this a little bit more narrowly so that it will not remain a mere linguistic convention. In any case, if we place separation in a direct relation with a novel, complicated, and spread syndrome as that of anorexia nervosa, we can verify how this second operation does not simply constitute a new speculative philosophy on the constitution of the subject—clinical remission is immediate and fruitful.

We next run into a series of associations, of breakdowns, starting from the word *separation*. In this wordplay—which is certainly not a divertimento—Lacan resorts to the Latin word *separare*, which when separated, scanned, renders *se parare*; in French, *se parer*, both to get dressed and to be on one's guard. Then, and again starting from a Latin word, Lacan shows another misunderstanding that derives from *separare*. It is the one that emerges from *se parere*, which alludes to giving birth to oneself, to begetting oneself—something that should not be confused with self-engendering, with the claim that the subject is *causa sui*. Despite the fact that determination lies in the field of the Other, it is possible to "beget oneself" thanks to separation. Some of the elements we are explaining we can already include in the columns so as to organize what corresponds to these two operations according to a higher degree of abstraction. Since there are several lines that gradually combine, we can punctuate, in a first approximation, four grids arranged as follows:

---

4. In Spanish the expression is "*te hago falta*," where the word *falta*, "lack," is present once again. (Translator's note)

	Effect in the $	Relation with the signifying chain, with the field of the Other	Logical operation	Mode of the lack
Alienation				
Separation				

In the first one we locate the effect produced in the subject, whom we write as $. In the second column we place the relation with the signifying chain, with the field of the Other. In the third one we see the logical operation at play. The fourth, and last, serves to register the mode of the lack that results from each operation. This table may help, at least temporarily, as a scaffolding that will allow us to think through certain issues. As it happens with every scaffolding, it must be dismantled once the building is finished. Concerning the effect on the subject, we mentioned two conjoint possibilities. Alienation produces a divisive effect: when meaning is chosen, the non-sensical [5] is inevitable. Meaning is found at the cost of its forced articulation with the unconscious, which is the nonmeaning. This divisive effect, on the other hand, involves the said aphanisis, which gives rise to the movement Lacan calls the fading[6] of the subject, insofar as it is an amputated materialization of his being:

---

5. In English in the original. (Translator's note)
6. In English in the original. (Translator's note)

	Effect in the $	Relation with the signifying chain, with the field of the Other	Logical operation	Mode of the lack
Alienation	dividing: aphanisis *(fading)*	meaning (non)		
Separation				

This fall, this vacillation or fainting, this finally "lethal" effect is the *fading*, the dissolution. If alienation provokes, as we said, a *knockout* of the subject, in separation we identify a begetting oneself. This *se parere*, as giving birth to the subject, is a function of freedom:

	Effect in the $	Relation with the signifying chain, with the field of the Other	Logical operation	Mode of the lack
Alienation	dividing: aphanisis *(fading)*	meaning (non)		
Separation	to beget oneself *(se parere)* function of "freedom"			

The quotation marks serve to have us keep in mind that this freedom, as we noted in our last meeting, has nothing to do with the absolute, all-encompassing freedom (in the Sartrean mode) that derives from the fact that existence precedes essence. This freedom brings about so many reflections and clarifications to deserve at least to be circumscribed with quotation marks. The function of freedom is limited, restricted; it works from the lack. It is not the one that is used to dictate, to conceive a "project" in the existentialist manner.

Let us move on to the second grid. As to the relation to the signifying chain, the use of a little gram that represents the minimum pair of signifying articulation will be very helpful. We will write them as S_1, S_2. We have pointed out that the effect in the relation with the signifying chain is that, in terms of at least two signifiers, an unknown quantity "x" is produced as a result, namely, that of the subject, speaking and petrified in accordance with the same movement:

	Effect in the $\$$		Relation with the signifying chain, with the field of the Other	Logical operation	Mode of the lack
Alienation	dividing: aphanisis *(fading)*	meaning (non)	$S_1 \longrightarrow S_2$ $\vert$ $x\$$		
Separation	to beget oneself *(se parere)* function of "freedom"				

We can see clearly here how at the time when the articulation S_1-S_2 occurs, the subject falls as an effect of it. Consequently, the subject is produced in alienation by the minimum signifying set, a pair. This formula is another way of saying that there isn't one signifier but at least two. The definition of this signifier must necessarily involve another signifier and yet another element, namely, the subject. That is why the Lacanian developments could never be confused with an "objective" linguistics, for the function of the subject is constantly interspersed in them in a decisive way. We may designate what takes place in alienation as capture:

	Effect in the $\$$	Relation with the signifying chain, with the field of the Other	Logical operation	Mode of the lack
Alienation	dividing: aphanisis *(fading)* │ meaning │ (non)	S_1———S_2 │ capture x$\$$		
Separation	to beget oneself *(se parere)* function of "freedom"			

We must recall that Lacan also uses the term *capture* in a different context, when he alludes to the imaginary capture called love. Here, instead, it is a signifying capture that belongs in the Symbolic register.

In the case of separation, the corresponding diagram will represent a crucial difference with respect to the former one. Circular (though dissymmetrical) return will imply the following:

	Effect in the $\$$	Relation with the signifying chain, with the field of the Other	Logical operation	Mode of the lack
Alienation	dividing: aphanisis *(fading)* │ meaning │ (non)	S_1———S_2 │ capture x$\$$		
Separation	to beget oneself *(se parere)* function of "freedom"	S_1--┬--S_2 ⋮ │ ⋮ x$\$$		

The dotted line introduced between both signifiers represents the fact that in the interval between S_1 and S_2 an attack on the chain takes place. This is the locus of the subject, who must burst into the signifying chain in order to attain separation there. This does not imply being left out of the chain, but rather making a place for himself in it. It is understood that here there is no dimension outside discourse, as happens in psychosis. To be outside the chain is something relative, dependent on that signifier we designated as Name-of-the-Father. Thus, in psychosis, its nonappearance conditions that "outside." The question here is different: it lies in making a place for oneself. It does not imply, however, a devastation, a sort of anarchic position, or anything of the kind. Regarding the analyst's interpretation, we will see later how in the latter this attack on the signifying pair at the weak spot of the interval, where, on the other hand, the Other's desire (yet to be found) "lies," also functions. Such a spot can be anywhere, although we conventionally graph it approximately midway into the journey:

	Effect in the $\$$		Relation with the signifying chain, with the field of the Other	Logical operation	Mode of the lack
Alienation	dividing: aphanisis *(fading)*	meaning (non)	$S_1 \text{————} S_2$ capture $x\$$		
Separation	to beget oneself *(se parere)* function of "freedom"		$S_1 \text{——⊢——} S_2$ attack $x\$$		

As you can see, the function of freedom lies in securing for oneself this place in the chain (*hacer-se ese lugar*). In the light of this operation, we may think of something I posited in my book *Pondering Psychoanalysis*[7] in connection with this seminar. For everyone who is claimed by Freud's and Lacan's teachings, a sort of path, of yearning, or *desideratum* emerges—after being alienated in Freud's and Lacan's signifiers, the attempt to separate occurs. In this way, the doors open

---

7. R. Harari, "*El constructo del discurso del Analista*" ("The Construct of the Analyst's Discourse"), in *Discurrir . . .* (Pondering . . .), *op. cit.*, pp. 23–26.

to these fevers of eclecticism that often invade our city and that involve, they say, the incorporation of a bit of each author or school. What is not at all clear is what is the rationale behind the evaluation of what is "good" in each author or school. In what locus of Other of the Other is the person making these propositions located, propositions that in fact imply rather a belief in nothing? According to the seminar, we can detect a problem here. Those who want to follow me, says Lacan, must alienate themselves in my signifiers, and not oppose them. What we usually try to do—as is the case with André Green, who can be seen here already debating with the exponent—is to search for the small difference, as if this ensured separation. In this way, as Laplanche once wrote, the little portable metapsychology belonging to each analyst is construed. There lies the difference thanks to which one seems to be taking a beneficial, creative distance from the signifiers that carry the masters' doctrine. I think, however, that the right attitude consists in trying to make these signifiers play, to play with these signifiers so that they will produce new effects. We must use them and alienate in them, yet in a way that will enable them to bring about unexpected effects by ex-tending them and in-tending them. One will thus be able to insert other signifiers, but always in the same field.

If this isn't the case, what often happens—and this is one of the risks we run with a teaching that is so elaborate, so rich, and still relatively unanalyzed—is that one falls into what I have called garglist (*gargarística*) echolalia. Since it is a gargle, one cannot swallow much; as in the case of echolalia, one only reproduces. There is nothing but alienation. If this is the case, the same will happen with Lacan as happened before with Freud—there is a sure danger of "death." If one insists on a punctual reproduction of the same, and not on a repetition (since the latter involves difference), we find pure alienation. Naturally, it is a challenge, for we must undertake something that is doubtlessly arduous and complicated. It would probably be better to opt for self-engendering, as the subject of representation proclaims. It is very appealing to try to build a theory of one's own from scratch. A paper by my colleague at this Center, Carlos Pérez, proves this point by means of a *reductio ad absurdum*, resorting to the ludicrous. In this text,[8] the author (fictionally) narrates the finding of letters and manuscripts by a certain Amaretto di Saronno (the name, as you know, of the well-known liqueur). Starting from this discovery he reconstructs a whole movement; how di Saronno starts his abstruse theories, carrying out complex elaborations that are later rectified, until he attains a system thanks to which he becomes a celebrated thinker.

With great perspicacity and mordant humor Pérez "shows" a variety of correspondence and texts that serve as testimony to the mentioned process. The problem is that anybody may prefer to emulate this imaginary Amaretto di Saronno rather than enduring the alienation in the masters' signifiers. The temptation to believe that we are our own children is always great. Why not? you will ask. Is it immoral? Does it mean that one is proclaiming a submission, an obeisance? Not at all. It means forgetting that if one intends to "escape" alienation in this way, the fact is that one falls into a much more effective alienation, it being unconscious. Doubtlessly, we are speaking here of the debt to the father, of the possibility either to recognize such a debt or, on the contrary, to believe oneself to be born from oneself. Briefly, it seems hard to conceive (not just in biological terms but also due to the true locus born by the field of the Other) a sort of illumination that starts from scratch. It is better to notice that one's own discourse finds its origin in the field of the Other, and that creation is possible due to the function of debt, and not to one's opposition to it. How to create-repeating, or repeat-creating?

The question of separation bears very significant consequences for the analyst's ethics; or, to be more precise, the question of enduring alienation and, in the movement of the twisting return, going toward separation. We will explore this point more thoroughly later on, when we approach again, as we announced before, the topic of interpretation. Prior to that we will attend to the logical operations in the table we are developing. As we pointed out in our last meeting, in alienation we find what set theory designates as joining:

---

8. C. Pérez, "El esquema α de Amaretto di Saronno" ("The Scheme α by Amaretto di Saronno"), in Del goce creador al malestar en la cultura (From Creative Jouissance to Civilization and Its Discontents), Paidós, Buenos Aires, 1987, pp. 231ff (previously published in 1986).

	Effect in the $\$$	Relation with the signifying chain, with the field of the Other	Logical operation	Mode of the lack
Alienation	dividing: aphanisis *(fading)* | meaning | (non)	S_1———S_2 | capture x$\$$	Joining	
Separation	to beget oneself *(se parere)* function of "freedom"	S_1—┊—S_2 ┊ | attack┊ x$\$$		

The procedure of joining is the one we graphed by means of the following Euler rings:

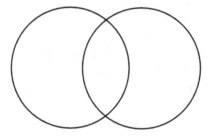

If there are X elements in each set, if there are common elements, they are counted only once. This is precisely what happens in the failed choice of "neither one nor the other," according to the *vel* of alienation; there is always something that is subtracted. The causative operation of the subject called separation, on the other hand, relates to the intersection or product. In modern mathematics, intersection designates what is included as common elements to both sets, in the same lunula we mentioned before:

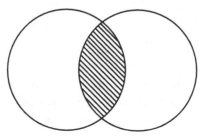

Whereas in the joining the common elements are eliminated as duplicates, what matters here are precisely those elements. We find ourselves before an operation that returns to the former one by means of a twist:

	Effect in the $\not{S}$	Relation with the signifying chain, with the field of the Other	Logical operation	Mode of the lack
Alienation	dividing: aphanisis (fading) | meaning (non)	S_1———S_2 | capture x$\not{S}$	Joining	
Separation	to beget oneself (se parere) function of "freedom"	S_1—-—S_2 | attack ⁝ x$\not{S}$	Intersection or product	

Finally, regarding the mode of the lack, in the case of alienation we will find the corresponding *vel* (as we saw in our last class). As we have already pointed out, there is no choice; whatever one chooses, a loss will occur:

	Effect in the $\not{S}$	Relation with the signifying chain, with the field of the Other	Logical operation	Mode of the lack
Alienation	dividing: aphanisis (fading) | meaning (non)	S_1———S_2 | capture x$\not{S}$	Joining	*Vel* (there is no choice, he loses)
Separation	to beget oneself (se parere) function of "freedom"	S_1—-—S_2 | attack ⁝ x$\not{S}$	Intersection or product	

In separation, in turn, what counts is the enigma in the face of the desire of the Other, which we illustrated with the case of the infantile "whys." We will write it with the Lacanian notation d(A)—desire of the

Other. Enigma in the face of the desire of the Other, translated as interrogative answer in a "Can he lose me?":

	Effect in the $\cancel{S}$		Relation with the signifying chain, with the field of the Other	Logical operation	Mode of the lack
Alienation	dividing: aphanisis *(fading)*	meaning (non)	$S_1 \longrightarrow S_2$ | capture x$\cancel{S}$	Joining	*Vel* (there is no choice, he loses)
Separation	to beget oneself *(se parere)* function of "freedom"		$S_1 \overset{|}{-} S_2$ | attack $\vdots$ x$\cancel{S}$	Intersection or product	Enigma of the d(A): "can he lose me?"

In this way, the subject works with his own lack, threatening, demanding, and intimidating the Other, trying to provoke in him the same lack. It is precisely in this "overlaying" (*recubrimiento*) of the lacks that we punctuate the shared, what is intersected in the lunula. We have thus completed this diagram that I hope may be useful to orient yourselves basically in the reading of such a decisive (and not easy) stretch of the seminar as is the one devoted to the causative operations of the subject.

In Chapters 17 and 19 of *The Four Fundamental Concepts of Psychoanalysis* some issues are developed that we must detail here, or at least two of them. The first one will be once again the problem of the signifying pair S_1 and S_2, which, as we can see, is located in the second column of our diagram. Lacan will stipulate that S_1 (which he calls unary signifier) is articulated as "a matter of life and death"[9] to S_2, or binary signifier. This S_2 is precisely the one that appears in Freud under the term *Vorstellungsrepräsentantz*, whose proposed translation is representative of the representation, and not representative representative (*representante representativo*).[10] Is it a matter of mere terminology? Not at all:

---

9. J. Lacan, *Los cuatro . . .* , *op. cit.*, p. 224. [*The Four . . .* , p. 218.]

10. This is the option adopted by J. Laplanche and J.-B. Pontalis in their *Vocabulaire de la psychanalyse* (P.U.F., Paris, 1967, pp. 412–414), who actually question Lacan's proposition. (There is a Spanish translation.) [*The Language of Psycho-Analysis*, tr. Donald Nicholson-Smith, W.W. Norton, New York, 1973, pp. 203–205.]

it is not just words at stake here. A crucial difference exists. *Vorstellung* is the traditional psychological representation, the idea, the perception one has of things in the world—subjectivity, in sum, with which gnoseology is linked. In a word, it is signification. This determines that *Vorstellung* must be understood separate from *Repräsentanz*:

> *Vorstellung:*   Signification
>
> *Repräsentanz:*

This is a very important point, because to conceive *Vorstellung* as the place where signification is at stake implies a firm step toward the comprehension of where repression is exerted. Let us recall that there is a certain psychoanalytic *Vulgata* that asserts that what is repressed are the affects, namely, anxiety, hate, and love. An elementary reading of Freud would convince us that he never wrote anything of the sort. The third point of the cited text *The Unconscious*[11] is titled "*Sentimientos inconscientes*" ("Unconscious Emotions"). To gloss, to denote this title, we should turn it into a query: unconscious emotions? They don't exist: emotions are felt. There is no possibility of any kind of repression. As Freud explains it, since they are bound to representations, affects undoubtedly suffer the effects of displacement, and they can also turn into anxiety, undergo the transformation into their opposite, be "suppressed," but none of this involves the action of repression, for the latter is exerted on the *Vorstellungsrepräsentanz*, the representative of representation. If *Vorstellung* is read through the slant of signification, *Repräsentanz*—like the ambassadors—is somebody who does not speak on his own behalf. He isn't but a representative, a signifier of the changing, the mobile significations it carries:

> *Vorstellung:*   Signification
>
> *Repräsentanz:*   Signifier

---

11. S. Freud, *op. cit.*, pp. 173–176. [pp. 177–179].

As the signifier does not signify itself because it responds from the locus of the Other, the same happens with the ambassador. He is there responding to interests other than his personal ones, since his own signification is not relevant—it must not intervene. He is saying: "I am the one who represents . . . ," regardless of his being a nice man or not. The term *representative of representation* is indicating then how a subject is constituted when this signifier, S_2, falls, founding the subject through his split, his aphanisis. Freud already taught this: it is primal repression that gives rise to the splitting of the subject, S_2 inscribing itself as a point of attraction toward the secondarily repressed. I take the opportunity here to allow myself a small observation to Lacan. He points out that in Freud's *Metapsychology*, his text on *Verdrängung* (Repression) follows that on *The Unconscious*.[12] If we look up the respective volume we will see that *Repression* precedes *The Unconscious*. The issue here is the following: How does Freud "put together" the essays included in the *Metapsychology*? His journey[13] is the following (in what concerns the first three articles):

Drive ⟶ Repression ⟶ The unconscious.

On the other hand, according to what we have been able to follow, how does the development of this seminar proceed? This is its itinerary:

The unconscious ⟶ Drive ⟶ Repression.

Consequently, with respect to Freud's discursive strategy, Lacan's consisted in situating the unconscious first:

12. J. Lacan, *Los cuatro . . .* , *op. cit.*, p. 223. The new edition, *op. cit.*, p. 225 does not point out the lapsus either. [*The Four . . .* , p. 217.]

13. S. Freud, *O. C.*, *op. cit.*, Vol. 14, pp. 105, 135, and 153 [pp. 109, 141, and 159].

Given that this is the Lacanian path in its practical state in accordance with the logical order of this seminar, it is reasonable that this path would give rise to a *lapsus*—that of changing the sequential order of a text. This is in no way attributable to an alleged ignorance of Freud's work. On the contrary, knowing how Lacan frequented and mastered the work of the father of psychoanalysis, this fact is doubly striking. For a start, it seems to indicate a strong inclination to place the developments on the unconscious in the first place. In this way, accounting for the unconscious as structured like a language, since the unconscious is not *causa sui*, allows him not to start from the drive as if it were an instinct. This is not an order of preference; it doesn't imply a hierarchy. It is a logical order of reasons that conveys, in the *lapsus*, the guidelines of a program.

In these almost concluding passages of the seminar a discussion is held with Jean Laplanche. Thus, another milestone of the debate will dwell on the relational issue metaphor-repression. Naturally, the latter follows the pattern of any metaphor, hence the importance, the decisiveness of being able to stipulate whether the substitution of the Name-of-the-Father for the Desire of the Mother has taken place in a subject, which configures the paternal metaphor. For this purpose, it is necessary to have an accurate comprehension of this structurating circumstance.

In these stretches of the seminar, Lacan refers quite viciously to a certain infatuated person who has taken a university position. We already know to whom he is alluding. Among other things, Lacan mentions how this professor tried to reduce his formula of the metaphor, a procedure that, if followed, would lead to a risky impasse of special importance in the delimitation of the question of interpretation.

In "The Agency of the Letter"[14] we see the following symbols:

$$F\left(\frac{S'}{S}\right) S$$

This reads as follows: the function of the signifier consists of being able to substitutively locate a signifier—with an apostrophe, as in S prime—on top of another signifier. It is as simple as that; this is the first propo-

---

14. J. Lacan, "*La instancia . . .*," *op. cit.*, p. 200. ["The Agency . . . ," p. 164.]

sition, the first part of the formula of the metaphor, which is presented as a congruence ($\cong$) of the former with a second term:

$$S (+) s$$

This implies that the signifier admits a crossing, a transposition, in the generation of signification. The sign that indicates the relation does not imply an addition but the crossing of the bar that resists signification. The complete formula of the metaphor will be written thus:

$$F \left(\frac{S'}{S} \right) S \cong S (+) s$$

Since it constitutes a spark of poetry or of creation, if there is metaphor the substitution must be fortunate enough so that what was substituted will be grasped by the substitute. If not, the metaphor fails. Hence, if a realization of what one is talking about through this resource, through this figure, does not take place, the metaphor is a failure. The transposition of the bar implies that something of the constitution, of the emergence of signification can be read in the substitutive signifier (or signifierness); it is "in the warren" where we can indeed apprehend, through the substitute signifier, the substituted one. Moving on to our specific case, this general consideration implies that the function of the paternal metaphor consists in being able to substitutively place the Name-of-the-Father over the Desire of the Mother.

This is what Freud states in a more empirical (or more imaginary) way when he explains the passage from the mother to the father in the case of feminine sexuality.[15] Lacan's attempt at formalization accounts for the fact that this transit does not occur only in women, for, qua operation of passage, it is characteristic of every *sapiens*. Now, we can resort (with reservations) to arithmetic fractions in order to formalize the issue. What takes place in this example (as in any metaphor) can be translated very simply into the following formula:

---

15. S. Freud, "*Sobre la sexualidad femenina*" ("Female Sexuality"), *op. cit.*, pp. 223ff. [pp. 225ff]

$$\frac{A}{B} \cdot \frac{C}{D}$$

It is a simple ratio, posited as a multiplication. If we replace the letters with the elements that are conducive to the constitution of the subject, we will obtain the following arrangement:

$$\frac{\text{Name-of-the-Father}}{\text{Desire of the Mother}} \qquad \frac{\text{Desire of the Mother}}{\text{signified to the subject}}$$

What is posited here is actually a product. The appearance of the same term in the middle terms of the ratio determines its reduction, that is, its elimination:

$$\frac{\text{Name-of-the-Father}}{\cancel{\text{Desire of the Mother}}} \qquad \frac{\cancel{\text{Desire of the Mother}}}{\text{signified to the subject}}$$

The formula is then limited to establishing the following: it is the Name-of-the-Father that grants a signified to the subject, a signified that will be phallic. Laplanche, however, complicated the terms of the metaphor—he conceived it as an operation of four strata and he evidently opted for postulating a not very clear juxtaposition of two signifiers in the unconscious. His proposition is written thus[16]:

$$\cfrac{\cfrac{A}{D}}{\cfrac{B}{C}}$$

In this way, we have A over D, over B, over C. The dot, indicative of the product, is replaced by the bar of division. Thus, as is well known, the relation of the product is reconstituted.

---

16. J. Laplanche-S. Leclaire, "*El inconsciente: un estudio psicoanalítico*," in H. Ey, ed. *El inconsciente (coloquio de Bonneval)*, Siglo XXI, México, 1970, p. 122. ["The Unconscious: A Psychoanalytic Study," in *The Unconscious and the Id: A Volume of Laplanche's Problematiques*, J. Laplanche, L. Thurston (trans.), L. Watson (trans.) and S. Leclaire, Karnac Books, 1999.]

If Laplanche's formula accounts for the structure of the unconscious, the long bar separates the manifest from the latent, understood as (pre) conscious over unconscious. This division is then understood as graphing any articulation, a capturing of two signifiers (here, B and C) in the unconscious. Thus, what is finally being said is that the signifier signifies itself, instead of (Lacanianly) marking a distancing, "expelling" substitution. Considering his observations as true, Laplanche goes as far as presenting, as a valid deduction, the notion that the interpretation is open to any meaning. So, as the binding among signifiers is absolutely arbitrary, whatever the analyst says, he will "touch" the chain of the unconscious, so that the pertinent interpretation may consist of saying anything.

Of course, this fosters the idea that any upstart can tell his patient whatever comes to his mind with the conviction that he is producing a psychoanalytic effect. One can undoubtedly produce effects—there are enough forms of imaginary effectiveness (as we have already seen), and there are many cases where one doesn't know why certain things happen during an analysis. And let it be clearly understood that we are not talking just about noxious consequences but also about those that are favorable to the end of analysis.

In the Lacanian formula, what is adopted is the convention, the fiction of a continuous ratio, that is, a ratio that has the same middle terms. It is just a particular form of ratio. On the other hand, the fraction model does not properly account for the signifier-signified relation (whose algorithm, $\frac{S}{s}$, seems in fact a fraction) for it does not contemplate the production of the effect of meaning. One thing then is to interpret the signifier if we think, with a minimum of rigor, that we are ruled by the laws of metaphor and metonymy, and a different thing is to suppose that one interprets the signifier according to a foolish playing with words that has nothing to do with the teaching that concerns us here.

When Lacan proceeds to link *separare* to *se parare* and *se parere*, for instance, he is not resorting to a sort of maniac delirium where words merrily articulate by means of a fast flight of ideas. Sometimes it would seem that it has been understood thus, especially on the part of some analysts who are always ready to play around with the signifier in a mad association. In sum, Laplanche's proposition fails from its inception to its last consequences. I repeat: it is not simply a matter of mathematical formulae but of their, sometimes unpredictable, clinical implications.

As to what happens with formulae—in the plane of algebraic notation—it turns out that in the Lacanian development, rather than the sole empirical outcome, the occurrence, punctuated in, and by its implicit logic, is particularly significant. If the possible outcome obtained with Lacan's formula of the metaphor ended up being coincidentally identical to the one produced by Laplanche's proposition, this would not indicate that both postulations were equally correct. We are thinking here about how the elements articulate. That is why the same outcome does not always ensure the legitimacy of the respective operations. Believing the opposite would mean not distinguishing the fact that one has reached a successful interpretation because it constitutes a signification related to the analysant, from having "found" a symptomal resolution by means of an inadmissible interpretation (I am using the singular in order to simplify). In this last case we must say that there was a transferential influx rather than a signifying work. This influx will undoubtedly provoke effects. Momentary remission might even occur in both cases. However, the possibilities of relapse are inexorable once the "hypnotic" effect ceases to exist.

An important point to remember, therefore, is that interpretation is not open to all meanings. It may fail relatively, but in any case, it must be founded on, and by, the signifiers provided by the analysant. We can't suppose then (and there is an ethical implication here concerning the analyst's desire) that by a sort of chain reaction, whatever we say we will be tackling the patient's problem responsibly.

In the Lacanian formulation there is an ethics of interpretation. We will return to this before we finish, but let us continue to reflect for a moment on the use of mathematical formulae. In the examples we have seen today, symbols are used in a very particular sense. In the same way as Lacan uses linguistics or topology, he uses arithmetic. His manipulation, let us reiterate, is similar to that of a *bricoleur* who takes what is suitable to him, resorting to an "I help myself because it helps me" (*me sirvo porque me sirve*). With respect to the formulation of the metaphor, his specifying search consisted of developing a formula capable of explaining the eclipse, the fall of the Desire of the Mother by virtue of its replacement with the Name-of-the-Father. On the other hand, if we read the part of "El inconsciente, un estudio psicoanalítico" ("The Unconscious: A Psychoanalytic Study") that bears Laplanche's byline, we can notice how what he intends is an implementation of the formula of the metaphor that will accept his invention of an unconscious in a primal state, which he considers as "condition for language." [17]

We can already notice the irreconcilable antinomy between Lacan's and Laplanche's conceptions in this essay's starting point. The first considers that language is a condition for the unconscious; the second, that the unconscious is a condition for language. Do we need to clarify that in the second proposition the Lacanian teaching is already lost? From this sort of primal unconscious, this axiom, Laplanche starts to design a model for the construction of language, a problem that almost belongs in the realm of developmental psychology. And I don't mean that this discipline deals with something erroneous. What happens is that everything that is construed in that field is alien to our specific interest, for its episteme is psychoanalytically unthinkable.[18] Its realm encompasses the acquisition of language as instrument, the development of the ability to master a vocabulary or to put phrases together correctly. From the point of view of psychoanalysis, this is the deflection cast when the paternal metaphor is ignored, namely, the conception of language as a repertory to be acquired, as an aptitude based on a preexisting entelechy.

QUESTIONS AND ANSWERS

Q: In "La metáfora del sujeto,"[19] Lacan writes that the metaphor is a four-term operation: A over B, times D over C. He then distributes a definition by Perelman in this way. I always thought that development was very strange when confronted with the three-term one that appears in the case of the paternal metaphor, and I still don't understand it.

---

17. J. Laplanche, *op. cit.*, pp. 118 ff.

18. J. Lacan, "*De una cuestión preliminar . . .* ," *op. cit.*, p. 240. ["On a Question Preliminary . . ."]

19. J. Lacan, *Escritos II*, Siglo XXI, México, 1984, pp. 867–870. [I have not been able to find an English edition.]

A: It's true: Lacan takes the four terms of Perelman's formulation, but if we notice how the text unfolds, it is possible to see how he asserts that the four terms are not homogeneous—three are signifiers, and one a signified. This is marking the fact that there does not exist a relation in the same plane. If you're interested, I published a paper last year in the journal *Imago*, number 12, *Lacan, diez años después* (Lacan, Ten Years Later). Its title is "*Metáfora: ¿tema y fora?*" (Metaphor: Thema and Phora?), and it refers precisely to the metaphor of the subject. My text attempts to be a tracking of the *princeps* places where Lacan talks about metaphor, and I explore the latter in particular in relation to Perelman's book,[20] which is not easily found in our milieu. Moreover, since you referred to this text, we should ask ourselves, What does the genitive mean when applied to the metaphor *of* the subject? Starting from alienation and separation, then: Is the metaphor of the subject the one the subject processes, or is it the subject as effect of the metaphor? If what counts is the second option, then we are thinking above all of the paternal metaphor, and not of a reduced, ultimately individualistic, unconscious in a primordial state.

Going back to what we were discussing, if we postulate the unconscious as a condition for language, we shift again to the individual as *causa sui*, who builds a language as he grows and develops. We thus fall into the problematic of the psychology of the individual, the one characteristic of the subject of representation, the focus of introspectionist, behavioral, or any other psychology. Lacanian theorization, of course, tries to subvert this episteme.

Q: What are the main discordant points between Lacan and Perelman's formula?

A: One of the nodular points of Lacanian criticism lies in the fact that for Perelman the metaphor is inscribed as one of the forms of analogy. For the psychoanalyst, analogy is located in the register of the

---

20. Ch. Perelman-L. Olbrechts Tyteca, *Traité de l'argumentation. La nouvelle rhétorique*, Editions de l'Université de Bruxelles, 1976, pp. 499–549. [*The New Rhetoric: A Treatise on Argumentation*, trans. J. Wilkinson and P. Weaver, University of Notre Dame Press, Notre Dame, 1969.]

Imaginary, while metaphor is located in the register of the Symbolic.[21]
The whole of Perelman's attempt—even though Lacan remarks that they
are "admirable" pages—is framed in the question of ratios comprised of
homogeneous terms, because he understands that this is how analogies
are constituted. Concerning this, the "leap" is quite marked; "*La metáfora
del sujeto*" ("The Metaphor of the Subject") pays homage to the rhetori-
cian but marks at the same time unbridgeable distances. One of the basal
discordances is located in the function of the subject. That is the crucial
point even, whereby, as we have explained, there is no "applied linguistics" in psychoanalysis—the introduction of the subject function.

Lastly, once some questions on the metaphor have been clarified, I
want to posit an important issue before we consider our reading of the
seminar to be over. We find in it a very simple formalization of interpretation by means of the inverted writing of the already-famous Saussurian
algorithm. Let us start once more from the relation of signification:

$$\frac{\text{Signifier}}{\text{signified}} \qquad \frac{S}{s}$$

With respect to interpretation, Lacan proposes its inversion. The outcome will then be:

$$\frac{\text{signified}}{\text{Signifier}} \qquad \frac{s}{S}$$

In the Spanish edition of Seminar 11 there are two diagrams (in
pages 242 and 255 of the first edition, and 245 and 258 of the second)[22]
that deserve much more time than what we have now to devote to their
analysis. Their base, their radical pillar, is this inversion.

This postulation indicates that interpretation is first of all a signification. This certain signification intends to isolate a signifier repressed
under the bar so that it can cross it. If we take Seminar 20, *Encore*, trans-

---

21. J. Lacan, "*Función y campo . . .*," *op. cit.*, p. 83. ["The Function and Field . . . ,"
p. 53.]

22. Pages 238 and 248 of the English edition. (Translator's note)

lated wrongly into our language as *Aun* (Still)—the Portuguese version's title is more pertinent: *Más, todavía* (More, Still)—we will verify how Lacan considered the possibility of the ejection of S_1 as the end of analysis.[23] This is interesting because it signals, as we have seen, another decisive differential point with positions such as the Kleinian. A Kleinian psychoanalyst will try to take analysis toward the introjection of the good object, to the reintrojection of everything that, due to massive projective identification, has impoverished (it claims) the subject. If we notice how Lacan speaks ironically of such a task of incorporation in "The Direction of the Treatment,"[24] we will agree that the point is, in the end, for the analyst to offer himself as food for the analysant. Not as a semblance but as food that will be taken as degraded, degrading, and even stinking. Thus, in the cited text Lacan goes as far as to compare the analyst in that "function" with pig feed. He will link that alleged incorporation ("eat my body, drink my blood," he will go as far as to parody) to an end of analysis understood as identification with the analyst, a stage that for us is solely a moment of arrest, of stagnation, which the analyst, by design, must cross.

In Lacan's view, instead of introjective identification, the goal will be to be able to eject the S_1 signifier, which he also calls nonmeaning. Interpretation has signification, it is a signification. It does not consist of a psychodramatically chaotic behavior that is now being called an act, and that some in our milieu, and on behalf of Lacan, have come to conceive as optimal analytic intervention—a sort of foolish and reactive *mise-en-scène* that surprises the analysant in vain, since he does not find any meaning to it. As they say, this leads the analysant to ask himself about the desire of the Other, and it grants certainty (?) concerning object *a*. In a different way, Lacan advocates a signification that seeks to isolate an irreducible signifier, nonmeaning, and designates it as interpretation, privileging its use by the analyst.

In the (already quoted) article "*Lo inconsciente, un estudio psicoanalítico*" ("The Unconscious: A Psychoanalytic Study") there appears

---

23. J. Lacan, *Encore, op. cit.,* pp. 129–133.
24. J. Lacan, "*La dirección . . . ,*" *op. cit.,* pp. 270ff. ["The Direction . . . , pp. 272ff]

an example classic in the Lacanian milieu. Even though both Laplanche and S. Leclaire appear as authors, it is the latter who expounds the clinical angle. He presents the case, which constitutes a customary reference in texts or courses of a Lacanian orientation. As you will see when you read it, Leclaire has done justice to his name. Indeed, he succeeds in isolating with "clarity" in the analysant that *Kern*, that nucleus of nonmeaning that has no possible lexical translation. The signifier at play there—said from the Other, evidently—is *Poordjeli*.[25] Leclaire's development is meticulous enough for us to note what it means to go from the signifying interpretation to the nonmeaning signifier.

Due to their complexity, the two mentioned schemata have given rise to doubts as well as to various versions, but we will leave their examination for another opportunity.[26] Now we have only to move on to the final questions.

Q: At a past meeting I asked about the operation in which sublimation is involved, since repression does not act there. What is the influence of the operations of alienation and separation on sublimation?

A: The first point to consider is that, if we recall the Lacanian definition according to which sublimation implies elevating the object to the dignity of the Thing, we mustn't attribute to sublimation an adaptive nature. As we have already expounded, *das Ding* bears an engorging, enveloping dimension. Through sublimation one refuses, renounces to, withdraws from love and sex. This is quite far from the simple image of the successful insertion in the social. Sublimation possesses a devouring side that is different from the adaptation to culture. Now, if sublimation is related to the possibility of the appearance of the metaphor as creating meaning, it is precisely there that we must find the operation of separation.

---

25. S. Leclaire, *op. cit.*, pp. 108–118 and 126–134.

26. This does not prevent us, however, from highlighting the fact that the crucial role Lacan assigns to interpretation remains so until the end of his production. Thus, in 1977 he insists that interpretation, if "exact," will succeed in quelling a symptom, showing that "truth is specified in so far as it is poetic" (J. Lacan, "La varité du symptome," in *Ornicar?*: 8/17, Lyse, Paris, 1979, p. 16, part of Seminar 24, *op. cit.*).

Separation works with the data provided by the wall of language in order to make a hole in it, to break something in this wall that rises before the subject and produces the aphanisic effect. In this way, every creative act linked to the metaphor—and hence to separation—must possess as necessary condition the capacity to subvert, to attack the signifying chain, logically, after having alienated itself in, and by, it.

Q: What would then be the relation between drive and separation? Because it seems as though separation worked in the signifying chain and the drive were located in a nonsignifying plane.

A: There is a mistake in that. We must not consider the drive as being outside the signifying order. Recall how we criticized the conception according to which the drive would be something irrepressible, allegedly of an energetic nature. It isn't so because the drive is taken by the signifying order, and furthermore, because of the term of the erogenous zone, the drive bears a topological homology with the structure of the unconscious. Due to this function of cut, of hiatusness (*hiancia*) that is present in both of them, the drive has a temporal pulsation. It is not that which bursts in bestially, but a circuited construction in which signifiers, and hence desires, are involved. The problem is that Lacan suggests two operations of constitution of the subject that are stipulated by the signifying action. Sometimes, placing this proposition in a strict correlation with the Freudian conceptual instruments proves complicated. The field is a shared one, but there is a whole articulating work to be done (in this respect, let us note how Freud postulated the drive inflections as data of the verbal conjugation, of the "verb").[27]

In any case, sublimation is more connected to separation than to the integration to social customs. I believe that the latter is rather related to alienation, but this must not be understood, however, in Hegel's or the young Marx's sense, as a process whereby somebody alienates something from himself. In Lacanian alienation there is no loss of an essence. Rather, the subject appears "domesticated" by the signifying chain.

---

27. S. Freud, "*Pulsiones* . . ." ("Instincts . . ."), *op. cit.*, pp. 122–128 [pp. 128–133].

Q: Would it be an attack on the demand of the Other?

A: Indeed. Due to the slant of separation, sublimation consists in a nonanswer to the demand of the Other. Since the opportunity is given to me associatively, I will make a comment about a different issue: that of understanding interpretation as the site where the analyst enacts the operation of separation. In other words, how we can find the action of separation in the analyst's sublimation.

When, for instance, we say re-petition, we are performing a scansion. By scanning the term, as we know, we create an effect of meaning. The following issue emerges here: where was that meaning before? It did not exist until this operation was performed. This is precisely the analyst's task—when he scans, he separates. He "attacks" and highlights an interval made of hiatuses (*intervalo hiante*) in the signifying pair (in this case, "re-petition"). In "Positions of the Unconscious"[28] it is possible to note that separation does not materialize once and forever, for we are structurally taken in, and by, this alienation-separation dialectic. Hence, we are not referring in any way to phenomena that take place in a certain developmental stage. This operation of separation, on the other hand, is reiterated often in analytic intervention, for example, in the passage from I to *a*. It also occurs, undoubtedly, when the session is cut. In this case, there isn't separation because two bodies say good-bye until the next meeting, but because a signifying cut is being punctuated. Working with sessions that end strictly after fifty minutes would imply remaining in the plane of alienation. What is striking is that, as you may know, the reason why they last that long is because that is how Freud did it empirically, and he didn't even consider such a norm as unconditionally mandatory.[29] What I just said, then, does not imply a criticism of Freud but of those who, in favor of an unheard-of belief in orthodoxy, maintain that such rigidity is inexorable as a requirement to claim oneself Freudian.

We have already said it: "Do as I do, do not imitate me," said Lacan at one point. In this brilliant aporia there is much to think about the

---

28. J. Lacan, "*Posición . . .* ," *op. cit.*, pp. 375–380.

29. S. Freud, "*Sobre la iniciación . . .*" ("On Beginning . . ."), *op. cit.*, p. 125 [pp. 126–127].

implications of alienation and separation. The work with these operations is highly fruitful, for they can indeed account for numerous psychoanalytic concepts.

We arrive thus to the end of our journey. I am very grateful to you for having made it possible with your presence, listening, and participation. Thank you very much.

Index

Printed in the United States
by Baker & Taylor Publisher Services